THE CRIMSON COWBOYS

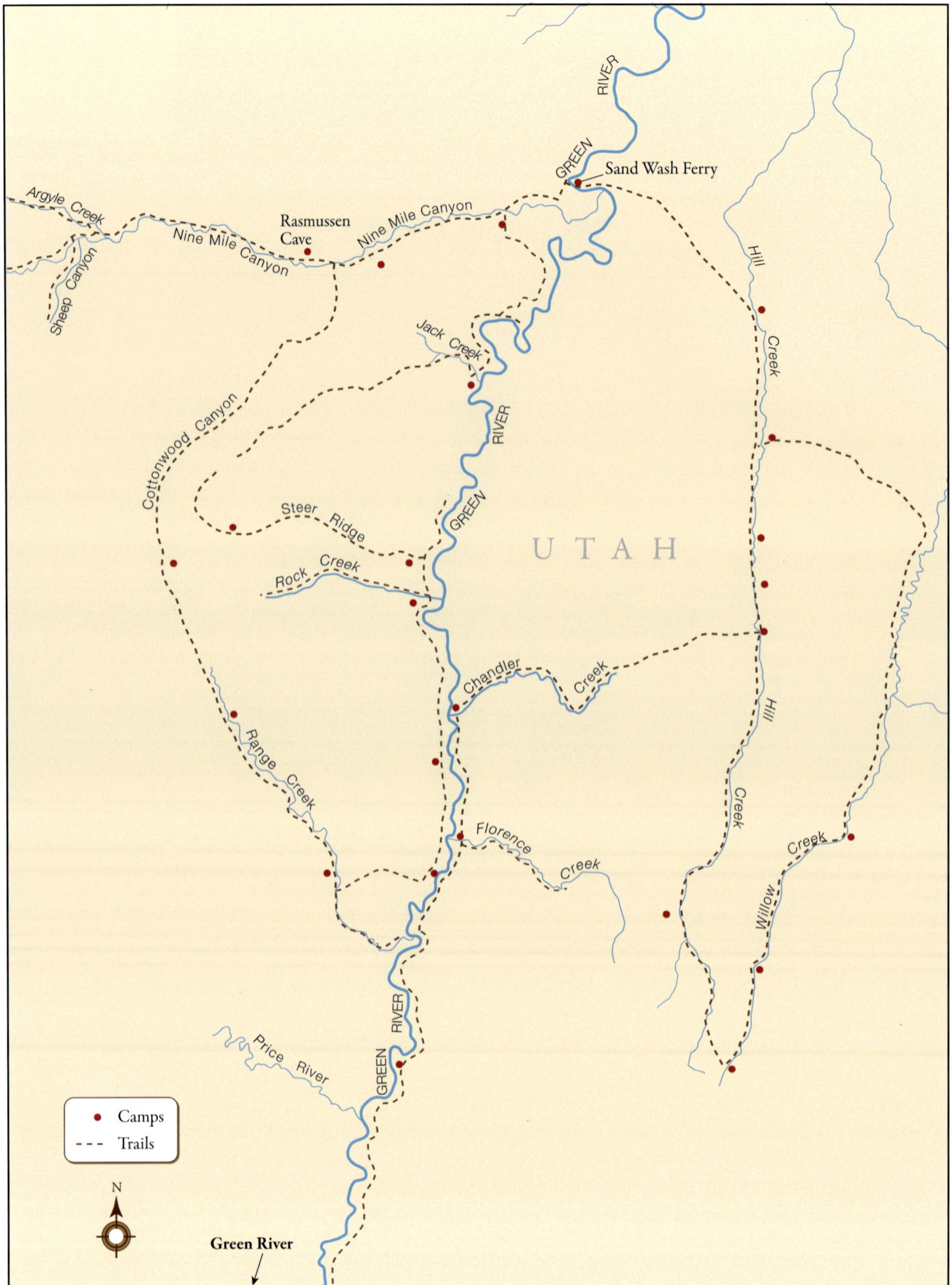

GREEN RIVER
Sand Wash Ferry
Argyle Creek
Nine Mile Canyon
Rasmussen Cave
Nine Mile Canyon
Sheep Canyon
Jack Creek
Cottonwood Canyon
GREEN RIVER
Hill Creek
UTAH
Steer Ridge
Rock Creek
Chandler Creek
Hill Creek
Range Creek
Florence Creek
Willow Creek
Price River
GREEN RIVER
Camps
Trails
N
Green River

THE CRIMSON COWBOYS

The Remarkable Odyssey of
the 1931 Claflin-Emerson Expedition

JERRY D. SPANGLER & JAMES M. ATON

THE UNIVERSITY OF UTAH PRESS
Salt Lake City

Ellen Emerson, Charlotte Forbes Wunderlich, Becky Dennison Sakellariou, and the Colorado Plateau Archaeological Alliance have generously supported the publication of this book.

The Defiance House Man colophon is a registered trademark of The University of Utah Press. It is based on a four-foot-tall Ancient Puebloan pictograph (late PIII) near Glen Canyon, Utah.

LIBRARY OF CONGRESS CATALOGING-IN-PUBLICATION DATA

Names: Spangler, Jerry D., 19957– author. | Aton, James M., 1949– author.
Title: The Crimson Cowboys : the remarkable odyssey of the 1931 Claflin-Emerson Expedition / Jerry D. Spangler and James M. Aton.
Description: [Salt Lake City, Utah] : University of Utah Press, [2018] | Includes bibliographical references and index. |
Identifiers: LCCN 2018032199 (print) | LCCN 2018041043 (ebook) | ISBN 9781607816508 | ISBN 9781607816492 (pbk. : alk. paper)
Subjects: LCSH: Claflin-Emerson Expedition (1927–1931) | Archaeological surveying—Utah. | Fremont culture—Utah. | Pueblo Indians—Antiquities. | Indians of North America—Utah—Antiquities. | Excavations (Archaeology)—Utah. | Utah—Antiquities.
Classification: LCC E78.U55 (ebook) | LCC E78.U55 S623 2018 (print) | DDC 979.2/01—dc23
LC record available at https://lccn.loc.gov/2018032199

Cover photos: *front* Harvard crew beginning their trek. Courtesy of the Peabody Museum of Archaeology and Ethnology, Harvard University (PM No. 971-21-1-/1--162.1.1028, file 99380318); *back* Red pictographs at Deluge Shelter in Jones Hole, by Ron Bauer.

Printed and bound in the United States of America.

Contents

Acknowledgments

When Jerry Spangler began this project, he had many supporters, but none more crucial than the Peabody Museum of Archaeology and Ethnology at Harvard University. Through their generous help with access to all the Claflin-Emerson materials—journals, photographs, and other records—the Peabody has, in a sense, walked every canyon with us and floated every river mile. In particular, we must thank Peabody Senior Archivist Patricia Kervick. Pat exemplifies everything an archivist should be—patient, friendly, efficient, generous, and helpful. We do not know how we would have accomplished the research without her.

But Pat was not the only librarian who assisted us. The following archivists responded to our many requests, always quickly and with good cheer: Ron Bitten (University of Utah), Ruth Chang and John Ulrich (Harvard Student Agencies Research), Michelle Fuller (Uintah County Library), Bill Goodrich (Union High School, Roosevelt, Utah), Harvard's Pusey Library staff who copied the Donald C. Scott records, Ryan Lee (Brigham Young University, L. Tom Perry Special Collections), Ken Rockwell (University of Utah), Alessandro Pezzati and Eric Schnittke (University of Pennsylvania Museum), Roy Webb (University of Utah Special Collections), and Janet Wile (Central Unified School District, Fresno, California). Special thanks go to Joanne Chandler of the John Wesley Powell River History Museum who went above and beyond to help us find photos at the museum on her day off. Joanne is always so excited about Green River history. The town is lucky to have her.

A number of scholars have shared information and expertise about various Claflin-Emerson–related subjects: Julianna Kelly Bratt, Kevin Jones, Michelle Knoll, Duncan Metcalfe, and Polly Schaafsma.

The best part of writing this book is that it required us to be in the field around the rugged but glorious Tavaputs Plateau. Sometimes that meant floating the Green River through Desolation Canyon. At other times it meant traveling to the backcountry on either side of the plateau and scrambling up cliff faces. All those trips allowed us to locate nearly all the sites that the Crimson Cowboys discovered, photographed, excavated, and recorded in the summer of 1931. Using the Harvard boys' journals and photographs, we had great assistance from many enthusiastic volunteers who helped us locate and redocument those sites according to contemporary scientific standards. The following individuals made the journey so much fun and shared our passion for this story; your great company around the campfire and wandering the canyons helped make this project sheer joy: Jonathan Bailey, Shannon Arnold-Boomgarden, Dan Bauer, Rick Chapoose, Mike Coffey, Laura Cotts, Emily Dean, Kate Grandison, Scott Hacking, Jayce Jenkins, Dave Karaszewski, Dave Lunt, Sue Lutz, Steve Lutz, Johnny Maclean, Mitch Marti, Tim Sweeney, Darlene Sweeney, and Peter Yaworsky.

Thanks to the wonders of the internet, we located four Claflin-Emerson descendants who shared valuable memories, photographs, letters, journals, and other records. Their help and enthusiasm for our project not only expanded the depth of our story. It made us ever more determined to tell the story well and tell it right. We hope we have justified their faith in us: Lynn Bowers, Ellen Emerson, Becky Dennison Sakellariou, and Charlotte Forbes Wunderlich.

A number of old-timers with deep family roots in the Tavaputs agreed to sit for interviews. They also shared maps, photographs, and other documents that enlarged our understanding of homesteading in the Tavaputs in the late nineteenth and early twentieth centuries: J. C. Brewer, Norma Dalton, Brownie Tomlinson, and the late Waldo Wilcox. Others listed in the interview section of the bibliography were interviewed for Jim Aton's Desolation Canyon book. Their insights and memories were no less helpful for this book.

The Bureau of Land Management's Price Field Office manages the Green River through Desolation Canyon and parts of the West Tavaputs Plateau. Through the years its managers and particularly its rangers have offered great support. They have accompanied us on trips down the river, searched out Claflin-Emerson sites on their own trips, and helped us with permits. They are all model public servants who help protect an invaluable natural and cultural resource: Skip Edwards, Katie Byrd Kalke, Amber Koski, Mick Krussow, Paul LaFontaine, Ahmed Mohsen, Dennis Willis, and Jim Wright.

Hunt Oil owns considerable property in Nine Mile Canyon and on the West Tavaputs Plateau. They have been good stewards and supporters of cultural resources. For many years, as we researched and surveyed in Nine Mile, they allowed us to camp at their ranch near the mouth of Gate Canyon and use one of their cabins to store our research and camping equipment.

Our editor at the University of Utah Press, Reba Rauch, has been a great advocate of this book from the get-go and has guided us well each step of the way. We thank her for her belief in this story.

Numerous scholars, colleagues, and Claflin-Emerson descendants have read this manuscript. We thank them for their careful attention to every aspect of the text: Dave Aton, Allisa White, Ellen Emerson, Don Fowler, Joel Janetski, Becky Dennison Sakellariou, Nathan Thomas, Gary Topping, and Charlotte Forbes Wunderlich. Each offered valuable insight and advice, as well as catching our many, many errors. Of course, any remaining errors are our own.

The *Utah Historical Quarterly* published an excerpt of this book in their spring 2018 issue. We thank editor Holly George for her help and insights.

Southern Utah University gave Jim Aton a year-long sabbatical in 2016–2017 to complete his part of the manuscript. The university also helped him with some travel and other research costs. Jim especially thanks President Scott Wyatt, Provost Brad Cook, Dean Jim McDonald, and his English Department colleagues: Lisa Arter, Kyle Bishop, Bryce Christiansen, Nozomi Irei, Caitlyn Jackson, Eben Thomas, and Jessica Tvordi. SUU also paid for numerous student research assistants who helped Jim with various book-related tasks: Chris Christiansen, Allyson Cole, Lexi Jocelyn, Carly Olsen, Gardner Stevenett, Jared Vanhille, and Charley Walquist. Special thanks go to Allisa White.

Dan Bauer generously volunteered his great photographic services to help us rephotograph the Claflin-Emerson sites in color. His many beautiful images help make this book special. Along the way, Dan has become our dear friend and fellow camp mate. Our lives have been enriched by his company.

Another photographer named Dan—Dan Miller—collaborated with Jim Aton on their 2009 Desolation Canyon book. For this Claflin-Emerson book he generously shared with us some of the many thousands of images he took of the Tavaputs from that earlier project.

Finally we must thank our wonderful and supportive spouses, Donna Kemp Spangler and Carrie Lynn Trenholm. They not only lived with this story for many years, but they also eagerly accompanied us on many field and research trips. What would we do without the loves of our lives? We are two lucky men.

Preface

I was a bumbling first-year graduate student when I stumbled upon my first Claflin-Emerson Expedition site in the spring of 1989 in Nine Mile Canyon. It was a fascinating site: a series of round, semisubterranean pit houses on a bench overlooking the valley floor. Below the floor of one, we excavated the remains of a child, an arrow point lodged in the chest area.[1] As radiocarbon dates later showed, these were homes of the ancient Fremont peoples, farmers and foragers who thrived in the Tavaputs Plateau region from AD 900 to 1250.

At the time, I did not know that it was one of the sites the Claflin-Emerson team first visited in 1931 in Nine Mile—no one did—because we did not have access to their 1931 field journals. And James Gunnerson's 1969 summary of those sites offered only vague clues as to their location. During the course of the next three summers, I inadvertently stepped onto at least ten of their sites, not knowing that Peabody Museum scholars had trod there more than a half-century before.

I didn't think much about the 1931 expedition in the years that followed, although my love for the history of Utah archaeology in general continued to mature. In 2002 I happened to be invited—along with Duncan Metcalfe, archaeology curator at the Natural History Museum of Utah, and Kevin Jones, at the time the Utah state archaeologist—to visit archaeological sites in Range Creek. We knew that the Claflin-Emerson Expedition had been there in July 1931, and we figured out some of the sites they had visited, in spite of the limited information Gunnerson had offered.

Sitting around the Range Creek campfire at nights, we spun out this idea: What did the Peabody Museum at Harvard actually have in its collection that would help us better understand the archaeology of Range Creek? And might they be willing to share that information with us?

Over the next few years, I made three trips to the Peabody Museum to work closely with museum staff to identify not just information relevant to

Range Creek but to the entire West Tavaputs Plateau. The amazingly gracious—and patient—museum staff provided me with copies of the original 1931 field journals, five of them in all, and of Donald Scott's unpublished report summarizing the expedition. I became thoroughly seduced by the words in those journals (long on archaeological data but short on interpersonal details), the sketches and photographs, and the sheer magnitude of what they had accomplished. But I was stunned to discover that Gunnerson's summary, part of his PhD dissertation at Harvard, had omitted perhaps as much as 30 percent of all sites visited in 1931.[2] I was even more surprised to find the museum had hundreds of 1931 photographs, a good share of them of excellent quality and ideal for research purposes.

What started as a simple attempt to learn more about Range Creek quickly became an obsession: The journals and the photographs were a road map to reidentify *every* Claflin-Emerson site. I am sure my Range Creek colleagues rolled their eyes a time or two at my giddiness when I discovered yet another 1931 site. Within two years, I had identified, redocumented, and rephotographed all twenty-nine Claflin-Emerson sites in Range Creek.[3] A comparison of the 1931 photographs to current site conditions was part of a groundbreaking research paper on archaeological site degradation, written with my esteemed colleagues Shannon Arnold and Joel Boomgarden.[4]

My obsession soon led me to search for Claflin-Emerson Expedition sites in Nine Mile and Desolation Canyon. And it was inevitable that my path would cross with Kentucky native James M. Aton, a kindred spirit and a fellow obsessive. Jim is a Fulbright scholar, an English professor at Southern Utah University, and an award-winning author. He wrote the definitive history of the Green River, *The River Knows Everything: Desolation Canyon and the Green*.[5] And he is just as passionate about the archaeological history of this wild land as I am. We have spent much of the past ten years together retracing the steps of the Claflin-Emerson Expedition.

I am an archaeologist and Jim is a historian—a perfect combination of skills to tell the story of one of the most remarkable archaeological expeditions in American history. It is a tale of mostly privileged young men who, at first blush, would seem ill-suited to four hundred miles on horseback into the wildest canyon country imaginable, all in the name of science. The fact that they accomplished it without a scratch speaks to the perceived immortality of young men everywhere, not to mention their skill and planning.

But how to tell this story? Neither of us wanted to write a day-by-day travelogue, nor did we care to burden the reader with endless descriptions of rock art and granaries and the sometimes spectacular architecture that dot this landscape. Although we necessarily must do some of that, we believe the story is rooted in the people: the scholars, the benefactors, the student participants, the guides and wranglers, the ranching families they met along the way, and those who walked these same lands before and after the Harvard boys' seven-week sojourn here. This is a story about archaeology, and archaeology is, or at least it should be, a story about people.

The Claflin-Emerson Expedition was actually a four-year project from 1928 to 1931 that explored much of the Colorado Plateau north of the Colorado River. This book focuses primarily on the 1931 expedition—the last one and certainly the most ambitious of all. In fact, the 1931 expedition dwarfed those of the previous three years, not only in geographic scope but in logistical difficulty. What they did in the summer of 1931 has not been duplicated since.

In July 1931, as the Crimson Cowboys set out from Green River, Utah, they probably had no idea that theirs would be the last great horseback adventure in the history of American archaeology. Why the Tavaputs Plateau? Probably because it was an unknown wilderness yet to be explored by archaeologists, one of the last in the West. By the following year, there were few places left where archaeologists had not already probed and prodded, and none with such a massive geography as the Tavaputs.

The 1931 expedition marked the end of an era when archaeologists endured privations and hardship in the spirit of new discoveries; it expanded the catalog of different cultures and how they related to one another. Within a few years, though, the entire discipline would undergo another theoretical shift. Archaeologists became preoccupied with understanding the context of artifacts and the human behavior behind them, the interrelation of features within sites and of different sites to one another, and the natural environment that influenced, as Gordon R. Willey described it, "the way in which man disposed himself over the landscape."[6]

In the following chapters, we unfold the remarkable story of the Peabody Museum expedition to Utah in 1931. We call the participants the Crimson Cowboys, a reference to Harvard University's official school color. Chapter 1 details the origins of the expedition itself, the benefactors who made it possible, and the family history of the participants. It is here we justifiably drop names like

Ralph Waldo Emerson, Henry David Thoreau, and various immortals in the business and political worlds. And here we introduce the reader to Donald Scott, a former publisher-turned-archaeologist who led the expedition. His attention to detail was most responsible for the expedition's success.

As we discuss in chapter 2, the expedition arrived in Green River, Utah, a tiny backwater of a town, where horses and mules awaited. The first leg took them along the east bank of the Green River where they explored Florence Creek and Chandler Creek—two areas that have escaped the scrutiny of modern archaeologists to this day. Aside from the time they got lost for a day and a half, the seventy miles on horseback warranted little attention in their journals.

Chapter 3 opens with the expedition at the Webster City Ranch in Hill Creek—a one-time haunt of rough-and-tumble cowboys and outlaws. At this point, three students split off from the main party to explore upper Hill Creek. They then crossed a divide to upper Willow Creek and descended most of that canyon before rejoining Scott and the others in Hill Creek. They were gone about a week, covering about 110 miles on horseback. They saw a lot of rock art and a couple of ruins, but little else to suggest the area had much in the way of archaeology.

That was not the case in upper Hill Creek. There the main party excavated at small village sites perched on mesa tops protected by defensive walls and at bizarre stone towers erected on top of mushroom-shaped rocks. Chapter 4 addresses the remarkable architecture of Hill Creek and the people who lived there. The Peabody crew rode through roughly thirty miles of Hill Creek Canyon before heading off to cross the Green River on a ferry. Ten miles beyond the ferry, they pitched their tents with the ranchers of Nine Mile Canyon.

In lower Nine Mile Canyon, as we discuss in chapter 5, the expedition found itself overwhelmed by the sheer numbers of sites: granaries everywhere, more rock art than they could ever hope to describe, towers and small villages, defensive walls, open circular residences, and more. These were the same kinds of sites as in Hill Creek, but a lot more of them. By sheer coincidence, this area of Nine Mile Canyon would, from 1989 to 1991, become the base camp for the Brigham Young University Field School.[7] We happened to pitch our tents in the same spot they did and followed in their footsteps.

At this point, Scott again dispatched three students on a long overland exploration. In chapter 6, the reader is introduced to Range Creek Canyon—today celebrated as one of America's crown jewels of unspoiled archaeology. And in chapter 7, the students made a miraculous overland journey up the west bank of the Green River into Desolation Canyon, a land so rugged that it is untamed wilderness to this day. Here, they explored myriad side canyons, yet they were stymied in their efforts to reach Flat Canyon, where rich archaeology had been rumored. They rode more than a hundred miles through the West Tavaputs Plateau during their two weeks there, much of it without trails or human residents.

As the students explored the wilderness, Scott and the rest of the crew set out to excavate Devil's Playground, a village site perched on top of a defensible butte, and Rasmussen Cave, a large rock shelter where looters had earlier removed mummies and other exotic artifacts. As we discuss in chapter 8, the Rasmussen Cave excavations, which turned up a "Basketmaker" burial, changed how archaeologists looked at the prehistory of this region, perhaps erroneously so. They hauled more artifacts back to the Peabody from this site than from any other in 1931.

After nearly four hundred miles on horseback, the expedition then loaded into a car and pickup truck for the last leg of the project in the Uinta Basin. As we see in chapter 9, locals had raved about the deep alcoves there loaded with mummies, baskets, and pots. However, when the Harvard boys strode into them, they found these alcoves already looted, and they had precious little to show for their own excavations there. One final horseback foray into Jones Hole revealed an undisturbed rock shelter, but they ran out of time to excavate it properly. Decades later, this site—Deluge Shelter—became one of the most important anywhere in the West, with deposits reaching back to the end of the last Ice Age more than ten thousand years ago. The Peabody team just hadn't gone deep enough.

In chapter 10, we examine the postexpedition lives of those who made the 1931 expedition a reality. We look at Donald Scott's rise to the directorship of the Peabody, and we follow the career paths of his students, some of whom had stellar careers in archaeology and others whose paths led elsewhere. Moreover, we examine how history forgot this remarkable adventure.

In a sense, the 1931 expedition marked the end of an era when archaeology was about adventure and discovery. Archaeology would eventually evolve into a structured science with laboratory analyses, mathematical formulas, predictive modeling, and other esoteric pursuits. Today, computers are more important to archaeologists than trowels. The Crimson Cowboys are a reminder of a bygone day when archaeology was rooted in the thrill of discovery. And young men didn't think twice about saddling up to find it.

1.1 View of the Green River that marks the center of the Tavaputs Plateau. Photo: Dan Bauer.

An Elephantine Endeavor

Preparations for the 1931 Field Season

1

HARVARD UNIVERSITY in Cambridge, Massachusetts, is a place that exudes boundless energy and excitement, as if each person envisions a future destiny as a scion of industry or science or literature. It is a place where men and women think bigger than what should be realistically possible, and then they make the impossible happen. Donald Scott was certainly a big thinker, and, as he proved in the summer of 1931, he made the impossible possible.

The previous winter while Scott was assistant director of the Peabody Museum of Archaeology and Ethnology—the preeminent anthropological museum of that era—he had assumed the helm of the museum's pet project: the Claflin-Emerson Expedition. It was a multiyear exploration of the unknown Utah canyon country north and west of the Colorado River. But the 1931 field season would be unlike any of the previous three seasons. Not only was it massive in geographic scope (the Tavaputs Plateau is bigger than the entire state of Massachusetts); it would venture into an unfathomably rugged canyon wilderness with no roads or towns, an area largely unexplored, unmapped, and uninhabited. It would also involve traveling at least four hundred miles on horseback, sleeping on the ground for nearly two months, and battling the ever-present demons of the desert—thirst, fatigue, and suffocating heat—all in the name of scientific inquiry.

An American archaeological expedition of such scale had never before been attempted. And no one to our knowledge has attempted anything similar since that time.[1] That Scott and his crew pulled it off should have been an exclamation point in the history of American archaeology. But it wasn't. The expedition, which produced remarkably detailed field notes, sketches, and hundreds of photographs of immeasurable wealth to modern researchers, was quickly forgotten. The anticipated monograph, to be written by project codirector Henry B. Roberts, was never published. Scott, who became museum director the following year, got distracted by other duties and responsibilities. Even though he managed a typewritten transcription of the 1931 field notes, scientists outside the museum never saw it. What should have been one of the greatest archaeological expeditions in American history was relegated to boxes and file folders hidden away in the Peabody Museum basement in Cambridge.

In the mid-1960s, a young scholar named James Gunnerson—a veteran of years of fieldwork under the iconic Great Basin archaeologist Jesse Jennings at the University of Utah—dusted off the Claflin-Emerson Expedition files for the first time during the course of writing his PhD dissertation at Harvard. He faithfully synthesized some of the field notes into concise descriptions of some of the expedition sites,[2] but for reasons not entirely clear, he ignored dozens of other sites found in those same field journals. He also largely ignored the photographs and paid scant attention to the individuals who made the impossible

1.2 Prehistoric rock art of the Tavaputs Plateau. Photo: Dan Bauer.

possible in 1931: the benefactors, organizers, students, guides, and Utah cowboys and families who eagerly gave the Harvard boys respite from their wilderness deprivations.

1.3 Scenic view of West Tavaputs Plateau rock art. Photo: Dan Bauer.

Gunnerson had visited a handful of the sites described in those field notes, all of them accessible by pickup truck, prior to his arrival at Harvard. But the vast majority had never been visited by archaeologists since 1931. There is a reason why archaeologists rarely ventured into Utah's canyon country: The waterless region can be nearly impassable without seasoned guides who know the hiding places of every small spring and seep. Places like the Kaiparowits Plateau, Waterpocket Fold, and the Tavaputs Plateau remain wilderness even today, largely untouched by the onslaught of human technology.

The stunning landscape of the Tavaputs Plateau makes the saga of the Claflin-Emerson Expedition into the region all the more remarkable. Imagine young Harvard University students, only one of whom was accustomed to the saddle and none of whom were hardened to the rigors of a Western cowboy, venturing into an unknown wilderness in pursuit of rumors and whispers of ancient ruins.

Three local wranglers/guides accompanied them, but none knew the territory all that well. Inexperience notwithstanding, the Crimson Cowboys were fearless when it came to accessing narrow cliff ledges, exploring many sites simply unreachable today without specialized climbing gear and considerable risk to life and limb. But they survived in the Utah wilderness without a scratch, leaving behind in the vaults at the Peabody Museum at Harvard a wealth of materials awaiting rediscovery.

The Benefactors

The Claflin-Emerson Expedition was by all accounts inspired by Alfred V. Kidder, the godfather of Southwestern archaeology who was curator of Southwestern Archaeology at the Peabody Museum. In the fall of 1925 he invited

William H. Claflin Jr. and his wife, Helen, and Raymond A. Emerson and his wife, Amelia, to join him in excavating at Canyon de Chelly in northeast Arizona. The two couples spent three weeks with him there between September 22 and October 15. All four helped Kidder and renowned archaeologist Earl Morris survey and excavate such famous ruins as Mummy Cave and Casa Blanca Ruin. Amelia Emerson later described Kidder as "the perfect leader, always interested in every aspect of the country and its inhabitants, never worrying, always cheerful and humorous and cloaking his wide knowledge under a gay and casual exterior."[3] According to Amelia's journal, the experience was transformative. Undoubtedly some time during the evenings as they sat around the campfire, talk turned to what Kidder called the "Northern Periphery," now known as the Fremont country.

Two years later, in 1927, Kidder suggested that they all take a horse pack trip through portions of that region, southern Utah north and west of the Colorado River. It was an area virtually unknown to archaeologists at that time. Their wide-ranging trip through the region helped them all recognize the archaeological importance of the Northern Periphery. Upon their return to Harvard, the Boston businessmen agreed to fund an extended reconnaissance to be carried out by the Peabody Museum.[4]

1.4 Alfred Vincent "Ted" Kidder. Courtesy of the Peabody Museum of Archaeology and Ethnology, Harvard University (PM No. 2010.1.5, File 99380316).

Kidder's motivation was pretty clear-cut: He had a long fascination with the Northern Periphery. He used this term in the 1920s to describe ancient peoples north and west of the Ancestral Puebloan centers of Mesa Verde, Chaco Canyon, and Kayenta. The very nature of the term implies that those living to the north were related, perhaps country cousins of the more "advanced" communities that consumed the lion's share of archaeological attention in those days. But just how far did that periphery extend? How prevalent was this sphere of influence? No one really knew.

The motives of Claflin and Emerson to fund the project can be surmised: They were both passionate about archaeology, and they had the economic means to support it. Plus, they were long-time patrons of the museum, supporting archaeological projects around the world. The fact that this expedition would carry their names into the hinterlands of Utah probably gave them a sense of pride and personal satisfaction, if not historical immortality.

William H. "Bill" Claflin Jr. graduated from Harvard in 1915, the son of a prominent Boston family. He served as a second lieutenant in France in World War I and in the fall of 1918 saw action in the Meuse-Argonne offensive, or the Battle of the Argonne Forest. It was the largest offensive to date in US military history and the bloodiest. Right before the war he had married Helen Atkins, the wealthy daughter of Edwin F. Atkins, a sugar magnate and owner of Soledad Sugar Company in Cuba, a firm Claflin himself would later run.[5]

WILLIAM HENRY CLAFLIN, Jr.

Born June 8, 1893, at Swampscott, Massachusetts. Home address, 269 Commonwealth Avenue, Boston, Massachusetts. Prepared at Noble and Greenough School. In college three and one-half years as undergraduate. Freshman Hockey Team; Manager Freshman Football Team; University Hockey Team, 1913-1915; Captain, 1915. Delphic Club, Phoenix Club, D.K.E., Institute of 1770, Hasty Pudding Club, Anthropological Society, Memorial Society, Varsity Club. Secretary-Treasurer Freshman Class; Student Council, 1913, 1915; Secretary-Treasurer Student Council, 1915.

1.5 William H. Claflin Jr. 1915 Harvard University Yearbook.

Claflin had acquired the archaeology bug early in life at his family's vacation spot near Augusta, Georgia, at age seven when he found an arrowhead. In 1965, looking back, he wrote, "This started me off as a collector of Indian objects, both archaeological and ethnological. I have a museum that now houses some 34,000 objects. My most interesting archaeological activities have been excavating cliff dwellings and ancient pueblos in northern Arizona." Besides his childhood experiences, Claflin's parents, William Sr. and Mary B. Claflin, influenced his developing passion. They had signed a successful petition in February 1889 to make Casa Grande Ruin in Arizona a national monument. Plus, their home in Augusta sat "adjacent to that of the Charles C. Jones family, who had excavated test units on Stallings Island [Georgia] back in the 1870s."[6] Claflin remained passionately devoted to archaeology—in the Southwest and in Georgia—the rest of his life.

Claflin took his first trip to the American Southwest in 1912 at age nineteen. He supported the Peabody Museum early on, funding Samuel J. Guernsey's work in northern Arizona from 1920 to 1923. There he met Alfred V. Kidder, who became one of the most famous archaeologists in the United States because of his work in the Southwest. He also supported Burton and Harriett Cosgrove's work in the Mimbres Valley, New Mexico, from 1924 to 1927; he then privately hired the couple to excavate Stallings Island in Georgia. Their work appeared as a Peabody Paper in 1931. The museum made Claflin the curator of southeastern archaeology in 1928, an honorific title that did not carry teaching responsibilities.[7]

1.6 Ralph Waldo Emerson, grandfather of expedition benefactor Raymond Emerson. Library of Congress Prints and Photographs Division, Washington, DC (Item 2003688869).

Claflin and his friend Raymond Emerson first traveled together to southern Utah in 1924. They spent time on the Kaibab Plateau in northern Arizona with legendary guide, hunter, and game warden James T. "Uncle Jim" Owens; Owens had also guided Theodore Roosevelt into the famed hunting region on the Kaibab Plateau, north of the Grand Canyon. There they met another man who would later become a Claflin-Emerson Expedition guide, Dave Rust. For the 1927 trip with Alfred Kidder, they contracted with Rust to guide them and their wives on the aforementioned pack trip through southeastern Utah, west of the Colorado River. They visited the well-known Coombs Village site in Boulder, Utah, as well as sites on the Kaiparowits Plateau and the Fremont River. This trip convinced the two Harvard friends that the Peabody should undertake a multiyear project to excavate and record sites north of the Colorado River that had largely been ignored by earlier researchers.[8] Originally scheduled for five years, the four Claflin-Emerson expeditions would help rewrite the prehistory of southeastern and northeastern Utah.[9]

1.7. Raymond Emerson as a young man. Photo: Emerson Family Archives.

Claflin's friend and cosponsor, Dr. Raymond A. Emerson, boasted an even more impressive lineage. He was the grandson of the preeminent American philosopher, essayist, and poet, Ralph Waldo Emerson. Raymond spent his childhood in the Emerson home on the Cambridge Turnpike in Concord. His father, Edward, a country doctor, grew up surrounded by the greats of the Transcendentalist Movement. Besides his father, Edward regularly saw Bronson Alcott, Ellery Channing, and especially Henry David Thoreau. The author of *Walden* lived at Emerson's house for a number of years and was a mentor and friend to the young Edward. He fired Edward's appreciation for nature, the outdoors, and ancient civilizations; the doctor later captured his relationship with Thoreau in his beautiful and insightful memoir, *Henry Thoreau, As Remembered by a Young Friend* (1917). He called Thoreau "the best kind of older brother." Edward Waldo Emerson passed along Thoreau's enthusiasms to his youngest son, Raymond.[10]

Aside from the Thoreau influence, Raymond Emerson's road to archaeology is not as clear as Claflin's. He followed his famous grandfather and father to Harvard where he was a classmate of another famous American writer,

T. S. Eliot; their pictures sit next to one another in the Harvard Class of 1910 yearbook. Like his friend Claflin, Raymond Emerson was an average student. In fact, he was on probation at various times during his Harvard years, and his student file contains a dozen or so letters between his father and the dean outlining Raymond's academic problems. In his third year, he earned less than passing grades in French, chemistry, Greek, Latin, and algebra. The grandson of the author of "Nature," Raymond passed English with a C.[11]

Like Claflin, Emerson married well in 1913 when he hitched his fortunes to heiress Amelia Forbes, the daughter of the wealthy capitalist John Malcolm Forbes. The two families intermarried more than once. Raymond graduated in engineering, and also served in France but did not see action. After the war he worked for his father-in-law's company, J. M. Forbes, an investment firm. His wealth afforded him many trips to the West with Claflin and others. Thus, Claflin and Emerson became the financial angels for these expeditions because of their friendship and shared interests in the West and in archaeology.

Like Claflin, Emerson was named a faculty member of the Peabody, but this was a nonteaching position, more akin to being a board member.[12] Even though Raymond and his father both helped edit and publish their famous relative's writings, he sometimes grew weary of the adulation. Dave Rust recounted that Claflin took him aside when they first met and told him not to mention Raymond's famous grandfather. It seems that Raymond himself had had too many compliments thrust upon him only because of his family connection to literary greatness.[13]

The Organizers

The expedition was indisputably the brainchild of Alfred Kidder, the master puppeteer pulling all the strings just out of view. But the actual planning fell to two other, less luminary personalities: Donald Scott, who would direct the 1928 and 1931 field seasons, and Henry B. Roberts, who directed the 1929 and 1930 field seasons. Both were highly capable, intelligent managers with the skills to tackle complex problems. And both were, despite their difference in age, rising stars in archaeology, a science then in its infancy.

1.8 Donald Scott as he appeared in the 1900 Harvard University Yearbook. He was fifty-two years old at the time he led the expedition into the Tavaputs Plateau.

In 1931 Donald Scott was assistant director of the Peabody under Edward Reynolds. But he was born in New York City in 1879 and prepped at Dearborn-Morgan School in Orange, New Jersey. He entered Harvard in 1896, played on the school football team, and graduated in 1900. He married Mary Channing

1.9. Some of the 1930 Claflin-Emerson Expedition crew: *front L-R*: Donald Scott, Henry B. Roberts, Waldo E. Forbes; *back L-R*: William B. Bowers, David D. Rust, Donald Scott Jr., James T. Dennison. Courtesy of the Peabody Museum of Archaeology and Ethnology, Harvard University (PM No. 2004.24.10494, File 120720015).

Eustis in 1908 and had two children, Donald Jr. and Douglas Channing. His wife died suddenly in 1917, and two years later he married Mary Louise Smith, a Simmons College graduate; she assisted him in his work in the Southwest. During those years before the war, he established a lucrative career in the cotton industry and then as a publisher with the Century Company and the *New York Evening Post*.

While working in publishing, Scott convinced Harvard president Lawrence Lowell in 1912 to found Harvard University Press. During that time, he also lectured on publishing at the Harvard School of Business Administration. When the United States entered World War I, he served on the US Shipping Board. After the war he joined his friend Edwin F. Gay, dean of the Harvard Business School, and a consortium of political and financial leaders that included Franklin Delano Roosevelt, to buy the *New York Evening Post*. As his obituary states, he also persuaded Henry Siedel Canby to start a literary supplement to the *Post* which became the influential *Saturday Review of Literature*.[14]

In the late 1920s, his wealth in place, Scott returned to Harvard to do graduate work in his true passion, archaeology. He was lured there by his classmate, the well-known archaeologist Alfred Tozzer. Scott said he loved "the freedom of action and of thought which is not only permitted but constitutes the essential atmosphere of the place."[15]

When Samuel J. Guernsey resigned as assistant-director in 1929, the Peabody replaced him with Scott. Scott had already been to southern Utah the previous year to excavate and work on his PhD research. But because he became so involved in the Peabody's administration and fieldwork, he never completed his doctorate, although Harvard awarded him a master's in 1930. He was fifty-two years old when he embarked on the last of the four expeditions. But he was already a seasoned archaeologist and a very thorough organizer. His correspondence with Rust, other archaeologists, and geologists, as well as with various vendors before the expedition, makes that abundantly clear.[16]

Born in 1904 or 1906 in Denver, Henry Buchtel Roberts was also a rising star in the Harvard anthropology program. From the tender age of eleven he had worked shoulder to shoulder with early archaeologists Jean Allard Jeancon and Etienne B. Renaud, earning a bachelor's degree from the University of Denver. Supported by a Hemenway Fellowship awarded to the best and brightest young scholars, he then enrolled at Harvard as a graduate student in 1927, three years after his more famous brother Frank H. H. Roberts. He never completed his degree.[17] Roberts was tasked with writing the monograph entitled "Peripheral Cultures of the Southwest with Special Reference to the Archaeology of Utah"[18]—a monograph that was either never completed or that was completed, readied for printing, and then shelved and eventually lost. Funding for such publications was in short supply during the Great Depression.

The Students

Scott's most experienced student on the trip was John Otis (J.O. or "Jo") Brew. "An experienced graduate student…who will be in charge of keeping our scientific record," as Scott described him, Brew was born in more humble circumstances than his fellow expedition members. His parents, Michael Parker Brew and Edith A. Fryer Brew, immigrated to the United States from Ireland. Michael volunteered for the Massachusetts Tenth Infantry in 1861 and fought at Gettysburg in 1863. He married Edith in 1902 at the relatively late age of fifty-one; she was thirty-five. It was Michael's second marriage. He was a carriage trimmer by trade, a decidedly lower- to middle-class social position. Michael and Edith had their only son four years later.[19] Social position notwithstanding, they managed to send him to Dartmouth.

1.10 John Otis "Jo" Brew would rise to archaeological prominence with his excavations at Alkali Ridge near Blanding, Utah. Courtesy of the Peabody Museum of Archaeology and Ethnology, Harvard University (PM No. 995-11-10/99994.1.23, File 99380255).

At Dartmouth he was seduced by classical archaeology, and when he graduated in 1928 he won a Thaw Fellowship, which the Peabody awarded to students to research Native Americans. He did his first field archaeology for the Peabody in Fulton County, Illinois, in 1929. By 1931, his master's in hand, Brew was on the cusp of achieving professional accolades for work he would begin later that year farther south at Alkali Ridge in San Juan County, Utah.[20]

Brew's fellow graduate student William Benton Bowers II was the only member not from Massachusetts. Born in Brooklyn in 1906, Bowers grew up in Scarsdale, New York, and also in France. His banker father, Henry S. Bowers, was a Massachusetts native and had graduated from Harvard; his mother, Margaret Thomas, hailed from nearby Connecticut. In fact, Bowers spent most of his summers in Scotland, Connecticut, where Margaret's family had a place. Every summer she brought scientists and artists such as James Chapin up from New York City to the valley. Bowers grew up in a very stimulating atmosphere.[21] Margaret's mother, Margaret Waldo, descended from the prominent Waldo family of Worcester, Massachusetts. Thus, Bowers was a distant cousin of Ralph Waldo Emerson. What all this points to is that Bowers, like Forbes, Kidder, and Dennison, had a family or friend connection with the Peabody team.

Bill Bowers graduated *cum laude* from Harvard in anthropology in 1929 and entered the graduate program there to study the same. He had worked with Alfred V. Kidder at Pecos Pueblo, New Mexico, in 1929. Scott had been very impressed by Bowers' excavation work with Kidder and named Bowers as chief excavator for the Claflin-Emerson Expedition.[22]

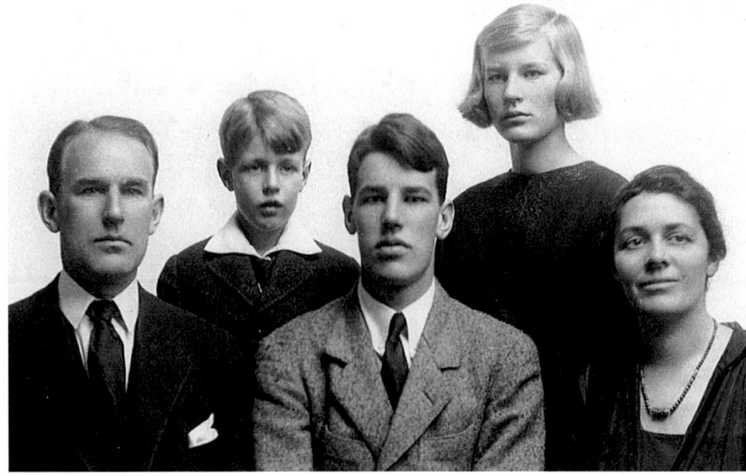

1.11 William "Bill" Bowers (*center*) between his parents Henry Smith Bowers and Margaret Thomas Bowers. Behind him are his younger brother, Paul Sachs Bowers, and sister, Margaret "Marge" Bowers. Photo courtesy of Lynn Bowers and the Bowers family.

Bowers no doubt met Alfred V. "Alfie" Kidder II at Pecos. Kidder Sr. had been working there since 1915, and his wife and children accompanied him on those excavations. Thus, Alfie Kidder had archaeology in his veins and on his hide; his mother, Madeleine, was also an accomplished archaeologist, a full partner in her husband's groundbreaking work in the Southwest and later in Central America.[23]

Alfie Kidder was the third generation of Kidders with ties to the Peabody Museum. Born in 1911 on Nantucket Island, he entered Harvard in 1929, and he worked on the 1929 Claflin-Emerson Expedition in the Robbers Roost area. The next summer, in 1930, he and two future members of the 1931 expedition, Waldo Forbes and Jim Dennison, joined a Peabody team led by Henry B. Roberts working around Moab and San Rafael Desert. Besides being immersed in archaeology, Kidder found time at Harvard to play football, run track, and perform in the Hasty Pudding theatrical comedies.

Kidder was not part of the original team as set out by Scott in April 1931. In fact, he had been turned down but was invited at the last minute to replace John Walcott, who mysteriously dropped

1.12 Alfred V. Kidder II, known as "Alfie," also participated in the 1929 and 1930 field seasons. This photo was taken in 1929 on his birthday near the Robbers Roost area. © President and Fellows of Harvard College, Peabody Museum of Archaeology and Ethnology (PM No. 2005.1.110.1.39, File 99380231).

out a week before their departure from Boston.[24] Kidder was clearly a man for all seasons, a standout in every way.

Alfie Kidder's 1930 fellow expedition member was James Thurber Dennison, whose father, Henry S., owned the Dennison Manufacturing Company, a paper and office products firm in Framingham, Massachusetts. Henry was a friend of Donald Scott's from Scott's days in publishing. He was known, as Rust biographer Frederick Swanson writes, "as a progressive employer who set up an unemployment insurance program to help workers he had laid off during the Depression. In the years that followed, he hired and mentored a young economist named John Kenneth Galbraith, who would go on to have a major impact on the nation's economic policies."[25] Galbraith served in the Roosevelt, Truman, Kennedy, and Johnson administrations.

ALFRED KIDDER, II

Born on August 2, 1911 at Nantucket, Massachusetts. Prepared at Noble and Greenough School and Phillips Academy, Andover. Home address: Highland Road, Andover, Massachusetts. In college four years as undergraduate. Dunster House. Freshman Football Team; Freshman Track Team; Freshman Class, Secretary-Treasurer; Second University Football Team, 1930, 1931; University Football Squad, 1932; University Track Team, 1932, 1933; Harvard College Scholarship; Hasty Pudding-Institute of 1770; Stylus; Signet Society; A. D. Club.

Field of Concentration: Anthropology — Intended Vocation: Archaeology

1.13 Alfred V. Kidder II as he appeared in the 1933 Harvard University Yearbook.

JAMES THURBER DENNISON

Born on July 17, 1912, at Roxbury, Massachusetts. Prepared at Noble and Greenough School. Home address: Edmands Road, Framingham Center, Massachusetts. In college four years as undergraduate. Eliot House. Freshman Glee Club; Freshman Instrumental Clubs; House Football, 1932-33; House Tennis, 1933; House Squash, 1933-34; House Golf, 1932; Inter-House Athletic Council Committee, 1933-34; Permanent Class Committee; Glee Club, 1931-34; Instrumental Clubs, 1932-33; Hasty Pudding Theatricals, 1932, President, 1933; Eliot House Dramatics, 1932-33; Hasty Pudding-Institute of 1770; D.U. Club.

Field of Concentration: Mathematics — Intended Vocation: Manufacturing

1.14 James T. Dennison as he appeared in the 1934 Harvard University Yearbook.

Jim Dennison spent two summers with the Claflin-Emerson teams, the first in 1930 right after graduating from prep school. His job on the 1931 expedition was "general utility," even though he had a year's worth of surveying and excavating under his belt.[26] He turned nineteen years old shortly after the expedition left Green River, Utah.

Dennison's mate for two successive summers was Waldo Emerson Forbes, nephew to the expedition's supporter and great-grandson to the famous Transcendentalist. Born a week before his friend and roommate Dennison, Waldo Forbes chose to major in anthropology, although as a youth he was interested in mechanical devices. He led an active outdoor life, riding, sailing, shooting, and playing football and baseball, according to his mother, Ellen, Raymond Emerson's sister-in-law. (Waldo's father died in 1917, seven years after he married Ellen.) Prior to Harvard and the first Claflin-Emerson trip in 1930, Waldo spent a summer in Europe and a summer working on the Forbes family ranch in Sheridan, Wyoming.[27] Being in the West got into his blood. After the expedition and his graduation, he spent the rest of his days there, living perhaps the most unusual life of any of the 1931 trip members. And he was the only one of the Crimson Cowboys who actually became an honest-to-goodness cowboy.

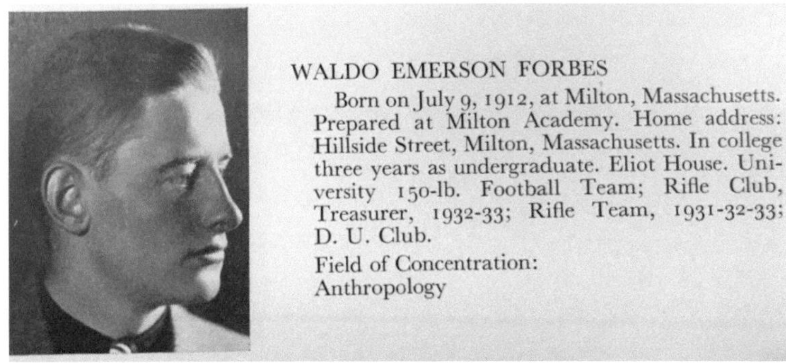

WALDO EMERSON FORBES

Born on July 9, 1912, at Milton, Massachusetts. Prepared at Milton Academy. Home address: Hillside Street, Milton, Massachusetts. In college three years as undergraduate. Eliot House. University 150-lb. Football Team; Rifle Club, Treasurer, 1932-33; Rifle Team, 1931-32-33; D. U. Club.

Field of Concentration: Anthropology

1.15 Waldo Forbes as he appeared in the 1934 Harvard University Yearbook.

The Guide

Perhaps the one individual most important to the success of the expedition was the man who actually knew the challenges of Utah's canyon country. David Dexter Rust was as seasoned a guide as the Colorado Plateau could offer. He was born near Payson, Utah, in 1874 to Mormon parents. He remained a devout Latter-day Saint all his life, and in his religious views he differed greatly from the New Englanders he guided around the Tavaputs Plateau and Uinta Basin between July and September 1931.

Rust grew up in Caineville, Utah, a tiny farming and ranching community on the Fremont River, just east of current-day Capitol Reef National Park. He received his secondary education at an LDS boarding school in Richfield, Utah. He attended Brigham Young Academy (now University) and Stanford but did not graduate. As Frederick H. Swanson writes,

1.16 David Dexter Rust with the Claflin-Emerson Expedition in 1929. © President and Fellows of Harvard College, Peabody Museum of Archaeology and Ethnology (PM No. 2005.1.110.1.129, File 99380232).

"Overcoming an impoverished upbringing and primitive schooling, he latched onto books like a lifeline."[28] That was enough for him to gain high school principal positions in Burley, Idaho, and then Fredonia, Arizona, where his father-in-law, Dee Woolley, lived. Woolley helped develop the tourism industry in southern Utah and northern Arizona in the early twentieth century. Through Woolley, Rust began to guide in the summers. In addition to careers in education and guiding, Rust published a newspaper in Kanab, Utah, for a few years, served as Kanab's mayor, and served for one term in the Utah legislature. He also did some mining and dryland farming.[29]

Rust was atypical of most guides. He could quote Shakespeare, John Dewey, and Susan B. Anthony. He had very progressive political views for a Utah Mormon, and he knew the landscape through both experience and reading. Rust also saw his guiding service in larger terms: The goal was not just adventure or scenery, although there was plenty of that; Rust sought to immerse his clients in the landscape of his beloved Colorado Plateau so they would leave loving it and understanding it.

His clients, who were often wealthy businessmen, scientists, writers, and world travelers, did not pay for a packaged tour that stopped at hotels. They roughed it on horseback and ate basic cowboy fare like beans, oatmeal, bacon, and biscuits. They savored the game they shot on the trip, and maybe indulged in some honey on sourdough bread for dessert. One client, a New York attorney named George C. Fraser, summed up Rust, speaking of his friend's "'knowledge of the plains and of woodcraft, his unfailing good temper and resourcefulness.... Besides being a good scout, he is an educated and cultivated gentleman and is as agreeable a companion as one could find.'"[30]

Rust hooked up with the Claflin-Emerson Expedition via three related events. In 1919, he took Donald Scott, then a New York publisher, on a trip around the Navajo Reservation and Navajo Mountain. Five years later, Rust met Bill Claflin on the Kaibab Plateau through hunting guide Uncle Jim Owens. Later, in 1927, Dr. J. P. Proctor, an ophthalmologist from Santa Fe, also recommended Rust to Bill Claflin, who was planning his own sightseeing trip to Utah with Emerson and their wives.[31]

When Claflin wrote Rust in May 1927, the guide was ready to put his considerable knowledge of the canyon country and its ancient inhabitants in the service of the science of anthropology. He was retained as an expedition guide every year through 1931, occasionally serving also as expedition photographer. As Donald Scott immersed himself in expedition planning during the winter of 1930–1931, it is not surprising that he turned again to Dave Rust for help with the trip logistics.

Rust carried the title "guide" into the 1931 field season, despite the fact that he was not familiar with the Tavaputs Plateau and might not ever have stepped foot there.[32] But he was smart enough to hire local men who professed to know the country, at least somewhat: Dafton Thompson and Oliver Rasmussen (more on them later).

1.17 Utah rock art photographed by the 1930 Claflin-Emerson Expedition. Courtesy of the Peabody Museum of Archaeology and Ethnology, Harvard University (PM No. 971-21-10/100162.1.620, File 122400123).

Origins of an Expedition

When Scott and Roberts first began planning their excursions to southern Utah in early 1928, the Tavaputs Plateau was not even part of their itinerary. The 1928 expedition—the first in what was hoped would be a five-year project—was focused on the Fremont River country near Torrey, Utah, the Boulder Mountains south of that, and the Kaiparowits Plateau south of Escalante, Utah. In 1929 and 1930, they explored the Dirty Devil River, Moab, and Barrier Canyon (now known as Horseshoe Canyon) in the San Rafael Desert.[33] Here, Scott and Roberts recognized that the prehistoric peoples north of the Colorado River differed decidedly from the Ancestral Puebloan cultures south of the river. These northern ancients seemed to depend more on wild plants and animals, their ceramics and architecture were simpler (mostly plain graywares and round house structures), and their rock art was different, perhaps even superior to the petroglyphs and pictographs found south of the river. The expedition leaders were undoubtedly excited at the prospect of being the first archaeologists to describe and define a new culture, what is today referred to as the

Fremont Complex.[34] But they still did not know the geographic reach of this new culture and how it related to peoples living to the south.

As the expeditions of 1928–1930 expanded farther north, the evidence of this new culture expanded with it. Donald Scott wrote to archaeologist Julian Steward of the University of Utah, observing,

> [W]e hardly thought that we would be in this area [the Tavaputs], but the Fremont culture picked up around the Dirty Devil, with the definite extension to the Barrier Canyon region, and with our knowledge that some pictographs exist at Jensen [in northern Utah], makes it certain that we must have an adequate survey much further [*sic*] north,

1.18 Crew members were certainly daring in their methods to gain access to cliff sites, something that characterized all four years of the expedition. Courtesy of the Peabody Museum of Archaeology and Ethnology, Harvard University (PM No. 2004.24.10208, File 99380327).

1.19 A 1928 crew member examining what appears to be a corrugated grayware pot while holding a basket fragment. Courtesy of the Peabody Museum of Archaeology and Ethnology, Harvard University (PM No. 2004.24.10209, File 121190012).

> and that we are now finding the peripheral southwest far further [*sic*] north than we were previously in the habit of thinking.[35]

Scott spent the winter and spring of 1931 furiously planning the trip and hand-picking the five Harvard students to survey and excavate. His first task was to acquire a research permit from the Interior Department because the Peabody team would be surveying and excavating on public land. He also ordered topographical maps from the US Geological Survey—fourteen to cover the area, all at a 1:250,000 scale (one inch equals four miles).[36] Much of the inaccessible territory they would visit had not been formally mapped by surveyors, although some mapmakers had inserted guesses as to the location of streams—guesses that frequently turned out to be wrong.

Scott was trying to glean as much on-the-ground information as possible about the wild and largely unexplored land—travel routes through the country and the availability of springs and feed for their animals. He corresponded with geologists and anthropologists who knew the region in one way or another like W. H. Bradley, E. M. Speiker, Neil Judd, D. J. Fisher, and W. H. Mendenhall, asking them if they had noticed any ruins that the group should make sure to locate and excavate. His most detailed, if not always accurate, response came from Bradley; he had researched in the area and had written professional papers on hydrocarbon potential there. The US Geological Survey geologist gave him valuable information about the towns where the team could resupply, as well as about the roads that were passable and useable. Amazingly, he did not remember seeing any Indian ruins, and his information about springs later proved inaccurate. As Dave Rust subsequently told him, there are plenty of springs in the region if you know where to look; plus, the heavy snow that winter meant all springs would be flush.[37]

In addition to those eastern scientists, Scott wrote to Julian H. Steward, inquiring about important sites in the area known to the University of Utah archaeologist. He asked Steward, though, not to talk about the Peabody's plans. Steward responded by urging the Peabody to focus on the Vernal area because vandals were looting important sites there at an alarming rate. Steward even proposed the 1931 expedition be a joint venture between the University of Utah and the Peabody. Steward would pay for a graduate student to accompany the Peabody, and Utah would get perhaps 25 percent of the specimens from the excavation.

Steward invoked, ever so subtly, the specter of states' rights—that is, Utah wanted artifacts to stay within the state and not be "colonized" by an eastern museum. Scott responded that his sponsors did not want to call it a joint venture and that the trip as planned did not have room for one more person. He did offer to give Utah some "opportunity to study the results obtained, and advance information of them, and a proportion of the material accrued." They ended their correspondence hoping to meet in the field that summer.[38]

Scott's refusal of Steward's invitation for a joint expedition might, in hindsight, smack of eastern elitism or academic hubris—why would an esteemed institution like the Peabody stoop to a partnership with a lowly state university? Also consider that just five years later, Scott collaborated with Steward's successor at Utah, John Gillin, a Harvard graduate and Scott student. Was Scott more willing to cooperate with Utah at that time because one of "his boys" was now heading up their archaeology program?

Regardless, Steward was simply mirroring a growing concern in Utah among politicos and policymakers that Utah's cultural treasures were being spirited away to distant museums when they rightfully belonged in Utah. In fact, the Claflin-Emerson Expedition might have been the proverbial straw that broke the camel's back. Within two years of Scott's correspondence with Steward, the Utah legislature had banned "all exploration and excavations for, as well as prohibiting the removal of, prehistoric relics from the state without a permit from the State Parks Commissioners."[39]

Besides gleaning information from other professionals who had traveled around the Tavaputs, Scott directed Dave Rust to conduct a reconnaissance trip that April. He wanted to know about trails, springs, pasturage, vehicle access, ferry crossings, resupply points, and potential horse wranglers.[40] With his usual efficiency, Rust reported he had driven over five hundred miles around the region and talked to geologist Ralf Woolley and riverman Bert Loper who had been in the area. Further, he also tracked down local cowboys, most of whom gave him good information. As Rust wrote, "Our best source seems to be the cowmen who know the country, when they prove reliable. You know how they run, some of 'em delight to hand out the bunk."[41] Scott was satisfied with Rust's report and so continued with his detailed plans for the trip.

Scott sent Rust eight typed, single-spaced pages listing every piece of equipment and food item to be purchased for the trip. Whether it was a nine-by-nine-foot Egyptian cotton wall tent from Abercrombie and Fitch or a twenty-cent ball of twine from the Harvard Coop, Scott seemingly thought of every detail, no matter how mundane or inconsequential. He was still buying supplies up until the day before the expedition left Green River. Some items were essential to any archaeologist's tool kit, such as trowels, shovels, pencils, and notebooks. But then there were more exotic items such as a movie camera, strychnine sulfate, and canned Royal Ann Cherries.[42] He also gave Rust a projected day-by-day itinerary.

1.20 David Rust leads the 1930 expedition along a narrow trail above the Colorado River. © President and Fellows of Harvard College, Peabody Museum of Archaeology and Ethnology (PM No. 2005.1.110.1.126, File 99380233).

Whistle Westward

By early July, the preparations were completed. Scott left Boston on July 6 and arrived in Green River four days later. His total cost for the train ticket, one way, which included a Pullman sleeper to Chicago, was about $120 (or $1,986 in 2018 dollars). Each of the students made his own way to Green River, although they arrived at the same time and probably traveled as a group. The Peabody may have paid their rather expensive fares, although there are no reimbursement notices in the files.[43] The pay scale for the students was $90 for the six weeks, except for J.O. Brew who was paid $100 because of his added responsibilities. Dave Rust earned $600 plus expenses for his horses, mileage reimbursements, and bonuses, which brought the total at the end of the expedition to about $1,275 (just over $21,100 in 2018 dollars).[44]

The team assembled in Green River, Utah, on July 10 and was joined by Dave Rust and his son, who had ridden into town from the San Rafael Swell area to the south. Two wranglers, Daft Thompson and Oliver Rasmussen, were already there. The Harvard crew stayed at the Midland Hotel while they purchased more supplies at the local stores W. F. Asimus and J. Beebe & Sons. By July 12 the packs, horses, and support crew had all been moved to the Beebe

1.21 A view of the Midland Hotel in downtown Green River, temporary quarters for the Claflin-Emerson Expedition in 1931. Photo courtesy of the John Wesley Powell River History Museum, Green River, Utah.

1.22 The Tavaputs Plateau is much different than those areas of Utah investigated from 1928 to 1930, both in terms of its geology and archaeological remains. Photo: Dan Bauer.

Ranch, ready for an early start the next morning.[45]

The students, all young and invincible, were probably grinning with anticipation. They ranged in age from nineteen to twenty-five, excluding trip leader Donald Scott, who was twice the age of the next oldest member, J.O. Brew. All had some experience in the field and all had at least some experience on horseback.

1.23 A scenic view of the Escalante River and Henry Mountains terrain from the Kaiparowits Plateau—the focus of the 1928 and 1929 investigations. Photo: James M. Aton.

But this adventure would not be a weekend ride on a New England farm. It would be four hundred grueling miles with no room for misstep or accident. Riding horses is a skill honed with continuous practice, one requiring leg strength and endurance. If you sit comfortably in a saddle, each step of the horse sends a jolt racing up your spine as your body weight slams against the horse's back (it is not uncommon for seasoned riders to suffer debilitating disk ruptures).

If you properly use the stirrups to raise your body weight out of the saddle to relieve pressure on the spine, it is like standing on tiptoes for hours on end. It becomes even harder on uneven terrain, which requires leaning forward or backward. Veteran horsemen can do it effortlessly, but except for Waldo Forbes, the Harvard crew were not seasoned riders, and the trail ahead would require eight to twelve hours a day in the saddle over some of the roughest terrain imaginable. Some of the Crimson Cowboys—Dennison, Forbes, and Bowers, in particular—would be in the saddle for thirty-three days straight. It was definitely going to be a once-in-a-lifetime adventure.

2.1 Sunset on the Green River, lower Gray Canyon. Photo: Dan Bauer.

The Adventure Begins

Probing the East Tavaputs Plateau

2

GREEN RIVER, UTAH, must have seemed a lonely backwater to Harvard boys accustomed to the finer accoutrements of life in New England. The town, now famous only for its watermelons and a rustic tavern boasting the best hamburgers in southern Utah, was in 1931 a remote outpost at the edge of the bleak Mancos Shale deserts sprawling to the south and the imposing Book Cliffs to the north. A mere 474 people called it home in the 1930 US Census, almost a third less than had lived there a decade before. The town's fortunes have not fared much better since that time, with city fathers eager for any kind of economic development.[1]

By 1931, the town's glory days were but a footnote to a long ago past. Early Spanish explorers had discovered a river crossing here in the late 1700s or early 1800s, and by 1829 the crossing had become part of the Old Spanish Trail trade route linking New Mexico to Catholic missions in California.[2] It was later used by Americans scouting routes for a transcontinental railroad. In January 1854, John C. Fremont reached the river crossing at the head of an expedition composed mostly of scientists and guides.[3] And it was a popular camp for Ute bands hoping to trade with travelers. Solomon Nunes Carvalho, an accomplished artist and daguerreotypist, wrote of the place in 1854:

> When we arrived at the river we saw on the high sand bluffs, on the opposite side, several Indians, whose numbers soon increased. As our party was much exhausted for want of wholesome food, we were buoyed up with hopes that we could obtain supplies from them. We crossed the river, and were conducted by the Indians to a fertile spot on the western bank of it, where their village was. We found that they lived on nothing else but grass seed, which they collected in the fall. Their women parch it, and grind it between stones. In this manner it is very

palatable, and tastes very much like roasted peanuts.... I made a hearty meal of it the night we camped among them.[4]

Later, in the 1880s, the Denver and Rio Grande Railroad crossed the Green River about four miles south of the old Ute camp before wending its way northwest to the coal fields in Price and Emery Counties and on to Salt Lake City. Even the coming of the railroad failed to establish Green River as anything more than a place to stop on the way to somewhere else. It never became a railroad hub or a railhead for cattle shipments.

The Crimson Cowboys arrived in Green River by this same rail line on July 10, 1931. Their support team, including wrangler Dafton "The Nebraska Kid" Thompson, had been hanging around the area for several days prior. According to the *Times Independent,* Thompson and two other cowboys organized an impromptu rodeo in Green River on July 4 as they "rode bucking broncos and mules for a large crowd that had gathered to watch them."[5] This certainly was risky behavior, considering an injury could have jeopardized Thompson's role in the expedition and sent organizers scrambling to find a last-minute replacement.

The second week of July 1931 must have been a chaotic exercise in organization and inventorying as the expeditioners busied themselves in Green River. According to Dave Rust's brief account, Donald Scott and J.O. Brew spent July 10 and 11 "making ready" for the grand expedition north,[6] although July 10 was probably a day for simply unloading boxes and gear from the train depot and moving supplies to a base camp to be packed and readied. The Harvard journals are silent on these preparations.

2.2 Cactuses in bloom. Photo: Jerry D. Spangler.

Over the course of three tedious days from July 10 to July 12, Dave Rust and his hired wranglers, Thompson and Oliver Rasmussen, a cowman from Nine Mile Canyon, had busied themselves repairing saddles and checking and double-checking the pack outfit. The paniers had been packed with food, camp tents, stoves, shovels, cameras and film, and other equipment. There were also dozens of other items that Donald Scott had deemed important: fifteen yards of cotton cloth, nearly four yards of burlap, a ball of twine, blank notebooks, protractors, scales, tape measurers, tracing paper, ink, maps, fiber cases to protect sensitive equipment, and four "yards" of something called Skookum Mustard. And four packages of snake antivenom, just in case.[7]

There would be no tolerance for error: Once they started into the wilderness there would be no going back for forgotten camp equipment or missing supplies. And resupply along the route was not an option until weeks later in Hill Creek.

In addition to the nine riders, the amount of gear was substantial and necessary for a six-week sojourn in the desert (Scott had paid a hefty overweight baggage fee to the railroad and additional supplies had been purchased in Green River). Thompson had provided two horses to the expedition and Rasmussen four. Scott rented more horses from a local rancher, Lafayette H. "Bud" Milton. The exact number of horses and mules is not indicated, but a fair estimate would be eighteen total, or one pack animal per rider.

Rust had been biding his time at the Howard Hastings Ranch outside of Green River, where the horses and mules were pastured at twenty-five cents per day and where Rust, Thompson, and Rasmussen could take supper at thirty-five cents each per meal. Rust indicates in his sparse journal that on July 12 they moved to the Beebe ranch for the night.[8]

2.3 *L-R:* Bob Beebe, George Beebe, Lloyd Beebe, and Grandpa Beebe. Photo courtesy of the John Wesley Powell River History Museum, Green River, Utah.

The Beebe Ranch, also referred to as the Hastings Ranch in some records, is located about eight and a half miles upriver near the mouth of Tusher Wash. There is a reference in the expedition's expense log to purchasing $7.20 supplies at J. Beebe & Sons in Green River, but there are no vital records for J. Beebe in Green River at that time. A photograph, archived at the John Wesley Powell River History Museum in Green River, depicts "Grandpa Beebe" and presumably his three sons, Bob, George, and Lloyd.

Only Robert W. Beebe, born in 1884 in Ainsworth, Nebraska, shows up in the census records. Beebe had come to Green River by way of Gooding, Idaho, with his wife, Edna, and two sons. In 1930, the year before the Harvard boys arrived, his occupation was listed as a clerk in a general store, and their house was located at the east edge of town near current-day Interstate 70. The Beebe general store was located about halfway down Main Street.[9]

Robert Beebe might also have had a ranch outside of town to which Rust was referring. Or the reference might have been to Warren Beebe, who had a hay farm in Green River in 1920, although in 1930 he was living in Vernal.[10] There is no indication that Robert and Warren were related, although it seems plausible given the shared surname in such a small town.

2.4 The interior of Beebe & Sons, a general store where the Claflin-Emerson Expedition made last-minute purchases in July 1931. Photo courtesy of the John Wesley Powell River History Museum, Green River, Utah.

2.5 Harvard crew beginning their trek. Gunnison Butte is in the background. This photo was taken on July 13. Courtesy of the Peabody Museum of Archaeology and Ethnology, Harvard University (PM No. 971-21-10/100162.1.1028, File 99380318).

The Harvard crew might not have joined Rust at the Beebe Ranch at that time. Based on an entry in the "Journal of Expenses," it seems they checked out of the Midland Hotel in Green River on the morning of July 13, paid their $14.50 bill for two nights and seven meals,[11] and then traveled to the base camp at the Beebe Ranch just outside of town, where the horses and mules were pastured and the wranglers were itching for the adventure ahead. At long last, the planning and inventorying and worrying over logistics were over. Departure day had finally arrived.

To the Cradle M

July days in Green River are brutally hot, usually in the triple digits, and July 13 was probably no different. But stifling heat was little deterrent this day or any other to follow as they reined their horses north and set out to do what no archaeologists had done before, probe the heart of the unknown Tavaputs Plateau. Their path was initially easy, more of a Sunday stroll through Harvard Square. From the town of Green River, they followed a well-defined wagon road along the east bank of the Green River towards the prominent feature on the western horizon known as Gunnison Butte, a sentinel guarding entrance to the Tavaputs Plateau and the wildlands beyond.

The first ten miles would have been monotonously uneventful: mile after mile of barren, undulating gray sand hills on their right and a ribbon of green cottonwoods along the lazy Green River on their left. Farmers had earlier begun to till the nutrient-rich, sandy soils along the broad floodplain that, according to community boosters, produce some of the finest watermelons and cantaloupes in the world today. The Fields were passed without comment.[12]

Eleven miles from town they arrived at Willow Bend at the base of the Book Cliffs. Here, the Green River spews out of the Tavaputs, marking the lower extreme of what John Wesley Powell had named Gray Canyon some five decades before, a reference to the coal-laden Cretaceous deposits that lend a twenty-million-year-old, blue-gray pallor to the cliffs and canyon walls.

In the early twentieth century, speculators had championed the idea of a private dam on the Green River at Coal Creek, called the Buell Dam after one of its chief promoters, O. S. Buell of Heber City, Utah. It was a grand plan, or more accurately, a pipedream. Not only would the dam have generated hydroelectric power, the impoundment would supposedly have irrigated 150,000 acres of farmland below the dam through a series of 337 miles of canals—enough to support a thriving community of 20,000 to 50,000 families, and transforming Green River into one of the largest cities in the state of Utah.[13]

A first-rate wagon road was constructed connecting the dam site to Green River; in places, the road was cut into the side of cliffs and buttressed with thousands of tons of stone. These buttresses survive to this day. The train of pack animals would have trod effortlessly along the existing wagon route, seldom used in 1931 but once a trail bustling with freighters hauling supplies to Coal Creek another fifteen miles upstream.

Construction was started in August 1906 and continued in fits and spurts through at least 1911 when Ellsworth and Emery Kolb, pioneers of modern river rafting, stopped for a visit and found a crew of eight to ten men drilling on the west side of the river and a full-time camp cook living in the stone

2.6 The expedition would have passed next to this rock art site on July 13, but it did not warrant a mention in the journals. Photo: Dan Bauer.

2.7 Expedition's first camp at the mouth of Rattlesnake Canyon. It was taken the evening of July 13 or the following morning. Courtesy of the Peabody Museum of Archaeology and Ethnology, Harvard University (PM No. 971-21-10/100162.1.416, File 99380214).

cabin constructed on the east side (she reportedly made excellent pies).[14] But by 1913, the dam project was in its death throes due to poor financing, much to the relief of modern river runners.

The Claflin-Emerson Expedition certainly benefited from that earlier road construction, allowing them to log twenty-two miles on the first day. At Nefertiti Rock, they passed close to impressive petroglyph panels depicting four or five large elk, but they did not pause long enough to note them in their journals or take any photographs. In fact, they recorded no journal entries of any kind during their first two days out of Green River, even though archaeological sites were clearly visible from the trail. For the most part, their journals are devoid of personal comments about landscape, people, or their ordeals. They camped the first night at the mouth of Rattlesnake Canyon where a small, clear creek enters the Green River. Exploring the creek and the archaeology that might be found there was not on their agenda.[15]

The crew rose the next morning with a more arduous sojourn ahead of them, at least comparatively so. Their objective was the Cradle M Ranch seventeen and a half miles farther upcanyon. In four miles, the party reached the abandoned stone cabin at the end of the wagon road at the mouth of Coal Creek, and from there they followed a pack trail that had been carved into the steep talus slope on the eastern margin of the river channel. In two more miles they reached Curry Canyon, named for the notorious outlaw George "Flat Nose" Curry, a member of Butch Cassidy's Wild Bunch who met his demise here in 1900 at the hands of lawmen.[16]

This pack trail was well known to cowboys of that day and to generations before them, although few beyond the most hard-bitten had ever traveled it. The trail was established in the early twentieth century, its primary and perhaps only purpose to provide overland access to a remote ranch known as the Cradle M Ranch at the mouth of Florence Creek, originally owned by Jim McPherson. The names of McPherson family members can still be observed etched into the cliff faces along this trail, a testament to their hundreds of overland trips to Green River to obtain supplies for the wilderness ranch.

The seventeen and a half miles from Rattlesnake Canyon to Florence Creek passed without comment, and the expedition probably arrived too late in the

2.8 The Cradle M Ranch at the mouth of Florence Creek is mostly in ruins today, but it was a welcome oasis in 1931. Photo: Dan Bauer.

day for any explorations. The ranch the Peabody team encountered sat about two hundred yards from the Green River, and as US Geological Survey geologist Ralf R. Woolley described it in 1922, it was "truly an oasis in a region of desolation."[17]

Euro-Americans had been here for over four decades. The first white person to stake claim at Florence Creek was the mysterious Trapper Jack, a recluse who drowned in the river on July 28, 1887.[18] Shortly thereafter, Jim McPherson, at the time only a teenager, and his uncle Alexander appropriated Jack's cabin and his squatters' rights three miles up Florence Creek from the river. They named the creek after their young cook, Florence Lorene Harris (later Fuller). A few years later Alexander drowned in the river, and young Jim was left to run the ranch by himself.[19]

In his early years, McPherson had to negotiate with various outlaws who also took a liking to this remote outpost. He was by most accounts an honest rancher, but he was also known to rub shoulders with lawless types that haunted the Utah wilderness in those days. As it happened, the ranch was roughly halfway between outlaw hideouts, one in Robbers Roost in the San Rafael Swell to the south of the ranch and the other in Browns Park on the Utah-Wyoming-Colorado border to the north. The trail not only afforded an isolated refuge between the two hideouts where outlaws could ride unmolested, but it was centrally located and within the easy reach of banks, payrolls, and cattle herds in Wyoming and Utah. Members of the Wild Bunch were frequent visitors, as were lesser-known miscreants from the Robbers Roost Gang.

Family recollections suggest the outlaws used the bottomland around Florence Creek to fatten up their rustled cattle and do a little brand altering. After local law enforcement killed outlaw Joe Walker, some outlaws believed—erroneously—that McPherson had tipped them off.[20] He cleared out for a bit, but in 1901 he returned to the Cradle M with his new bride, Tora Seamount, whom he had married the year before in Provo. They had probably met at a Seventh-day Adventist Church.

He continued to build up his herd, specializing in Hereford bulls that he sold to ranchers from central Utah to western Colorado. In 1909, they moved from Trapper Jack's old cabin above "the slough" down to the river where they built a beautiful sandstone house. It had two large rooms, a bathhouse, and a summer kitchen. It boasted the latest plumbing features: hot water and a flush toilet. Woolley said it was the most modern house imaginable.[21]

Besides the handcrafted stone house, McPherson planted fruit trees: apricots, cherries, apples, and peaches. The four apricot trees were named after his four daughters, Zelpha, Ione, Fern, and Pearl; McPherson also had a son, Jim Jr. Visitors floating down the river often commented about the family's great hospitality. The McPhersons wintered first at Woodside, then in Elgin on the east side of the river across from the town of Green River.[22]

Besides raising Hereford bulls, McPherson was known as a master blacksmith, a skill he picked up from his father, David, a mechanic for the Denver and Rio Grande Railroad. He made the largest bear trap locals had ever seen. He killed a number of grizzlies over the years, and probably contributed to the extirpation of that subspecies from the Tavaputs region. His wife, Tora Seamount, played the organ and was involved with the ranch operations, in addition to raising the children. She read her Bible regularly and was known as an excellent cook.[23]

In 1930, the year before the Crimson Cowboys arrived, McPherson sold the ranch to his son-in-law Ray "Budge" Wilcox, who had married his daughter Pearl. No member of the expedition recorded meeting anyone at the ranch when they arrived on the afternoon of July 14, 1931, although Dave Rust noted in his journal, "apricots, bath, spring water, pasture, milk." By assumption, someone must have been present to at least milk the cows.[24] But none of the journals mention anything about their hosts. Most likely, the Wilcoxes, or at least the menfolk, were busy at that time of the year tending their cattle across the Green River on Valley Mountain on the West Tavaputs Plateau.

The Claflin-Emerson archaeologists took one photo of the picturesque ranch but said nothing about it in their journals. Nonetheless, the Wilcox family operated the ranch successfully for another decade, and in 1940 or 1941, the Bureau of Indian Affairs purchased the ranch on behalf of the Ute Indian Tribe as part of the Hill Creek Extension.[25] The purchase was part of a belated effort by the federal government to compensate the Utes for lands stolen from them by Congress during the Gilsonite hydrocarbon boom of the 1880s.[26]

The Wilcoxes were pleased to sell their ranch at what they thought was a good price; they had always wondered if they would get out of their ranch what they had put into it. Thereafter they focused their ranching efforts on Range Creek and the West Tavaputs.[27] Meanwhile, with the reestablishment of tribal land, Ute tribal member Ouray McCook began to run cattle and horses at the Cradle M along with his wife, daughter, three sons, and two other relatives. In the fall of 1945 or 1946, the family returned after a short time near reservation headquarters in Fort Duchesne to find it ablaze. They suspected arson.[28]

The McCooks abandoned the ranch, and it remained decaying when the tribe constructed the Florence Creek Lodge next to it in 1970. With motel rooms and a central dining area, the lodge functioned as a destination for big-game hunters. From there, tribal guides horse-packed the hunters to the East Tavaputs Plateau to hunt deer, bighorn sheep, elk, and bison. The lodge also sold cold soft drinks to river runners. Thomas Chapoose, the Ute Tribe fish and game official, ran it with his wife, Clarice, and their children. It was not a financial success, and the Chapoose family abandoned it in the 1990s. It now sits decaying alongside the old Cradle M Ranch buildings.[29]

In 1931, however, the stone ranch house and immaculate grounds would have been a wonder to behold with its hot baths and flush toilets in the middle of nowhere. Two days into their adventure, the expedition had traveled uneventfully nearly forty miles, they had enjoyed fresh water at both camps, and they had even feasted on fresh milk and apricots. It was hardly typical of what was to come. To this point, the adventure had been little more than a pleasant summer houseback ride in the countryside on well-established trails.[30]

2.9 Fremont petroglyphs in Florence Creek Canyon. Photo: Dan Bauer.

Florence Creek

The following morning, July 15, saw the expedition split into two groups. Donald Scott and Waldo Forbes made a brief foray east into Florence Creek to explore for ruins,[31] while the remainder of the party loaded the pack animals and headed forthwith to the mouth of Chandler Creek about eight river miles to the north. Scott and Forbes, according to Forbes's account, ventured about four miles into Florence Creek before turning around to rejoin the main party at Chandler Creek. In reality, Forbes and Scott might have ridden well beyond four miles into Florence Creek because none of their sites are located in the four-mile range indicated.

Florence Creek is one of five permanent creeks draining west out of the East Tavaputs Plateau into the Green River. Unimpeded by dams or irrigation diversions, the creek ranges from four to eight feet wide most times of the year, except where beavers have worked to create willow-choked ponds. Patches of cottonwoods line the banks, part of a tapestry of green that clings to a creek that meanders timelessly through the reddish-brown canyon walls that tower hundreds of feet above. The canyon bottom is relatively flat—ideal for prehistoric agriculture—but it is not especially broad.

It is not known how Florence Creek, an unassuming small stream, came to Scott's attention as worthy of the expedition's first investigation. It was certainly known to local cattlemen, many of whom probably worked for the Cradle M over the years, and cowboys had most certainly whispered about the Indian ruins there prior to 1931. But Florence Creek is sufficiently isolated that archaeologists had never before ventured there, and the ancient ruins had never warranted any earlier mention in newspapers or periodicals. Scott and Forbes's horse ride into Florence Creek marked the first time anyone had directly observed the remarkable archaeology of the Tavaputs Plateau with scientific intent.

Both men had previous experience identifying archaeological ruins in the deserts of southern Utah, but the architectural remains of the Tavaputs

2.10 Scenic view towards the mouth of Florence Creek. Photo: Dan Bauer.

are different. For one, there is a predominance of stone and adobe masonry granaries tucked onto cliff ledges and natural nooks and crannies. But there are no cliff dwellings in the traditional sense; the residences are actually open circular structures along the edge of the floodplain and not always visible in the overgrowth of sage and greasewood.

And as any archaeologist seasoned in the unique characteristics of the Tavaputs Plateau can attest, it is not always easy to recognize the granary sites tucked on cliff ledges. The ancients often took great pains to construct their granaries to blend seamlessly into the surrounding sandstone—a prehistoric camouflage, of sorts. Little wonder that the pair rode past numerous granaries without even a mention, and they never noted a single residential structure anywhere in the canyon.

At this point, we should forgive Scott and Forbes for their failure to notice sites or accurately describe them. It was their first exploration of the 1931 adventure, and they might have been rusty in terms of a synchronized system of identification, documentation, and photography. Also, seeing sites from horseback is much more difficult than finding them on foot. This will be a recurring theme. For example, it seems that Forbes wasn't sure what he was supposed to be recording in his journal. Scott's journal, if he kept one, has not survived.[32]

The first site they encountered was a rock art site a mile and a half east of the river. Forbes wrote only this: "Florence E 1.5 mi above river. Site on the way up. Leica 2 views pictographs, 5.5 1/25 11 o'clock, bright some shade, E.E 7 hat for scale. Voigtlander 8-9-10 same subject 1/25-4.5. Photos V 1/25-8-2X, L 1/30 3-8-2X,"[33] clearly a reference to exposure settings on two different cameras. But he never bothered to mention what it was he was photographing. There is a very prominent petroglyph panel that would be impossible for them to miss, given its location next to the trail. But the images depicted in Forbes's photos are not found at this site.

2.11 One of several rock art sites visited in Florence Creek on July 15. This site (ET9-5) has not been reidentified. Courtesy of the Peabody Museum of Archaeology and Ethnology, Harvard University (PM No.971-21-10/100162.1.275, File 99380221).

Another problem they had was judging distance when riding on horseback,

2.12 Waldo Forbes on horseback investigating ET9-7, a granary tucked into a crevice, inside Florence Creek on July 15. This site has not been reidentified. Courtesy of the Peabody Museum of Archaeology and Ethnology, Harvard University (PM No. 971-21-10/100162.1.261, File 99380319).

something neither Scott nor Forbes was very good at. Forbes, who had spent summers on the family ranch in Wyoming, was an experienced horseman, but Scott's experience was probably limited. Our attempts to relocate the Florence Creek sites based on their mileage estimates were entirely unsuccessful, whereas we were able to identify more than ninety percent of their sites in other drainages.

For example, a granary (ET9-7) was described and photographed a mile and a half east of the river, but no such granary exists anywhere near that location.[34] In fact, there are no cliff formations even remotely similar to the one depicted in the 1931 photograph until about three miles into the canyon. Other granaries and rock art sites were noted at three and a half and four miles into the canyon, but a thorough inspection of the canyon walls to a distance of about five miles failed to identify any of the sites they described. In all, Forbes's field journal mentions four cliff granaries and three rock art sites—none of which we have reidentified.

This number of sites certainly represents a tiny fraction of the sites actually located here. During our informal reconnaissance, we noted nearly a dozen granaries and another dozen or so rock art sites, none mentioned by Scott and Forbes. Albert Reagan, a self-taught archaeologist out of Vernal, later visited the canyon in 1933 or 1934 and mentioned twenty-three granaries,[35] which is probably also an underrepresentation of what is actually there. This canyon, located on the Ute reservation, has yet to be formally investigated by modern archaeologists.

Chandler Creek

Scott and Forbes probably spent about a half-day exploring Florence Creek before riding upriver to rejoin the others at Chandler Creek. It is not known if they had a guide at this point, but probably the cow trail between the Cradle M

Ranch and Chandler Creek was obvious in 1931. Today, the trail is obliterated by a rough four-wheel-drive road constructed by the Ute Tribe to access their Florence Creek Lodge, although the road requires constant maintenance to clear the rock falls and landslides.

Beginning at Florence Creek, as one heads upriver, the main Green River canyon becomes progressively deeper and the canyon walls more sheer and forbidding and in some instances impenetrable to the north. This is the lower end of what John Wesley Powell first referred to as Desolation Canyon or, in his words, "a region of wildest desolation."[36] In places, the chasm is more than a mile deep and half that wide. The canyon walls are split and rended at regular intervals by side canyons, each testifying to millions of years of magnificent flash flooding that sliced channels into the soft sandstone plateau, debouching countless tons of boulders and sediment into the river channel to be carried south towards Arizona, Nevada, and California. Dozens of rapids—some mere ripples and others roaring cacophonies—shatter the wilderness tranquility in Desolation Canyon.

Upon leaving the creature comforts of the Cradle M, the Claflin-Emerson party followed a narrow cow trail along the eastern side of the Green River, at times clinging to narrow cliff ledges and other times breaking out onto broad river flats. They rode past places that now bear monikers such as Red Point, Joe Hutch, Moonwater, and the bone-dry but prettily named Bluebell Creek. There were undoubtedly blue herons, pelicans, and Canada geese cavorting in the river, maybe even mule deer and black bears crashing through the willows. The wilderness panorama here is undeniably stunning, but apparently not enough so that it warranted any description in the journals.

The crew camped the evening of July 15 in a grove of cottonwoods at the mouth of Chandler Creek; the grove is still there more than eighty years later. Chandler Creek is a small, shallow stream, smaller than Florence Creek at only two to six feet wide. In dry years it

2.13 The Harvard crew relaxing at a camp at the mouth of Chandler Creek on July 15 or 16. The area remains a popular camp for river runners to this day. Courtesy of the Peabody Museum of Archaeology and Ethnology, Harvard University (PM No. 971-21-10/100162.1.296, File 99380223).

2.14 Chandler Creek is one of only five flowing creeks on the east side of the Green River in this region, although it disappears underground in many places. Photo: Dan Miller.

often disappears underground only to re-emerge farther downstream. But it is a perennial, predictable water source that drains a very large area on the East Tavaputs Plateau. As such, the canyon carved by this unimposing brook is broader and deeper than most others in the region. The floodplain is also steeper, which lends itself to down-cutting and debris flows during flood events—conditions that would not have been well suited to prehistoric farming.

The creek and canyon acquired the Chandler name during the second Powell expedition in 1871, named for a family member of expedition participant John F. Steward. But the Powell groups of 1869 and 1871 were not the first Euro-Americans to stop at Chandler Creek. During the fur-trapping era between 1825 and 1844, trappers fanned southward out of the Uinta Basin and most likely headed down Desolation Canyon. One such trapper, Denis Julien, left his inscription at many places along the Green and Colorado Rivers. He may have scratched his distinctive "DJ" at the mouth of Chandler Creek, although no date is affixed, and some historians question its authenticity.[37] But Chandler is the perfect place to trap beaver. If Julien did not trap there, surely his fellow trappers did.

The first cowboys to move into Chandler were probably outlaws who rustled cattle and then hid them in the bottoms of Florence Creek and Chandler to fatten them. The earliest dated inscriptions here are in the mid-1880s, a time when the East Tavaputs Plateau was overrun by cattle barons and rustlers. An outlaw could easily disappear in the labyrinth known as Desolation Canyon, and Chandler Creek was a remote refuge far from the bounds of civilization. And it offered relatively quick egress east and north through Hill Creek to Browns Park, a famed outlaw hideout at the nexus of Utah, Colorado, and Wyoming.[38]

Jim McPherson probably used the bottoms at Chandler for his own cattle. At least one of his son-in-law's ranch hands, Harry Tomlinson, squatted there in the 1930s and built a cabin with his brothers Art and Alton. The log cabin sported a stone chimney and sat near the mouth of the creek about fifty yards from the river. Built after the Harvard boys passed through, the cabin is now gone, but the chimney has withstood almost nine decades of flash floods coming down Chandler.[39]

Another ranch hand who squatted near the mouth of Chandler about the same time was Lew Ackland. He also worked for the Wilcoxes downstream and the Downards upstream at Rock Creek. At the beginning of World War II, he used Chandler's remoteness to dodge the draft. He succeeded for a while, but eventually the army found him and shipped him to the Pacific. Ackland survived the war and returned to the canyon just long enough to retrieve some cows from the Downard brothers at Rock Creek.[40] In 2009 or 2010, Ackland's cabin burned, a victim of arson. No one knows the reason or motive, but there is a road down Chandler from the Ute Reservation. For years that road provided the Chapoose family and Ute Tribe access to their lodge at Florence Creek. Although the lodge has been closed for nearly two decades, the tribe grades the road occasionally, and anyone with a four-wheel-drive can access the Chandler bottoms today. Only tribal members can do so legally, however.

Chandler Creek was undoubtedly home to hundreds if not thousands of prehistoric farmers over the centuries. Unlike the rest of Chandler, the mouth of the canyon next to the Green River featured the optimal combination of conditions for farming: a broad, flat river floodplain with sandy soils renewed annually by river flooding; a permanent creek with fresh water for drinking and irrigation; and plenty of fuel wood to abate the brutally cold winters. Modern archaeologists have not investigated evidence of their sojourn here, but it can be seen everywhere, from the rock art on the cliff walls to massive stone and adobe granaries on the cliff ledges.

It is not known if Donald Scott knew this before his arrival here on July 15, or whether Chandler Creek was merely the best access route to Hill Creek where archaeologists had marveled for decades at the stone towers and defensive fortresses high on rock outcrops. Based on the sparse journal entries, it appears the expedition spent very little time actually exploring the Chandler's ruins, barely scratching the surface of what was there. They may have spent more time getting lost and backtracking than they did actually exploring for ruins.

The Chandler Creek camp also presents another interesting mystery, of sorts, which we refer to as "the missing site." The Peabody Museum collections house several artifacts recovered "at the mouth" of Chandler Creek. These include a piece of worked bone with lateral incisions, two biface tools, and two pieces of white chert. The museum assigned these to a site labeled ET9-2. The only problem with that notation is there is no ET9-2 at the mouth of Chandler Creek mentioned in any of the participant journals (nor is there an ET9-1, for that matter). Rather, ET9-2 was assigned retroactively and inexplicably to a completely different site in Hill Creek discovered and described several days later. Adding to the mystery, the journals for Chandler Creek, which use a numbering system of A, B, C, etc., skip from Site A to Site C with no mention anywhere of an intervening Site B.

2.15 Rock art site "Chandler A" is located close to the expedition camp and was probably investigated on July 15. Photo: Dan Bauer.

In all likelihood, the pack train with camping gear arrived at the mouth of Chandler Creek several hours before Scott and Forbes had finished their Florence Creek reconnaissance and set out to catch up. This window of time probably allowed Brew, Kidder, Bowers, and Dennison to go exploring inside Chandler.

For some reason, they did not notice (or did not mention) a prominent petroglyph panel on an outcrop next to their camp, nor the petroglyphs around the mouth of the canyon. But about a half-mile up they discovered a rock art site, labeled Chandler A, next to ground level with four rows of short, parallel white lines and petroglyphs of a concentric circle, meandering lines, and a solid-pecked human figure.[41] They somehow never saw the two-chambered stone granary just above this site.

On the morning of July 16, the reunited team packed their horses and mules for the long ascent of Chandler Creek with an end goal of reaching Hill Creek. At about two miles (they thought they had ridden four and a half miles into the canyon, but they greatly overestimated the distance traveled), they seemed to have stopped for a break. And as they began scanning their surroundings, they noticed granaries on almost every ledge. Across Chandler Creek to the south sat two inaccessible granaries a hundred twenty feet above the canyon bottom with no obvious means of access (ET9-8).[42] To the north of the trail, a long, narrow rock shelter beckoned, and on the inside they found four partially subterranean cists carved into a soft shale substrate (ET9-9).[43] And as they returned from that site, they found four more granaries on a different cliff face nearby (ET9-10).[44]

2.16 Waldo Forbes posing at ET9-9 in Chandler Creek on July 16. Courtesy of the Peabody Museum of Archaeology and Ethnology, Harvard University (PM No. 971-21-10/100162.1.457, File 99380321).

In other words, they had found no fewer than ten storage structures, some of them quite large, within a hundred yards of each other—an exceptionally high density by any standard of measure. These granaries probably "appeared" because the crew stopped long enough to look. At this point, they had already passed more than a dozen granaries without seeing them, some of them impressive and hard to miss.

2.17 One granary at ET9-10 in Chandler Creek taken on July 16. Courtesy of the Peabody Museum of Archaeology and Ethnology, Harvard University (PM No. 971-21-10/100162.1.459, File 99380248).

About a quarter-mile beyond the three granary sites, the trail cuts in close

2.18 This granary is located above the Chandler A rock art site, but the 1931 expedition apparently did not see it. Photo: Dan Bauer.

2.19 One of many Chandler Creek granaries that escaped the attention of the 1931 expedition. Photo: Jerry D. Spangler.

to the north canyon wall, where Kidder paused to describe Chandler D, a small and unremarkable petroglyph panel opposite the mouth of a major side canyon on the south.[45] This latter site illustrates the difficulty we encountered in reidentifying Claflin-Emerson sites when the field numbering systems are (sometimes) not sequential. And there were many problems with the five Chandler Creek sites.

For one, Chandler A is located just inside the mouth of the canyon. And Chandler B, as noted, is not mentioned in any of the field journals. Chandler C (PR9-8) was confidently reidentified about two miles inside the canyon on the south canyon wall. In theory, Chandler D should have been next in the spatial ordering of things. Instead, Chandler E (PR9-9) and Chandler F (PR9-10) were both discovered on the north side of the canyon and close to Chandler C. And Chandler D was found another quarter-mile or so to the east. Confused? We were.

At this point, just as the archaeologists' journals go silent, Dave Rust's journal offers insight into an expedition that wasn't certain where it was or how it intended to get to Hill Creek. The Chandler Creek trail, well traveled from the 1880s to 1900s by cowboys and rustlers, was not particularly obvious in 1931, and it appears that none of the wranglers—Rust, Thompson, and Rasmussen—knew this country. Rust mentioned that they "detoured into wrong canyons," forcing them to make an unexpected camp in the "south fork" of the canyon.[46]

The following day, on July 17, they dispatched Rasmussen to find a trail out of Chandler Canyon, saying, "and we removed to [the] top of East Tavaputs and stop[ped] at sheep camp."[47] This stop was about sixteen miles from their camp at the mouth of Chandler Canyon, but it had taken them two days to get there. On July 18, they descended about six miles down Big Doggie Canyon,[48] arriving finally at Hill Creek and a new camp at the Webster City Ranch.

2.20 Chandler Creek pictographs. Photo: Dan Bauer.

Put another way, the crew had spent one or two hours exploring the archaeology of Chandler Creek and a day and a half getting lost before finally making their way out of the canyon. They probably had no inkling that Chandler Creek is home to hundreds and hundreds of sites, perhaps a site density akin to better-known Nine Mile Canyon to the west. Scott, in particular, seemed unimpressed, writing only that "crude stone and adobe granaries were found in Florence and Chandler Canyons, as well as a few pictographs, but numerous finds were not encountered until the party had passed over the East Tavaputs Plateau."[49] They might have encountered "numerous finds" if they had simply bothered to spend time looking for them.

Scott's casual dismissal of Florence Creek and Chandler Creek was later echoed by James Gunnerson, whose 1969 synthesis of the Claflin-Emerson Expedition became a benchmark for later researchers.[50] It is still a truism today that these drainages are rich in granaries, but nothing much else. A cautionary postscript to that assumption is Range Creek (discussed later), which was also dismissed by Scott as little more than a few granaries. Over the past decade, research by the University of Utah has demonstrated a rich tapestry of open and sheltered residential sites and a variety of granaries and storage cists—more than five hundred sites in all—reflecting all aspects of prehistoric farming and foraging.

Could the same thing be true in Florence Creek and Chandler Creek? Probably, but we don't know for sure. Formal research there has not yet been conducted. But we have learned a lot in recent decades about the behavior of these

2.21 Inaccessible granaries in Chandler Creek. These are probably the same ones labeled ET9-8 and visited on July 16. Photo: Dan Bauer.

ancient Tavaputs farmers. For example, the large granaries were constructed on inaccessible cliff faces where they are meant to be seen but not accessed. GIS analysis suggests they were constructed in such situations so as to be monitored and protected by a resident population.[51] In other words, if there is a massive granary on a cliff ledge, chances are a prehistoric residence or small village lies within line-of-sight of the granary. And if that is the case in Florence Creek and Chandler Creek, an awful lot of residences are waiting to be discovered.

There is little doubt that Scott underestimated the importance of Chandler Creek, and Florence Creek for that matter. When Albert Reagan arrived here a

2.22 Scenic view of the Green River. Photo: Dan Bauer.

couple years later, in 1933 or 1934, he described twenty-eight storage structures, mostly beehive-shaped granaries two and a half feet to three feet in diameter, three feet in height, and capped with a flat stone lid. Others were constructed by "walling up the fronts of natural caves or crannies; their floors are not leveled, their roofs are seldom smoked, and there is little in the way of rubbish or potsherds in or about them."[52]

Our own informal pedestrian foray revealed a continuous series of granaries on both the north and south sides of Chandler Creek at almost every level from the valley floor to skyline hundreds of feet above. The Harvard boys had ridden through but scarcely noticed them. The bottom line is that Chandler Creek has not been formally studied by archaeologists since the 1930s, and those were cursory.

It seems that Scott was determined to get to Hill Creek where he knew there were plenty of ancient ruins ripe for excavation. They had ridden some seventy miles from Green River (not counting their detours to explore Florence Creek and getting lost in Chandler Creek) to get to Hill Creek. And for all intents and purposes, Florence Creek and Chandler Creek were given short shrift in light of this greater objective.

3.1 Scenic view of the desert country between Hill Creek and Willow Creek. Photo: Dan Bauer.

Divide and Conquer

The Exploration of Willow Creek

3

On Saturday, July 18, the Crimson Cowboys broke camp on the high plateau at the head of Chandler Canyon and descended Big Doggie Canyon,[1] a short ride of about seven miles to its intersection with Hill Creek, a south-to-north drainage long known for its ghost towns of prehistoric inhabitants (see next chapter). Within a few hours, the crew was lounging and napping at Webster City, no longer a city in any sense of the word but a collection of ramshackle buildings swaying under decades of decay.

The Hill Creek country is an area referred to by locals as "The Book Cliffs," or sometimes just "The Books."[2] As local historian George Long describes it, "For those who have never been to the Book Cliffs, one cannot imagine the vastness of the area. There is mile after mile of ridges and canyons of which much is covered with juniper and pinion.... If you were not familiar with handling livestock...you had no place in this locality. This was cowboy country in its fullest."[3] The Harvard boys, far from being experienced cowboys, probably had no business in this wild land. But the next morning, on July 19, a crew of four—Alfred Kidder, Waldo Forbes, and James Dennison, along with wrangler Oliver Rasmussen—set out into the backcountry on a horseback adventure into Willow Creek that would cover more than a hundred miles.

Rasmussen apparently did not know this country prior to his arrival here in July 1931, but he was the designated guide nonetheless. Over the next week, the exploring party ascended Hill Creek to its headwaters, then crossed a divide to the head of Willow Creek, a parallel sister drainage to the east, and finally back to the main base camp in Hill Creek. In terms of archaeological discoveries, the trip was largely a bust. Yes, they described nineteen sites during their foray, but most of them were small rock art panels or rock shelters with very minimal evidence of human occupation. Not surprisingly, Scott's subsequent report[4] and James Gunnerson's later synthesis of some of the expedition field

3.2 Claflin-Emerson crew lounging at the Webster City Ranch on July 18. Courtesy of the Peabody Museum of Archaeology and Ethnology, Harvard University (PM No. 971-21-10/100162.1.463, File 99380249).

3.3 Waldo Forbes (*left*) and J.O. Brew after their arrival at the Webster City Ranch on July 18. Courtesy of the Peabody Museum of Archaeology and Ethnology, Harvard University (PM No. 971-21-10/100162.1.465, File 99380250).

notes paid scant attention to the Willow Creek investigations.[5]

The real question never addressed by those previous researchers is *why* Willow Creek had a dearth of impressive architecture. Hill Creek, by comparison, is teeming with those kinds of prehistoric sites: granaries, stone towers, villages, and rock art localities with hundreds of images representing a rich tapestry of human experience. Willow Creek has mostly small clusters of rock art images. Yet both Hill Creek and Willow Creek are indistinguishable from one another. They are both parallel south-to-north drainages more than fifty miles long located only a few miles apart, both with headwaters in the high East Tavaputs Plateau at about 9,500 feet elevation. Both have broad and relatively flat floodplains that would have been suitable for prehistoric agriculture below 7,000 feet elevation. The geology, hydrology, and vegetation communities are the same. So why the difference in how prehistoric groups utilized this particular landscape? We still don't have those answers.

Scott's desire to split the expedition into two groups—one an exploring party and the other focused mostly on excavations—was probably rooted in a desire to investigate as much of this unknown landscape as possible in the short time allotted. He already knew that Hill Creek had impressive architectural sites, and he would remain there to lead excavations. But Willow Creek was unknown to archaeologists. Scott might have assumed that Willow Creek would have the same rich archaeology as Hill Creek, and hence the decision to dispatch the four-member team to investigate.

A serendipitous byproduct of the seven-day expedition into the backcountry is that it provided the young archaeologists with plenty of experiences in horseback archaeology—a good test of the Crimson Cowboys' equestrian mettle. They would need it for a much longer and more dangerous exploration yet to come, in Range Creek and Desolation Canyon.

Cowboys and Indians

The upper Hill Creek and Willow Creek areas were well known to generations of cowboys. And there were even a few scattered ranches about, some actually serviced by a rough two-track road connecting them to towns farther north in the Uinta Basin. But these ranchers were latecomers here. Fur trapper Antoine Robidoux had established a trading post in the area, and another fort was erected at the mouth of the White River just north of Hill Creek. Licensed out of Santa Fe, New Mexico, Robidoux was a middleman who bought up furs from free trappers and used Willow Creek as his transportation route to haul the furs to Santa Fe; in turn he would resupply his trading post on the fringes of Mexican territory.[6] The inscriptions of various fur trappers and traders can still be found along this Willow Creek route. By 1844, Robidoux had been driven out of the area by Utes, just as the fur-trapping business everywhere was collapsing.[7]

The Ute Indians had roamed this country, hunting and gathering for centuries, if not longer. They filled the void left behind by the abandonment of the farming communities attributed to the earlier Fremont Complex. The Ute presence in the Book Cliffs intensified, however, with the so-called Meeker Massacre in Meeker, Colorado, in 1879. Coloradans successfully lobbied the federal government to remove all Utes from western Colorado to the wastelands of eastern Utah: the Yampatika Utes (or White River Utes) involved in the Meeker affair and the Tabegauche (or Uncompahgre) Utes farther south who had no involvement in the matter. The Uncompahgre Reservation, established in 1880 and joined with the Uintah Reservation in the Uinta Basin, comprised two million acres from the Utah–Colorado Ute border to just west of Desolation Canyon.[8]

When shown their new homes, the two Colorado tribes viewed it as a wasteland compared to their Colorado homeland.[9] Yet settle they did, mostly along the permanent waterways such as Hill and Willow, and with them they brought their own rich rock art tradition. Petroglyphs found in this area depict a stunning array of images: trains, horses, warriors riding into battle, bison, and owls. Collectively, these images constitute perhaps the largest concentration of historic Ute rock art in North America, and certainly some of the finest.

In the mid-1880s, trespassing miners discovered Gilsonite,[10] a black hydrocarbon found only in the Uinta Basin north of Desolation Canyon. The government promptly reneged on its agreement with the Utes and withdrew from the reservation those lands richest in this mineral. Gilsonite development, along with the later Dawes Severalty Act of 1887, had stripped the Utes of most of their lands by 1897. Moreover, big ranching operations such as Preston Nutter and the Webster City Cattle Company had begun moving cattle onto the high-country ranges by the late 1880s. So had smaller operations like those of Jim McPherson and Charley Hill, after whom Hill Creek was named. Many Ute leaders like Red Moon, Ole Santio, and Alfred Pawwinnee, however, stayed in the area, along with their families.

The very first rancher in Hill Creek was Charley Porter Hill. He originally filed on a homestead in Ashley Valley near present-day Vernal, but also ran cattle in the Hill Creek area prior to 1880 and the establishment of the reservation.

3.4 An example of the historic Ute rock art common to Willow Creek. Photo: Dan Bauer.

He sold out a few years later.[11] Then in 1886 Preston Nutter pushed his herd of cattle out of Colorado and into the southern Book Cliffs, where he competed with the Webster City Cattle Company, a ranching syndicate headquartered in Webster City, Iowa. As Utah ranching historian James H. Beckstead says, Webster City was "the most mysterious of all big corporate cattle companies in Utah."[12]

By 1931 when the Harvard expedition arrived, the ranch had changed hands several times. Dave Rust noted in his expedition journal that it was owned at that time by Harry Mohlares and Sam Sabeus, both Greek Americans and the last Anglo owners of the ranch.[13] But in its prime in the late nineteenth century, it was a large ranch with all the trappings of a town. Located near the Uintah–Grand County line, the company employed so many cowboys it had to build a bunkhouse so elaborate that ranch hands began calling it "the Webster City Hotel." There were also cabins for married cowboys, a general store, a saloon that doubled as a school for the ranch hands' children, and a post office. Managed by Clarence Knight, Webster City brought in the best Hereford cattle to the Book Cliffs. They eventually bought out Preston Nutter's five thousand cattle in 1893 for $58,740; this brought their herd to an estimated 25,000 to 35,000 head.[14]

Webster City, though, was hardly a "happy valley" town. It sat squarely on the Outlaw Trail between Brown's Park in Wyoming and Robber's Roost to the south in the San Rafael Swell, and, as mentioned previously, like it or not the settlement became a stopover for outlaws. The company initially had trouble with cattle rustlers, so rather than fight them, the Webster City ranch foreman hired them. Reported on the Webster City payroll at one time or another were Butch Cassidy and his Wild Bunch cohorts Elza Lay and Harry Longabaugh, who went by the moniker Sundance Kid. Rustling mostly stopped after that.

Another outlaw who worked for the company was Tom Dilley. Webster City fired Dilley when he reportedly killed a man, and in retaliation Dilley took to rustling their cattle. When Sheriff Jesse Tyler killed the infamous Wild Bunch bandit George "Flat Nose" Currie in April 1900, it was Dilley they were actually looking for.[15] A month later, Sheriff Tyler and Deputy Samuel F. Jenkins were gunned down just upstream from Webster City while still in pursuit of Tom Dilley; according to one unverifiable account, the perpetrator of the deed was Harvey "Kid Curry" Logan, another notorious member of the Wild Bunch who had vowed revenge for the killing of his mentor, George Currie.[16]

By the late 1890s, Webster City was out of business. It sold off its holdings to the Taylor family out of Moab and two men named Carpenter and J. M. Cunningham. Nowadays beaver have dammed up the creek, and a willow-choked pond covers what was once a "lively town," as Doris Karren Burton describes it.[17] Some in the Claflin-Emerson Expedition crew referred to this area as "The Willows."[18]

The Taylor family was among the original settlers of Moab in Grand County to the south. Four Taylor brothers had ranches on the old Webster City range in Hill Creek, but foremost among them was Norman "Jik" Taylor; Rust had even suggested him as a guide to Hill Creek but ended up not hiring him.[19] Born in 1873 in Juab County, Jik married Veone Jensen sometime before 1920. They had two sons, Lorin and Charles, and a daughter, Norma. Waldo Wilcox, a grandson of Jim McPherson of Florence Creek's Cradle M Ranch, said that his family always looked up to the Taylors. They had so much money, Wilcox joked, that they could afford an entire roll of toilet paper for their outhouse. Despite being wealthier than most of their neighbors, the Taylors got along with them and vice versa.[20] In fact, a common theme in all the stories told by Hill and Willow old-timers is how well all the ranching families got along with each other, as well as with their Ute neighbors. Oddly, the Harvard boys never mentioned any Utes being in the area.

3.5 Scenic view of the Willow Creek country. Herds of wild horses proliferate on federal and Indian lands in the area.

As noted above, many Ute families stayed along the two drainages even after they officially "lost" their reservation. Shortly before that, however, encroaching Anglo ranchers sometimes clashed with Utes living around Hill Creek. In the summers, many Utes, like Red Moon, (or Com-matt-too-its) ran horses on the Book Cliffs. In 1893 he had a run-in with Preston Nutter near Bull Prick (now B.P.) spring. Red Moon accused Nutter of trespassing on the Uncompahgre Reservation (he was correct). Nutter, in turn, accused Red Moon and his companions of rustling. One day the Ute and his group ambushed Nutter in front of his cowboys. He whipped Nutter with a bull prick whip. The cattle baron forbade his men to retaliate, saying it was better to let the Indians save face than to start an armed conflict between Natives and white cattlemen.[21] Red Moon, though, was one of the most assertive Utes in the area. Most did not confront the ranchers, especially after reservation status was revoked. By the 1930 census, close to seventy Utes were recorded as living in the Book Cliffs.[22] And there were probably more because locating them for a census would have proved particularly difficult. Many Utes moved between the Book Cliffs in the summer and Ouray, a trading post and reservation headquarters, in the winter.

The Anglo ranchers in the area said they got along with their Ute neighbors, as long as one treated them fairly. As George Long writes, "If Indian people liked you, they would do anything for you. It was a matter of befriending and sharing, as this was home to all." This sentiment was echoed by the daughters of Pawwinnee, a prominent Ute leader in the Willow Creek area. They said that "the white [*sic*] lived out there, they used to camp in the Indian camps, they'd eat their meals with them...and the same way when the Indians would go to a white home—they'd feed them."[23] Long described how the Utes would come to ranchers' homes to trade and barter for deer skins which they made into buckskin for three dollars per hide. They also loved to trade or barter beadwork, knives, blankets, and their prized possession, horses. Long names a number of Ute families who lived in the Book Cliffs; one of the most unusual, however, was Auggussaw. According to local historian George E. Stewart Jr., he wore a dress, by tribal fiat, because he showed cowardice as a teenager during the Meeker episode. At the other end of notoriety was Chipeta, the most famous and revered Ute on the reservation. She was the wife of Ouray, the great Uncompahgre Ute leader. She accompanied him to the White House in 1868 and was as respected and influential as her husband. She died in Bitter Creek, an eastern tributary to Willow Creek, in 1924.[24]

Despite large numbers of Utes in the two canyons, the Claflin-Emerson participants said little about them in their journals. This oversight was unfortunate. Interviews with local Utes might have provided keen insights into the archaeology of the two drainages, perhaps even clues as to which sites could be attributed to their own ancestors and those that were the remains of other people long ago vanished. As the Crimson Cowboys traveled and recorded sites, perhaps they did not encounter any Utes.

3.6 Crew member (perhaps Dennison) holds a slab metate at ET9-1 in upper Hill Creek. Photo was taken on July 19. Courtesy of the Peabody Museum of Archaeology and Ethnology, Harvard University (PM No. 971-21-10/100162.1.305, File 99380225).

The Trek Begins

In July 1931, the Great Depression was unleashing its fury on Europe, and Germany was on the brink of economic collapse. International emergency sessions were being held in London to find a way to prevent the total collapse of the German government, just as the National Socialist Workers Party—the Third Reich—was causing jitters with its inflammatory rhetoric. The Harvard boys knew nothing of the world events unfolding around them. They were insulated by vast expanses of Utah wilderness, their thoughts directed singularly at the archaeological discoveries that awaited them. The exploring expedition into upper Hill Creek and Willow Creek was their first serious test.

On July 19, James Dennison, Waldo Forbes, and Alfred Kidder mounted their horses and set course south from Webster City to first investigate sites in upper Hill Creek. Kidder, soon to be a college junior, was placed in charge; he was the most experienced archaeologist because of the many years he had worked alongside his father at Pecos Pueblo in New Mexico. Forbes was called on to create a map of the route. But whoever took the photographs was not very good at it because most of the images from this trek are underexposed and are of minimal research value.

The ride was apparently uneventful because they mentioned nothing until about twelve miles above Webster City.[25] There they discovered a large rock shelter with considerable smoke staining on the ceiling and litter from recent sheepherder camps (ET9-1). Excavations revealed only two metates, a single flint flake, and a few pieces of unworked animal bone.[26] Another half-mile up canyon they investigated another large rock shelter (ET9-2). This one had layers of charcoal two to three centimeters thick, a single black potsherd, and a few pieces of white chalcedony, but again the excavations did not reveal much to get excited about.[27] Both sites seemed to be short-term camps. They photographed the sites and then called it a day, setting up camp next to a spring. This might have been the "large spring" they observed in a draw about one hundred fifty yards to the northwest of ET9-1,[28] but this would have meant they backtracked a half-mile or so to the spring rather than dry-camp farther upcanyon.

In the morning, on July 20, they continued up Hill Creek south towards its headwaters. As the elevations increased, the vegetation changed from scattered pinyons and junipers to a more woodland environment, with dense patches of scrub oak, pine, and eventually quaking aspens. They apparently spent some time exploring the side canyons that drained into Hill Creek because they found another cave site (ET9-3) about three hundred yards inside one of these drainages about three to four miles above their camp, or fifteen to sixteen miles above Webster City. A boulder with worn depressions from grinding seeds, called bedrock slicks, and smoke staining on the ceiling drew their attention, but excavations revealed nothing.[29] They must have spent a fair amount of time here, enough so that they made their evening camp in this area, having only traveled three or four miles from their previous camp.

The expedition route from upper Hill Creek over the pass to the head of Willow Creek is not known for certain. Forbes indicated they traveled by way of Simmons Draw, but a draw of that name is not indicated on current topographic maps. The location can be surmised based on the limits of the local topography. Hill Creek Canyon in this area is deeply entrenched, in places more than 1,500 feet deep, with heavily wooded, steep slopes that would have made cross-country passage extremely difficult. Furthermore, if they attempted to cross over to Willow Creek too soon, they would have faced a difficult lateral crossing of other steep south–north drainages, such as Spring Creek, Pioche Canyon, and Corral Creek.

In the Walker Point area, Hill Creek splits into two major forks, east and west. The crew probably ascended the bottom of East Fork about three miles to its headwaters. They then made a difficult ascent of what is today the Sunset Dugway about twelve hundred feet to a ridgeline that divides Hill Creek from Floy Canyon on the south and Pioche Canyon on the east. This ridge is now called Wagon Road Ridge, and it is passable to vehicles, trending east–west and northwest–southeast, skirting the heads of several drainages, including Pioche Creek, a major tributary to Willow Creek. The trail today wends its way down the Corral Creek tributary, intersecting with Willow Creek about three miles below the West Willow Creek headwaters.

The trail in 1931 might have been altogether different than the trail today. They could have arrived in West Willow Creek by way of any of three tributary canyons: Clear Creek, Corral Creek, or Potato Creek. All three would have required unimaginable horsemanship because those routes would have taken them from a high of 9,400 feet elevation to a low of 7,800 feet elevation in less than a half-mile's distance.

But Forbes's journal indicates that they descended from the head of Willow Creek. It was only an eight-mile ride from their camp at the head of Hill Creek over the divide to the head of Willow Creek. But this rough ride consumed most of the day. If the Harvard boys indeed reached the head of Willow Creek, rather than descending one of the tributaries already mentioned, they would have detoured to the southeast, following the broken ridgeline to the Hells Hole area, where the descent into Willow Creek would have been much easier but the route much longer. Forbes indicated they descended about three miles from the head of Willow Creek before making camp, which would place the camp at or near the mouth of Corral Canyon. The eleven-mile ride had taken them through some of the roughest country anywhere in the nation. Their only comment was the notation, "cattle country," confirming what George Long wrote about the area many years later.[30]

On July 22, the crew continued to ride down West Willow Creek, observing nothing until about six miles below their camp, or about nine miles from the head of Willow Creek. There they investigated another rock shelter on the west side of the canyon (ET10-1). Excavations revealed pretty much the same thing they had noted at the previous three shelters: a lightly worn sandstone metate and a layer of charcoal eight centimeters below the surface.[31]

After taking lunch, the Harvard boys rode another five miles downstream where they found several modern images pecked into the eastern wall of the canyon (Site Willow B), although a few "seem older than others."[32] One of the images in Dennison's sketch appears to be a typical Fremont trapezoidal anthropomorph. At a little more than a mile above the mouth of Pioche Canyon, they noted a cleft in the east canyon wall with wooden poles and small willow branches resting inside, "unworked, apparently quite old, no ax marks," which they labeled ET10-2.[33] By the time they arrived at the mouth of Pioche Canyon it had been a long day in the saddle, at least fifteen miles from the head of Willow Creek. All they had to show for it was a metate, some rotting wooden beams, and a few pecked images that might or might not have been prehistoric.

3.7 Modern view of the Willow Creek floodplain. Photo: Dan Bauer.

Middle Willow Creek

Their camp that evening was at the mouth of Pioche Canyon. Their journals refer to an upper ranch here belonging to Walter ("Dutch") and Pauline Hazelbush, but they were mistaken. The upper Hazelbush Ranch was at least another ten miles down canyon as the crow flies. Pioche Creek is a major tributary to Willow Creek, with headwaters located about twelve to fifteen miles to the south of their camp and very near the head of Hill Creek. Compared to the other small side canyons they had already passed—Supply Canyon, Clear Creek, Potato Creek, and scores of others with no names—Pioche Creek was broad, and at 6,800 feet elevation it might have seemed suited for prehistoric agriculture. On the morning of July 23, the crew explored into the canyon, and about a half-mile inside they found a rock shelter with six or seven pecked images and a red "smootchy" line. They also noted a long, narrow groove worn into the sandstone surface and a single piece of flint (ET10-3).[34]

Apparently convinced the canyon offered minimal potential for impressive sites, the archaeologists returned to the mouth of Pioche Canyon and continued to follow the creek downstream.[35] They soon began to encounter an abundance of rock art sites on both sides of the canyon. At about two and a quarter miles below their camp, they stopped to photograph a rock art site (ET10-4), described only as "pecked deer, sheep,"[36] and a half-mile below they

3.8 View of petroglyphs at ET10-4 in upper Willow Creek just below the mouth of Pioche Canyon. The photo was taken on July 23. Courtesy of the Peabody Museum of Archaeology and Ethnology, Harvard University (PM No. 971-21-10/100162.1.258, File 99380220).

3.9 View of petroglyphs at ET6-15 in upper Willow Creek. The photo was taken on July 23. Courtesy of the Peabody Museum of Archaeology and Ethnology, Harvard University (PM No. 971-21-10/100162.1.257, File 99380219).

stopped to visit, sketch, and photograph yet another rock art site, this one with images painted in red and yellow, and with hand and toe holds carved into the cliff face nearby (ET10-5).[37] Another quarter-mile below that was a panel of red pictographs (ET10-6), mostly indistinct shapes too faded to photograph.[38] And just below that was another cluster of pecked figures: "mountain sheep, a man with a bow-arrow, male figures, stars, [and] irregular peckings" (ET10-7).[39] It is puzzling that the crew noted no prehistoric architecture of any kind because rock art sites usually appear near granaries and residences.

The crew camped on July 23 at an unspecified ranch either seven or ten miles below the mouth of Pioche Creek, depending on whose mileage estimates are used. In the camp area, located about thirty miles below the head of Willow Creek, they described and photographed another cluster of petroglyphs (ET6-15)[40] and a nondescript cave with a crude stone wall thirteen feet long erected across the front of the shelter (ET-6-16).[41]

Willow Creek is noted today for its abundant rock art sites, and it appears the crew was diligent, at least in the beginning, to note everything they saw. But the number of rock sites seemed to have overwhelmed them, and they were making little progress as they inched their way downstream. At this point, they appear to have pocketed their journals and rode another ten miles without writing a word before they stopped to photograph another pictograph panel (ET6-17). They described it as "red and white painted figures, three red cross shaped men, white man and animal head, buffalo, two red crosses, blue cross-like figure, one red man [with] blue marks."[42]

In this same area, located near the Hazelbush Ranch at the mouth of Dry Gulch, they discovered an outcrop—locals call it Mushroom Rock—with a commanding view of the valley (ET6-18). On the top, the ancients had erected a dry-laid stone wall defining the outer perimeter, in places nearly three feet high, which limited easy access. This site, the first substantial architecture they had encountered, is commonly referred to in this country as a "fort." Archaeologists, who prefer the more neutral term "tower," tend to agree they were defensive in nature. With only a few exceptions north of the Colorado River, they are unique to the Tavaputs Plateau. They usually stand on the bedrock surface of a prominence high above the valley. Their dry-laid rock walls block or greatly limit access to them, and in most instances they have very few artifacts. This suggests they were used only temporarily, perhaps as places of refuge during times of perceived threat. Most tower sites feature a single room, although a few might have three or four rooms on the pinnacle top.

3.10 View of the stone tower at ET6-18 in middle Willow Creek near the mouth of Dry Gulch. This photo was taken on July 24. Courtesy of the Peabody Museum of Archaeology and Ethnology, Harvard University (PM No. 971-21-10/100162.1.313, File 99380226).

This particular tower site—Kidder called it a "lookout"—perched three hundred feet above Willow Creek on a thirty-foot-high pinnacle top. Access required a steep climb up a slippery shale slope to the base of the pinnacle. The crew then leaned a pole into a crevice and shinnied up the natural chute to the top of the forty-six-by-seventy-five-foot pinnacle. Here they found courses of overlapping sandstone slabs lining the outer edge. Unlike other tower structures in the region, traces of adobe still held the wall matrix in place. They also found an arrowhead, a triangular stone blade, and flint flakes[43]—certainly a meager assemblage given the amount of energy that was expended to build the tower.

Returning to Hill Creek

After a long day in the saddle, the crew camped that night at the Hazelbush Ranch at the mouth of Dry Gulch. Pauline Hazelbush first came to the Book Cliffs in 1908 as the twenty-year-old bride of Charles Turner. They settled where Dry Gulch enters Willow Creek, just north of the Uintah-Grand county line. As she wrote in her autobiography, "I was the only white woman for miles."[44] Ten years and two children later, Charles died from the infamous 1918 influenza epidemic. Pauline was still a partner in the ranch and part of a large sheep deal with one of Charles's hands, Dutch Hazelbush, who was four years younger than Pauline. She sold her sheep to Dutch in the spring of 1920 and then married him. Dutch was born in Germany as Hasselbush, but the family Anglicized their German name during World War I when anti-German sentiment was running high. To further hide their German background, Dutch and his brother lied by calling Nebraska their birthplace when they enlisted in the U.S. Army. Pauline described Dutch as "quiet, but like any young man pretty sharp."[45]

She and Dutch had four children and continued in the sheep business. By then the couple was good friends with their Ute neighbors, such as Ole Santio. They were also close to the well-known African-American cowboy in the area, Charlie Glass. Her oral history tells many stories of life in Willow Creek, but none more harrowing than that of her son, Chuck Turner, almost drowning under a frozen Willow Creek.[46]

Dutch and a neighbor to the north were building a bridge across Willow Creek one winter. The creek was frozen except for a few air holes, over which both men's children were jumping. All the children cleared a pretty large hole except Chuck, who fell in and then disappeared under the ice, barreling downstream. The children screamed to Dutch who ran a quarter-mile downstream to find the next break in the ice. When Chuck's body came into sight, Dutch pulled him out of the freezing water. He was still breathing, and Dutch rushed him home in a wagon. His clothes were frozen stiff. It took all day to warm him up so that he ceased shaking. As Pauline told the story, "the next morning, he woke up singing and was just fine."[47]

The Hazelbushes sold their ranch to the Bureau of Indian Affairs (BIA) in 1939 as part of the Hill Creek Extension of the Ute reservation. They purchased the West Uintah Motel in Vernal and a large home next to it. They had two good years running the motel until gas rationing started with the advent of World War II. Later Dutch operated heavy equipment for a while in Dugway, Utah. Pauline was active in many civil organizations in Vernal. Dutch died September 29, 1959, in Salt Lake City at St. Mark's Hospital from a pulmonary embolism aggravated by emphysema. He was sixty-seven.

Pauline lived another two decades, dying in Fruita, Colorado, in 1980 at age ninety-one.[48] At the end of her life, she marveled that she had begun married life in a cabin with a dirt floor and now saw that telephones, automobiles, airplanes, and mechanized farm equipment had become necessities of life. She wrote, "Men have landed on the moon and plan to visit Mars. All these modern miracles are a long way from the horse and buggy days of my youth. I wonder what changes will come in the next 90 years.... I have led a full and interesting life."[49]

3.11 Recent view of petroglyphs at ET6-20. Photo: Dan Bauer.

One can infer that someone in the Hazelbush family was present to welcome the Harvard boys. On the following morning, July 25, they returned up canyon about a mile to investigate a relatively intact stone-and-adobe granary with intact wooden poles (ET6-19). The fact that they backtracked a mile to find it might have been because someone at the ranch told them about the granary, which is tucked away and difficult to see.

The granary was sitting in a side canyon that archaeologists called Big Water (it is probably the eastern tributary to Willow Creek called Meadow Creek today). Accessing it involved another steep scramble 250 feet above the valley floor. There were indications the interior had been plastered with a thin coat of adobe, but there was nothing on the inside but scattered stones and "rat shit."[50] It was the only granary they described in all of Willow Creek Canyon.

3.12 Recent view of the red and white "shield" at ET6-21 in middle Willow Creek. Photo: Dan Bauer.

At this point, the overland explorers rode north from Big Water Canyon about five and a half miles before stopping to describe and sketch a site with petroglyphs, including an unusual human figure (ET6-20),[51] and then they repeated the exercise a half-mile beyond that with a site with "red and white painted men and small white figures" (ET6-21).[52] Two miles farther, they stopped to describe another rock art site (ET6-22), this one with red, white, and yellow images.[53] By midday, they had already made an arduous climb to a granary and stopped and sketched three rock art sites, all while traveling ten miles on horseback.

They dallied to explore for sites and sketch rock art, and they didn't seem to be in a big hurry, even though their plan was to rejoin the main expedition later that day in Hill Creek. They stopped for lunch at a "Ute ranch" about seventeen miles below the Hazelbush Ranch, perhaps the ranch of Ole Santio previously mentioned, a long-time neighbor of the Hazelbush clan. If Santio was home at the time, the crew never mentioned it. At this point they crossed a divide between Hill Creek and Willow Creek, riding another seventeen and a half miles to the Aus Wardle Ranch on Hill Creek where Donald Scott and the rest of the expedition was base-camped. In all, they had logged at least 35 miles on this leg of the adventure—and roughly 115 miles in seven days.

Their decision to cut west up and over a divide to Hill Creek, rather than continue descending Willow Creek to its confluence with Hill Creek, certainly

3.13 The 1931 notes did not mention nor did they sketch these red, white, and blue-green figures next to the shield at ET6-21 in middle Willow Creek. Photo: Dan Bauer.

saved them several miles of trail riding. But that shortcut also meant they never saw the spectacular historic rock art panels in lower Willow Creek—some of the finest examples to be found anywhere.

Post Script

At this point, we return to the question posed earlier in this chapter as to why the overland exploration party discovered so little in Willow Creek, at least compared to Hill Creek. As noted in the previous chapter, their explorations of Florence Creek and Chandler Creek had also revealed only a few sites, but the archaeologists had clearly missed far more sites than they had described. Was the same thing true in Willow Creek and they simply didn't notice them? That is probably the case to some extent, but not entirely.

As part of our reidentification efforts, we re-examined a state database of all Peabody crew sites documented in Willow Creek over the years. Unlike Florence Creek and Chandler Creek, which have not been revisited by archaeologists since the 1930s, Willow Creek has seen dozens of archaeological investigations over the past four decades. These were not formal university research projects, but rather surveys in advance of oil and gas exploration. Under provisions of Section 106 of the National Historic Preservation Act, developers must first identify significant archaeological sites that might be directly or indirectly impacted by the development. During the course of these Section 106 projects, archaeologists have examined an estimated 20 to 25 percent of middle and lower Willow Creek. This should give a fairly good sample of the entire canyon.

If the Crimson Cowboys had simply missed the granaries and residential sites, then the later surveys should have identified them. But that is not the case. Only thirty-two prehistoric or historic Ute sites have been documented between the mouth of Willow Creek on the north and the lower Hazelbush Ranch on the south, a distance of at least thirty-five miles. Most of these were rock art sites, and only two were granaries. Not a single prehistoric residence has been formally documented anywhere in the drainage.

That leaves us with two possible scenarios. One, even though archaeologists have examined a good chunk of Willow Creek, the restricted nature of those investigations—they investigate only those sites directly in the path of development—means there might have been dozens or even hundreds of sites

3.14 Waldo Forbes near the end of the Willow Creek investigations. Photo taken on July 22 or 23. Courtesy of the Peabody Museum of Archaeology and Ethnology, Harvard University (PM No. 971-21-10/100162.1.467, File 99380251).

just outside their narrow corridor of investigation. In other words, the sites are actually there, but because they sit outside the small development area, they were not documented. Support for this comes from the fact that none of the sixteen Willow Creek sites described in 1931 have been documented since that time, even though several are clearly visible from the road in the bottom of Willow Creek.

The second scenario is that prehistoric farmers might not have utilized Willow Creek to the same extent or in the same manner as Hill Creek. It should have been. Almost everywhere in this arid region, vibrant agricultural communities sprang up anywhere there was permanent water. Permanent water flows here, and today ranchers easily divert the stream onto the flat, verdant floodplain. And there are plenty of nooks and crannies ideal for granaries, and plenty of terraces and bluffs and ridgelines that would have been suited for residences. But evidence for these is minimal, at best.

Exploring the "why" is a question for future generations of archaeologists. Maybe soil qualities are different here, and maize simply doesn't grow well here. Maybe Willow Creek was deeply entrenched in prehistoric times and the limited engineering skills of the early corn farmers did not allow them to dam the creek and raise the waters high enough to water their fields. Maybe flash flooding in the summer months was more prevalent here, and crop losses to flooding far exceeded the cost of planting, tending, and harvesting. Or maybe there are other reasons no one has thought of yet.

4.1 Massive stone towers at Fort Rocking Chair above the Taylor Ranch in Hill Creek Canyon. Photo: Dan Bauer.

Castles in the Sky

The Hill Creek Excavations

4

THE PREHISTORIC architecture of Hill Creek Canyon is spectacular by any standard: Stone towers top what seem to be inaccessible mushroom-shaped outcrops. Clusters of stone rooms—perhaps small villages—are perched high on defensible mesa tops with commanding views of the valley floor. And the canyon walls boast hundreds of pecked and painted images depicting the natural world and the supernatural. In some instances, the tower walls stand twenty feet high or more, inspiring awe and myriad questions. Who were these ancient builders? What was the purpose of these buildings that have stood the test of time? If indeed defensive, who were they afraid of and why?

The Hill Creek ruins were no secret in 1931, but they had never really been studied, and no trained archaeologist had ever sunk a shovel into them. Donald Scott was determined to change that. In fact, excavating the Hill Creek ruins appears to have been one of two overriding priorities of the Claflin-Emerson Expedition that year (the other was excavating Rasmussen Cave in Nine Mile Canyon, discussed in chapter 8). Hill Creek might very well have been a measuring stick by which the success—or failure—of the 1931 expedition would be gauged.

Hill Creek came to Scott's attention through two brief reports written by Dr. J. Walter Fewkes, chief of the Bureau of American Ethnology at the Smithsonian Institution. Scott might even have communicated with the respected archaeologist and anthropologist prior to his death in 1930, the year before the expedition. In 1916, Fewkes was leading efforts to stabilize and preserve ruins in Mesa Verde National Park, but when funding ran out at the end of September of that year he began a search for "undescribed buildings" that were "new to science."[1]

4.2 A modern resident of Hill Creek Canyon. Photo: Dan Bauer.

A. H. Kneale, the government agent at the Ute reservation in Fort Duchesne, wrote to Fewkes about the Hill Creek ruins, and in October of that year Fewkes made a circuitous journey from Mesa Verde to Ouray, where he was joined by T. J. Lemmon of Dallas, Texas; the expedition guide, a Mr. Owen, who was described as "the official farmer" of the reservation; and an unnamed Ute teen who served as the expedition driver. They base-camped at the Taylor Ranch—the same ranch that would serve as a two-day camp for the Claflin-Emerson Expedition fifteen years later.

Fewkes was steeped in the archaeology of the Ancestral Puebloans of Mesa Verde, and it is not surprising that he would compare Hill Creek's ruins to that region. In fact, he saw little difference, except that the quality of Hill Creek architecture was not as good and there were surprisingly few artifacts of any kind. The latter point led him to question whether or not the sites were even residential. As Fewkes observed, the Hill Creek ruins were typically of two types: (1) "true mushroom rock ruins, as their name implies... perched on top of isolated rock pinnacles," and (2) defensible structures on narrow mesa tops overlooking the valley.[2]

Fewkes offered detailed descriptions of eight different sites, supplemented by excellent drawings and photographs, of the unusual ruins found in Hill Creek. He then proceeded to ask questions that have bedeviled archaeologists ever since. He said, for example, that their locations suggest

> that these towers were constructed for lookouts and for defense, but the questions might very pertinently be asked why should either of these uses necessitate three or four almost identical buildings grouped together, when one would be sufficient? Why are some of them in places where there is no broad outlook? The massive character of the walls suggests a fortification, but why if defense were the only explanation of their use would not one large building be preferable to many, especially as it would be more easily constructed?[3]

Fewkes's questions probably whetted Scott's appetite to study the ruins more closely. By 1931, most places in the Southwest had already been pilfered and picked over by museum expeditions from all over the world, as well as by looters. Hill Creek had probably escaped attention because of Fewkes's observations that there were no artifacts of any kind, something that would have deterred earlier expeditions interested in artifacts and curiosities for their collections.[4]

Another character also had his sights set on Hill Creek at this same time: Dr. Albert B. Reagan, a schoolteacher with the U.S. Indian Field Service in Ouray and a geologist by training. Reagan was not a trained archaeologist, but he had spent decades exploring and excavating archaeological sites, publishing scores of short reports in natural history journals as he went. He somehow cajoled the Secretary of Interior into giving him an excavation permit for public lands, which he pursued with gusto under the umbrella of the Museum of Anthropology in Santa Fe. By his own account, he first investigated Hill Creek sites in 1930 (and most years after that through 1935), using Fewkes's report as a road map to find those sites described in 1916. In some instances, the Harvard boys arrived at sites only to find that someone, probably Reagan, had beat them to the punch.

4.3 Pedestal Rock (ET6-4) as it appears today. Photo: Dan Bauer.

Pedestal Rock

On July 19, Donald Scott and his company—John O. Brew, William Bowers, Dave Rust, and Dafton Thompson—began to make their way down Hill Creek Canyon to the north toward the mouth of Horsecorn Canyon. They must have started late in the day because they only traveled a few miles and visited only two sites before camping at the Elery Wild ranch about a mile above Horsecorn.

Wild had arrived here some years before with his wife, Jennie, their toddler son, and Elery's brothers, Gilbert and Leo (or Les), the latter of whom had his own place a few miles up canyon

4.4 John "Jo" Brew leans against a stone wall at ET6-2. This photo was taken on July 19. Courtesy of the Peabody Museum of Archaeology and Ethnology, Harvard University (PM No. 971-21-10/100162.1.344, File 99380227).

4.5 Recent view of ET6-2. Photo: Dan Bauer.

at the mouth of Post Canyon.[5] With his brother Gilbert, Elery had purchased his ranch from what remained of the Webster City holdings.[6] Their grandparents were Mormon converts from England who settled in American Fork near Provo, Utah. Their father, Earnest, moved his ranching family to Ferron, Utah, in Castle Valley.[7]

Sometime in the 1920s, the brothers came to the Hill Creek country to ranch. As Waldo Wilcox recalls, "Gilbert was a big fat guy, and Elery was a little skinny guy." Wilcox thought Gilbert didn't take care of himself and believed he wasn't going to live very long.[8] In fact, Gilbert was very large—only five feet five inches but weighing in at 228 pounds—but he served in the U.S. Army in World War I and even registered for the draft during World War II. He died of a heart attack in 1946 at the age of fifty-one. Leo died in 1969 at age seventy.[9] Not much is known about Elery, but Waldo Wilcox said the family ran a good ranch. The Peabody group paid Wild and others two to three dollars per day for pasturage,[10] although they seem to have stayed here only one night before moving to the Wardle Ranch at the mouth of Horsecorn where they would base-camp for the next week.

The first site encountered on July 19 (ET6-1), located about two miles above Horsecorn and a mile above the Wild Ranch, was a rock shelter with smoke staining on the ceiling. It was a loosely constructed stone wall across the front, and charred juniper beams lying about. They excavated in two areas of the floor, encountering reddened earth from old fire hearths and small chunks of charcoal, but nothing else. Elery Wild told Brew at this point that "Utes were in the canyon for a considerable time, and remains of their camps are all over, both on the cliffs and the flats."[11] But the Harvard boys seemed to have dismissed Ute sites altogether; their interest was directed towards the corn-growing Fremont peoples.

A half-mile farther downstream they investigated a narrow ledge about one and a half to five feet wide and eighty feet long (ET6-2). Two walls had been constructed across this ledge, and looters' pits sat exposed "but apparently not to bedrock," Brew wrote. Excavations revealed little beyond rat dung and refuse brought to the ledge by packrats. Brew's curiosity, however, was piqued by two willow sticks about five inches long with bark still on them, lying horizontally behind one of the walls. He wrote, "The area behind the wall seems altogether too small for living purposes. The area at the base of the cliff disclosed no remains or refuse heaps of any sort."[12]

The following day, they excavated a small storage cist in a side canyon about a half mile above the Wild Ranch (ET6-3), recovering corncobs, a willow tube, greasewood sticks, and "wild rice twigs." They found a fire hearth below the cist at a depth of fifty-four centimeters, suggesting that even more ancient residents had occupied the shelter previous to the construction of the cist used to store maize.[13] The excavations consumed most of the morning, and by afternoon they had moved on to Fortification Rock (ET6-7) above the Wardle Ranch at the mouth of Horsecorn Canyon. At this point, Scott observed that

> Pictographs were found with increasing frequency along the walls as we proceeded down the creek until, upon arriving at Fortification Rock (ET6-7) we found the faces of the cliff at the base of the butte almost covered with them. These pictographs present certain new features, as well as distinct southern types including those characteristic of the Fremont region.[14]

Scott noted that the images were carefully photographed, and he promised he would analyze them in the near future—something that he never completed.[15] The photographic images are of high quality and certainly deserving of future study. The remainder of July 20 they focused on the rock art here.

4.6 Excavations at ET6-3. These occurred on July 20. Courtesy of the Peabody Museum of Archaeology and Ethnology, Harvard University (PM No. 971-21-10/100162.1.336, File 99380320).

At the Wardle Ranch, the expedition found itself surrounded by ruins and rock art on every side—they were in the thick of it. They would remain here through the morning of July 27. Their hosts, long-time locals Austin and Hazel Wardle, would have been excellent informants to the expedition, but Scott makes no mention of them. Austin's father, Jedidiah, a convert to Mormonism, brought the family from Fort Bridger, Wyoming, to the Uinta Basin in the early twentieth century. Shortly thereafter, he established a ranch near where Willow Creek enters the Green River.

Born in 1901, Austin, or "Aus," grew up with Utes as his neighbors and spoke their language fluently.[16] He met his future wife, Hazel Ivor, when she was just eleven years old and was visiting her relative, Jik Taylor, from her Salt Lake City home. She returned in 1923 when she was seventeen and promptly fell in love with him in Ouray, where he was working at Matt Curry's store. Aus proposed, and she did not return to Salt Lake, much to her mother's displeasure. Her mother later changed her mind once she met her daughter's fiancé.[17]

A few years after their 1924 marriage, the Wardles bought the Hill Creek Ranch from her uncle, Ernie Taylor, for the cost of the taxes; Taylor had defaulted and for $102 the newlyweds got a log cabin and 160 acres. They lived there for at least a decade and a half. Their herd size, which grew to 385 head, grazed in the uplands above their ranch at the head of Chandler Canyon.[18]

Aus Wardle's fluency in the Ute language was so good that he once landed a job interpreting for some English businessmen negotiating with the tribe. His Ute friends called him "Too-ti-gaw," or "Brown Butt," because he swam naked in the Green River regularly with them, becoming very tanned. The Wardles got along very well with the Utes who lived in the area, in part because they spoke the language. They gave freely of their food and other goods, and they never had any problems with theft whatsoever. As Hazel later recalled, "We had just as many Indian friends as we did white friends and there was no distinction."[19]

The Wardles hired Utes such as Milton Jenkins to work for them, and also grazed their cattle alongside the Ute herds of Wallace Tabee and Buster Patterson. During the fall roundup they all helped each other. Later, after they sold the ranch as part of the Hill Creek extension, Hazel compiled a dictionary of Ute words. Brownie Tomlinson, who grew up in Willow Creek, claimed that the Utes preferred Hazel's dictionary to the one the US government compiled.[20]

When Hazel and Aus left Hill Creek they bought the store in Ouray and ran it from about 1939 to 1951 when it burned down. They lost everything, including some beautiful Indian baskets and rugs. During their days running the store, they witnessed many Bear Dance and Sun Dance gatherings nearby. Hazel just watched, but Aus participated in the Bear Dance, which happened in early spring. He was one of the few Anglos who dared do so.[21]

From their base camp at the Wardle Ranch, the Harvard crew backtracked on July 21 to investigate ruins on and around Pedestal Rock (ET6-4) at the mouth of what they called Tom's Canyon, located about three miles above Horsecorn Canyon.[22] This site is typical of what Fewkes had earlier referred to as a mushroom-rock ruin, and in fact it might be the same site Fewkes called Inverted Cone Ruin.[23] Reagan had also visited the site in 1930 (Reagan's Site 10) and accessed the pinnacle top by a ladder. He doesn't say if he excavated here, but locals previously told him that "several artifacts have been obtained from this site, among which were beans, bark, string, a milling stone, and a spinning stick."[24]

4.7 Some of the rock art photographs taken in 1931 at the base of Fortification Rock. Note the images have been chalked to enhance their contrast in the photos. Courtesy of the Peabody Museum of Archaeology and Ethnology, Harvard University (PM No. 971-21-10/100162.1.220, File 99380263).

4.8 The Claflin-Emerson crew used ropes to gain access to the top of Pedestal Rock (ET6-4). This photograph was probably taken on July 21. Note Dave Rust walking into the frame on the left. Courtesy of the Peabody Museum of Archaeology and Ethnology, Harvard University (PM No. 971-21-10/100162.1.303, File 99380224).

In addition to the structure on top of the pinnacle, obvious to all, there were three circular structures around the base of the outcrop. Over the next two days and again on July 24, all four structures were excavated. They did not discover much, but enough to lay to rest Fewkes's idea that the structures were not residential. All three structures at the base of the pinnacle had charcoal layers, along with animal bones from cooking fires, and a mano and a metate that implied seeds were being processed into meal.[25]

Accessing the fourth structure on top of the pinnacle at ET6-4 involved "throwing a rope over the rock and anchoring it to a tree,"[26] something Elery Wild and probably others had done before; he probably instructed the Harvard boys on how to anchor the ropes and swing onto the pinnacle tops. Wild told them the only thing he found on top was a human jaw.[27] Scott and Dafton Thompson hoisted themselves to the top and discovered a dry-laid stone wall around the perimeter. The walls were about a half-meter high in 1931, and the amount of wall rubble on the interior suggested they were once much higher. Scott and Thompson promptly began "digging around and throwing down rocks."[28] At bedrock, they found a fire pit that had been excavated into the bedrock and was filled with charcoal, ash, burned bone, and charred wood.[29]

Later on July 22, the archaeologists found time to explore up Tom's Canyon at least as far as three hundred feet where they found a rock shelter with a stone wall constructed across the front (ET6-5). Although they did not enter it, they wrote "the exact nature of the structure indeterminable."[30] They might have noticed this site while working on Pedestal Rock. They noted a similar rock shelter near the mouth of Tom's Canyon on the west side of Hill Creek (ET6-6), but after getting into it they doubted whether it was an actual wall or a natural roof collapse.[31]

Fortification Rock

By the following day,[32] they had begun to investigate the impressive ruins at Fortification Rock (ET6-7),[33] situated on an isolated, narrow mesa top at the mouth of Horsecorn Canyon just above the Wardle Ranch. The mesa was created when Hill Creek changed course, eroding what now looks like an island that guards the entrance to Horsecorn. Isolated mesa tops are common in this part of the world, and small villages often perch on top of them, many with defensive walls blocking access to the main living area. One sits at the mouth of the White River just north of here called Breaking Wind Butte and another called Desolation Village at the mouth of Nine Mile Canyon, a short distance to the west. Both are strikingly similar to Fortification Rock.

The Harvard boys were the first trained archaeologists to plant shovel and trowel in these ruins, but they weren't the first to dig here. They found that someone had already left their mark, or "gophering" as the crew referred to it. And the site—Brew called it an acropolis[34]—was certainly a tempting target. The north half of the mesa top was littered with debris from the collapse of at least three and maybe five or more large rooms, as well as a lateral rock wall constructed to limit access to the settlement to a single entry point.

Fewkes had earlier visited this site, calling it Long Mesa Ruins, but he did not dig there.[35] The "gopher holes" might have been Reagan's excavation pits from the year before; he recovered animal bones, potsherds, red ocher, and "pieces of tomato-colored red rocks which probably had some religious significance, as similarly colored rocks have been found in shrines in other parts of the Uintah Basin."[36] He also described rock art at Long Mesa Ruins.

Like Fewkes, Reagan interpreted the architecture as "forts-lookouts which also served as religious edifices" and commented on the paucity of pottery and mortuary remains, suggesting the early inhabitants of this region practiced cremation.[37] In a colorful bit of speculation, Reagan surmised that sites like this one served as refuges "to ward off the murderous attacks of the head-hunting enemies to the northward who now and then made forays into the Region,"[38] and as "religious buildings being constructed in as nearly a circular kiva-form as their perched locations would permit."[39]

The Claflin-Emerson crew observed one large circular structure subdivided into two rooms, with walls more than six feet high, and "from the number of stones which have apparently fallen off, it must have been considerable higher."[40] Once subdivided, the two smaller rooms were quite small, seemingly too small for habitation, yet when they excavated through the debris, they found a hearth pit bored into the bedrock floor. Artifacts included a mano, a hammerstone, an arrow straightener, a stone drill, a stone bead, a spindle whorl, plain gray potsherds, and lots of charcoal from ancient cook fires—a catalog "relatively prolific for the region."[41] In other words, the site had all the trash items characteristic of a residential site.

Upon descending from the mesa, they also found another residential site within a shelter at the base of the cliff. Here they noted abundant artifacts, including potsherds, flint chips, corncobs, corn husks, a bean pod with three

4.9 View of the structures on top of Fortification Rock (ET6-7). The photo was taken sometime between July 23 and July 25. Courtesy of the Peabody Museum of Archaeology and Ethnology, Harvard University (PM No. 971-21-10/100162.1.391, File 99380209).

beans still inside, a pierced bone tube, another hammerstone, and more charcoal. They could not determine "from the character of the finds whether or not there was any connection between the habitation of this level and the occupiers of the houses on top."[42]

Neither the journals nor Scott's report mention that they collected at least four large chunks of charcoal and burned beams at Fortification Rock. The Peabody Museum later submitted these to the Tree-Ring Laboratory at the University of Arizona, and all revealed outside tree-ring dates between AD 957 and AD 1073,[43] or the height of the Fremont Complex occupation throughout the East Tavaputs and West Tavaputs Plateaus.

Besides Fortification Rock itself, the number of easily visible sites is impressive, but these did not warrant a description in any of the journals. Reagan did note at least three "cave" sites with artifacts; the sites guarded both sides of the canyon mouth. Another site he called a "cliff house," and nearby was an isolated promontory crowned by "the much dilapidated remains of an ancient house. Beneath the projecting rocks of the toadstool-shaped top of this promontory here are also parts of walls of rectangular rooms that are still standing, especially on its east front."[44]

At this point, the Peabody Museum journals become confusing due to the absence of definitive dates for various entries. The crew probably excavated at Fortification Rock on and off from July 23 to July 25, although Brew (and perhaps others) returned to Pedestal Rock on July 24 to continue excavations there. The overland horseback crew of Bowers, Dennison, and Forbes had returned from Willow Creek by the evening of July 25, and Waldo Forbes was dispatched to map the site—a task probably completed on the morning of Sunday, July 26, given that Forbes would have been exhausted by the marathon ride the day before. What is more puzzling is that Scott and company spent the better part of four days here, but the field journals indicate they only excavated two small rooms.[45]

While Forbes was busy mapping Fortification Rock, others set about exploring Horsecorn Canyon. At the mouth on the north side they investigated a large stone-and-adobe granary (ET6-8). Dennison scaled forty-six feet of cliff face to get into it. His field notes for this site represent an exceptional attention to details—seemingly overkill given the sparseness of his earlier entries.[46] Gunnerson, in his later synthesis, condensed Dennison's 440 words into a mere three short sentences.[47] It is not known why Dennison labeled this a "granary" when there was no trace of adobe, no corncobs were noted, and it had a side doorway, something rare for granaries in the region.[48]

Kidder then described a site about a mile inside Horsecorn Canyon on the south side. On a point about one hundred fifty feet above the canyon bottom, he found an oval structure and another in a shelter in the cliff face just above (ET6-9).[49] The vagueness of the description and absence of any photographs makes it difficult to ascertain exactly what this site was, but it might have been an open, circular residential structure. These are commonly situated on points and benches above the floodplain. The Crimson Cowboys would later observe many of these open residential sites during their explorations of Nine Mile Canyon, but they had not yet encountered any in Hill Creek and might not have recognized it for what it was.

The crew then returned to the mouth of Horsecorn Canyon, stopping to describe three granaries perched on a ledge (ET6-10) about a half mile inside the canyon.[50] Photographs depict crew members walking on a narrow ledge with a sheer drop of a hundred feet or more to the canyon bottom. They reported abundant corncobs, willow sticks, a piece of string made of juniper bark, and black-on-white potsherds.[51]

4.10 View of Claflin-Emerson crew members walking on a narrow ledge at the mouth of Horsecorn Canyon. This photo was taken on July 26. Courtesy of the Peabody Museum of Archaeology and Ethnology, Harvard University (PM No. 971-21-10/100162.1.433, File 99380216).

Rocking Chair Ruins

According to Rust's journal, they spent the night at the Wardle Ranch, then packed their horses the next morning to move to a new camp at the Jik Taylor Ranch downstream.[52] They passed two mushroom-rock ruins, High Perch Ruin and Leaning Pinnacle, without taking note of them. About a mile below the mouth of Horsecorn Canyon, they stopped long enough for Brew to jot a single sentence description of "a fort on a narrow prominence" (ET6-11),[53] and "faint traces of a wall on a point directly across the canyon from this [suggesting] the possibility of a second one over there."[54] They did not cross the canyon to investigate.

About a mile above the Taylor Ranch they stopped at a site known locally as "The Jugs"—twin pinnacles with a structure on top of each and another structure at the base (ET6-12).[55] Fewkes had earlier described these, calling them the "Twin Towers."[56] Reagan also had been here, noting a large depression, "probably a kiva."[57]

Despite the difficult access, the Harvard crew apparently reached the top of the pinnacles because they provided detailed measurements and descriptions,[58] though no artifacts were mentioned. On the opposite side of Hill Creek were two granaries (ET6-23) tucked into a side canyon with a typical array of corncobs and willow sticks.[59]

They continued their march north to the mouth of West Squaw Draw and the Taylor Ranch where they visited what they called Fort Rocking Chair (ET6-13), one of the largest and most enigmatic of all sites they encountered.[60] Fewkes and Reagan had both visited there, calling it Ruin A and

4.11 This site, located about a mile below Horsecorn Canyon, might be the one to which Brew made a passing reference (ET6-11) on July 27. Photo: Dan Bauer.

4.12 A partial view of "The Jugs" (ET6-12), visited on July 27. Courtesy of the Peabody Museum of Archaeology and Ethnology, Harvard University (PM No. 971-21-10/100162.1.435, File 99380322).

4.13 Recent view of "The Jugs." Photo: Dan Bauer.

4.14 Massive stone tower at Fort Rocking Chair (ET6-13) above the Taylor Ranch. This photo was taken on July 27. Courtesy of the Peabody Museum of Archaeology and Ethnology, Harvard University (PM No. 971-21-10/100162.1.27, File 99380244).

Ruin B.[61] There is a photograph of Albert Reagan and his "crew" at the site, implying they excavated here, as well.

Fort Rocking Chair was a massive stone tower on a point 250 feet above the ranch, with finely coursed stone walls extending about 20 feet high. The amount of wall rubble suggested it was once even higher. On the interior, a stone bench six to ten feet wide and about twenty feet long rimmed one side of the room. Looters, or perhaps Reagan, had tunneled into the bench only to find it was solid stone. And above the bench a doorway offered access to the interior by first stepping onto the bench and then the floor.[62]

A structure rimmed by a bench is unique in the Tavaputs country, although structures with interior benches are quite common in the Ancestral Pueblo world in the Four Corners, commonly in ceremonial structures or kivas. This probably led Fewkes to conclude this was, in fact, a kiva. The tower itself is probably the largest, certainly the highest, stone structure anywhere in the region. They found only a corncob.

But once upon a time there might have been a lot more here. Reagan commented that Veone Taylor (Jik's wife) and another man, Clifford Broom, had discovered several caches here. In one they found a water-tight basket that contained the bones of a child. In another they found a cedar-bark sack filled with corn, rawhide, and animal skin. Others had corncobs, resin, and something Reagan insisted was a "cloud blower," a clay pipe used by Pueblo peoples for sending symbolic puffs of smoke in different directions during religious ceremonies.[63]

The Harvard crew then investigated the south edge of the mouth of West Squaw Draw in an attempt to reach the mesa top. A large defensive wall (ET6-14) blocked their ascent. It was more than thirty feet long and almost six feet high, breached only by a small doorway. Behind the wall sat a pie-shaped room roughly ten feet to a side; excavations revealed only a single potsherd on the surface.[64] They camped that Sunday night at the Taylor Ranch.

Scott's Detour

At this point, the journals become increasingly confusing as to what occurred on which day. Rust's sparse journal indicates the move to the Taylor Ranch occurred on July 27, but that he and Donald Scott had departed. The expedition was in serious need of resupply, and Scott and Rust decided to motor to Ouray and then Roosevelt for supplies; they camped on a hill overlooking the Roosevelt High School. The two men stocked up on about seventy-five dollars' worth of groceries at Lambert's Grocery and fresh meat at Cash Meat Market, both in Roosevelt, and an unnamed grocery in Ouray.[65] While Rust stayed in Roosevelt awaiting repairs to the car, Scott and a local teacher and archaeology enthusiast, Walter Atwood, traveled to visit ruins near Myton about five miles outside of Roosevelt. By that evening, Rust was on his way back to Hill Creek with the supplies (although an electrical malfunction on the way prevented his arrival until the next morning).

Of course, this begs the question as to where Rust and Scott got a car to travel from Hill Creek to Roosevelt. The answer probably lies in an obscure notation in Dave Rust's journal that the expedition had been joined at the Wardle Ranch by Nelson Rust, Dave's adult son.[66] There is no indication Nelson was part of the overland expedition that departed from Green River. In all likelihood, he brought the vehicle—a pickup truck rented for sixty dollars—to Hill Creek to rendezvous with the expedition. By July 31, Rust was back in Roosevelt picking up more supplies.

Scott spent several days dallying in Roosevelt and Vernal, meeting with Albert Reagan to examine his photographic collection, and taking side trips to visit archaeological sites north of Vernal and in Brush Creek near the Green River. He then determined to travel to Salt Lake City to meet with Julian Steward, a brilliant young scholar recently named to head the new anthropology department at the University of Utah. The trip was a waste of time—Steward was nowhere to be found.

Because of Steward's important place in the history of American anthropology and because he was at the University of Utah at the time, his Utah story and correspondence with Scott about the expedition and about archaeology in the region bear scrutiny.

Steward had recently finished his PhD in anthropology in 1929 from one of the few doctoral programs in the discipline, the University of California at Berkeley. He had been Alfred L. Kroeber's and Robert Lowie's star student and had just taught two years at Michigan.

But University of Utah president George Thomas had lured him to Salt Lake City, partially at the urging of Steward's fiancé, Dorothy Nyswander. She was a psychology professor at Utah and a horseback-riding friend of the university president. Steward not only wanted to marry Nyswander, but he missed the Great Basin and the West. Thus, he ignored the misgivings of some colleagues who thought he was moving from a top-tier school to a provincial one. Steward, though, followed his heart. Plus, his salary was higher than at Michigan and his teaching load was half. Thomas hired him to create an anthropology program and revamp the natural history museum. His time at Utah, as at Michigan, would be short-lived, and again it was because Steward followed his heart.[67]

Even before his tenure in Utah, Steward had established contact with the Peabody when he met Alfred Kidder twice in Ann Arbor, in 1928 and 1930. No doubt as Kroeber's and Lowie's best graduate student, Steward gained peer stature in Kidder's eyes. And no doubt Kidder mentioned Steward to Scott. Then, in the summer of 1930, six months into his tenure at Utah, Steward traveled with Nyswander to the mouth of the Dirty Devil River where they met up with the 1930 Claflin-Emerson Expedition, led at that time by Henry B. Roberts.

Thus, when Scott began planning the 1931 field season around the Tavaputs Plateau and the Green River, he knew who Steward was and wrote him for advice. The tone of Scott's communication with Steward is clearly peer to peer. Plus, there is an obvious warmth. Steward had evidently impressed Kidder as well as Roberts and the other Claflin-Emerson people the season before. Scott even told Steward, who was just then overhauling Utah's museum, to come see what the Peabody had just done: "If you could come on, you may be sure of a royal welcome."[68]

Scott's and Steward's letters during the spring and summer of 1931 discussed current archaeology work in Utah led by amateur archaeologists like Frank Beckwith and Albert B. Reagan, as well as previous work in the region by Jesse

Fewkes and Henry Montgomery. They also bemoaned the increase in looting in the Uinta Basin. They exchanged photographs of rock art, and Scott promised to send Steward a list of Peabody publications. Then, as previously mentioned, Steward made a bold request. He asked that the Peabody partner with Utah for the 1931 season.[69]

4.15 Julian Steward records a Barrier Canyon Style rock art site in Hogup Canyon, about 1932. Photo: Utah State Historical Society, all rights reserved.

Steward was new in his job and had been told to make sure that prime cultural artifacts stay within the state. He explained this to Scott, along with other advantages of the arrangement. He admitted that "it would save my face in my own state, for I have been embarrassed more than once in trying to explain my failure in the Green River drainage and the lack of specimens from that part of the state." He went on to mention "state pride" and the urgency to acquire representative material of Pueblo culture from all areas of Utah "for educational purposes."[70]

Scott apparently seriously considered Steward's proposal (Steward wanted to call it "the Peabody–University of Utah Expedition"). But after talking to William Claflin and Raymond Emerson, Scott reported to Steward that the two patrons had shot down that idea. Still, Scott was sensitive to Steward's position. He thus offered to give the Utah professor "a representative collection of material found." Scott thought that it would appear as a coup if Steward could announce to President Thomas that the University of Utah had negotiated such an arrangement with the Peabody. Steward had to be disappointed, but he said he could see the sponsors' point of view. He told Scott that he hoped "this had not put you in an embarrassing position."[71]

Scott and Steward tried to connect when the Claflin-Emerson group was in Utah, but they missed each other. Steward had been working in the Uinta Basin in July before the Claflin-Emerson group arrived there. Then in early August, Scott came to Salt Lake City to find Steward, but the Utah anthropologist forgot to inform his department of his whereabouts. By the time Steward and his wife traveled to the Uinta Basin in early September to study Ute children, Scott and his team had just left.[72] And in the midst of all this, Steward's personal life with his wife was unraveling.

Although he and Nyswander worked together on projects such as a study of Ute children (combining the practices of anthropology and psychology had been fashionable for over a decade), they had a hard time reconciling their two active scholarly lives. She was at least as engaged a scholar as Steward, and she was further along in terms of publications. Also, Steward was a traditional male. He wanted his wife's full attention, as his second wife, Jane Cannon, confirmed to Steward's biographer, Virginia Kerns. Nyswander did not have the time or inclination to do so. Then another woman entered the scene, the abovementioned Jane Cannon.[73]

Jane Cannon was the well-educated, independent-minded, liberated daughter of Joseph Cannon. Her father was not only the editor of the *Deseret News*, the LDS Church–owned daily, the Cannon family loomed large in Utah political, cultural, religious, and business circles. Steward knew he was playing with fire. He had met Cannon in late March of 1931 when he was observing a Ute Bear Dance at Whiterocks, Utah; she was there on a lark with a girlfriend. Jane later said that "she remembered trying not to stare at him." He was by all accounts a handsome man. The two started seeing each other socially in Salt Lake City. By the summer of 1932, he asked Nyswander for a divorce; in the meantime, he had told Cannon he was divorcing his wife and "would she marry him?" She said yes.[74]

Steward knew that a divorce would end his career at Utah. First, two married professors divorcing at any university in those times, especially at conservative University of Utah, usually meant the dismissal of one of the spouses. Second, Nyswander was the more established faculty member and was also friends with President George Thomas. Third, another woman was involved, who just happened to hail from a prominent Utah Mormon family. Steward made the hard choice, made even harder because 1932 was the height of the Depression. Anthropology jobs were as scarce as snow in Los Angeles, so Steward had to be worried. Nonetheless, he submitted his resignation letter in January 1933. Through Nyswander's intervention, Thomas allowed him to teach out the year while searching for another job. But it took him another two years of grants and other part-time work before he found a permanent job at the Bureau of American Ethnology in Washington, DC.[75]

After he left Utah, Steward continued an association with Kidder and the Peabody. He visited Kidder in Santa Fe in May 1934 at the Laboratory of Anthropology. Then a few days later, Kidder took Steward and his second wife, Jane, to Pecos ruins where he was working.[76] The Peabody contributed in a small way to Steward's groundbreaking work in the Great Basin, especially his classic statement of his theory of cultural ecology, *Basin-Plateau Aboriginal Sociopolitical Groups* (1938). They gave him "one hundred dollars for collecting" in 1935 as he conducted field work among the various Shoshonean groups in the Great Basin.[77]

4.16 Fremont-style rock art common in Hill Creek Canyon. Photo: Dan Bauer.

Julian Steward would rise to become one of the most prominent anthropologists in the history of the discipline—renowned to this day for his groundbreaking approaches to understanding how human beings behave. But a visit with Donald Scott in the summer of 1931 was not to be. After a few days of waiting around in Salt Lake City, Scott rejoined the expedition, by that time camped in Nine Mile Canyon.

Rock House Ruins

The expedition, led by J.O. Brew in Scott's absence, was camped at the Taylor Ranch on the evening of July 27. After this, the sequence of events becomes muddled. This is due in large part to a photograph of the expedition at the Sand Wash Ferry dated July 28. If this is accurate, then the crew rode eleven miles to the Seeley Ranch, then excavated the village site, and then traveled another twenty miles or so on horseback to the ferry in a single day, a highly improbable feat.

We believe the date on the photograph is in error and the actual crossing occurred on July 30. This assumption is based on several factors: (1) there is an expense notation that the Seeley Ranch, the site of the village excavation, was paid seven dollars for hay, implying the crew actually camped there;[78] (2) Rust's journal entry for July 29 indicates they were camped at the Seeley Ranch, and the following entry on July 30 contains the simple notation "packs go to Hank's Ferry and cross";[79] and (3) any amount of excavation conducted carefully and properly, even by standards of 1931, would have required at least half a day,

4.17 Scenic view of Hill Creek Canyon. Photo: Dan Bauer.

leaving little time to make the remaining twenty- to twenty-five-mile ride on a rough pack trail to the ferry on the same afternoon.

We defer to Rust's journal entries, which state the expedition camped at the Taylor Ranch two nights and then at the Seeley Ranch one night. The crew departed the Taylor Ranch on July 29 to investigate one more site about eleven miles downstream, which they called Rock House (ET6-26), although Fewkes had earlier named it Eight Mile Ruin.[80] Reagan had also explored this site the year before. The impressive ruin was located above the Seeley Ranch, where they made their final Hill Creek camp. Not much is known about the Seeleys, who do not show up on the 1930 Willow Precinct census. According to Wilcox, they ended up in Colorado after the BIA purchased their ranch around 1940. Their property, however, was the site of a notorious confrontation between a cattleman/moonshiner and a Basque sheep man—Ben Morris and George Avjares, respectively.

The year before the Peabody Expedition arrived at the ranch, Ben Morris rode a mule into the Seeley Ranch, which Avjares was leasing at the time. Morris was bucked from the mule and accounts differ as to what happened next, but Morris's injured arm ended up in a sling. For some reason, probably part of a long-simmering animosity between cattleman Morris and sheep man Avjares, the two men fired at and wounded one another. Morris took a bullet to both his left lung and right arm. Avjares was hit in the right hip. Jik and Veone Taylor drove both men to the hospital in Vernal (Taylor had been one of Morris's best moonshine customers). A local court found Morris guilty of armed assault, and he spent at least three years in prison.[81] This was just one of many clashes that the affable and well-liked Oklahoman had with the law. During his lifetime he was charged with horse-stealing and various other infractions, but the law never nabbed him for moonshining. He later married a young girl from Maybell, Colorado, Becky Boan, and moved to Dinosaur, Colorado, where they lived in a cave and then a tent. He died in the early 1970s in his nineties. His wife was too destitute to pay for his burial, so the town's citizens took up a collection and buried him in an unmarked grave.[82]

Ben Morris was undoubtedly familiar with the ancient ruins of Hill Creek and Desolation Canyon, including the one above the Seeley Ranch. The ancient village (ET6-26), located opposite the mouth of Johnson Canyon, was the largest the Crimson Cowboys had yet investigated, with nine rooms perched on the edge of the mesa overlooking the valley some two hundred feet below. Some of the walls stood eight feet high. Littered about the surface were corncobs, and below the surface they found an arrow point, a stone bead, and animal bones.[83] It was hardly a rich haul of artifacts, but something they were probably getting used to at Hill Creek sites.

It appears the Peabody crew excavated only one of the nine rooms (Structure E), a rectangular room about eight-by-sixteen feet in size with walls nearly five feet high.[84] They carefully mapped the rest of the site but left it undisturbed. They apparently spent the entire day there. By the next morning, however, with pack animals in tow, they headed toward Nine Mile Canyon, an area even richer in ruins and artifacts than Hill Creek.

4.18 View of the Seeley Ranch from the mesa top to the west. They camped at the ranch on July 29. Nothing remains of the ranch today. Courtesy of the Peabody Museum of Archaeology and Ethnology, Harvard University (PM No. 971-21-10/100162.1.438, File 99380246).

4.19 View of the structures at Rock House or Eight Mile Ruins (ET6-26). The photo was probably taken on July 29. Courtesy of the Peabody Museum of Archaeology and Ethnology, Harvard University (PM No. 971-21-10/100162.1.358, File 99380228).

Maybe they were fatigued at this point, or maybe they were simply eager to get moving, but there are many other sites in this area that they either ignored or never noticed. As Reagan noted, at the foot of the mesa stands a large circular structure "five paces in diameter," and less than a quarter-mile to the northeast of that sit two smaller circular structures, and just beyond those lies a knoll with "an ancient village, three rooms of which still show in foundation." In the same area, Reagan noted a prehistoric irrigation ditch a half-mile long and an "ancient altar, built of rock that had been carried from the adjacent mesa."[85] Archaeologists have yet to identify or document these sites.

The overland route from Hill Creek to the ferry crossing at Sand Wash is not known for certain, but it undoubtedly followed a trail established by sheep men who used the ferry to move their livestock back and forth across the Green River. The ferry typically did not operate in the summer, but Scott, through Rust's pretrip planning, had arranged in advance to have ferryman Vern Muse there to move the expedition and all of its accoutrements to the west side of the river.

As discussed above, there is some confusion as to when the expedition actually crossed the Green River to begin their trek by horseback to Nine Mile

4.20 Claflin-Emerson crew excavating at Rock House or Eight Mile Ruins (ET6-26) on July 29. Courtesy of the Peabody Museum of Archaeology and Ethnology, Harvard University (PM No. 971-21-10/100162.1.361, File 99380229).

4.21 View of the ET6-26 today. Note the amount of wall collapse downslope. Photo: Dan Bauer.

4.22 Alfred Kidder, Daft Thompson, and Oliver Rasmussen loading the pack horses for the ride to the ferry at Sand Wash. © President and Fellows of Harvard College, Peabody Museum of Archaeology and Ethnology (PM No. 2005.1.110.1.155, File 99380253).

Canyon. This uncertainty is rooted in a photograph taken at the ferry which is dated July 28, 1931. But on that date, they were still working in Hill Creek. Based on notes in Dave Rust's journal, the expedition probably crossed the Green River on the afternoon of July 30. At this point, the horses and nine men made the crossing. Scott and Rust were not among them because they were purchasing supplies in Roosevelt.

Almost four months before the expedition left Green River, Donald Scott rightly worried about river crossings, especially one in the vicinity of Nine Mile Canyon, or "Minnie Maud," as he called it.[86] He knew that he wanted to spend considerable time in Hill Creek, east of Green River. And he knew that Nine Mile Canyon, to the west, was a priority. The question was: how to get from one side of the Green River to the other most efficiently. The nearest bridge across the Green River was in Jensen, Utah, more than thirty miles north of the mouth of Willow Creek. Dave Rust knew the answer to Scott's question, though, and the news was good; the "Hank Stewart ferry" at Sand Wash, two miles above Nine Mile, was still in business. And, as stated above, Rust had arranged to have ferryman Vern Muse float the team and their horses over.[87]

The Hank Stewart ferry had been a fixture at Sand Wash since the spring of 1920. The previous fall John Henry "Hank" Stewart had floated the ferry nearly thirty miles downriver from Tia Juana Bottom where he had operated for almost ten years. The once-divorced fifty-one-year-old was moving to Sand Wash with his new, fifteen-year-old bride, Elsie Wardle (by all accounts, their eighteen-year marriage was a good one). That same winter, the newlyweds took apart a four-room cabin, numbered the logs, and towed them on the ice to their new home. The reassembled cabin still stands today. The reason for moving the ferry? Local sheep men felt Sand Wash was a better, less contentious spot than Tia Juana Bottom to cross sheep between their winter pasture west on Pariette Bench and their summer pasture on the East Tavaputs Plateau. For a good decade or more, the ferry thrived.[88]

Stewart charged three cents a head, and in his best year, he made $2,700. Elsie was a full partner in the operation. Local stockmen noted that "she worked like a man." She was also an excellent cook, and her cabin sometimes served as a boarding house for ranchers passing through. She kept a detailed record of all business transactions. The Stewarts had one son, Arden, who was born in 1925; he later became Uintah County sheriff, a cowboy poet, and a historian of the region. Hank Stewart had a mining background through his father, Simeon, and his own past digging for Gilsonite. Thus, when times were slow in the winter, he hand-dug tunnels into the cliffs nearby, looking for oil shale in the magnesium sandstone in the Parachute Creek Member of the Green River Formation. Subsequent diggers followed Stewart's lead, but nothing came of their efforts.[89]

A few years before the Peabody team came through, Stewart sold the ferry operation to Chuck and Iola Sands who ran it for a few years. They may have sold it to Vern Muse, who was running the ferry in 1931, or Muse may have been working for the Sands. Nonetheless, the Harvard crew paid Muse ten dollars for crossing on July 30 and for pasturage for their horses.[90]

The Peabody boys would not recognize the crossing today. More than six thousand people every year use this launch point to float ninety miles of the Green River through Desolation and Gray Canyons. On summer days, one can see as many as a hundred people scurry about getting their rubber rafts ready for the adventure to come.

Postscript

By the time the Crimson Cowboys reached the crossing, they had documented seventeen sites and excavated nine of them over the course of eleven days. They had investigated roughly forty miles of Hill Creek and its tributaries. If artifacts for the Peabody collection were a priority, then they did not have much

4.23 The Claflin-Emerson Expedition preparing to cross the ferry at Sand Wash on July 30. © President and Fellows of Harvard College, Peabody Museum of Archaeology and Ethnology (PM No. 971-21-10/100162.1.24, File 99380238).

to show for their efforts. Gunnerson's catalog of Hill Creek artifacts currently in the museum lists fifty-five corncobs, a few corn husks, eight sticks, sixteen potsherds, two pieces of cordage, three manos, two metates, five hammerstones, seven chipped-stone tools, and assorted other artifacts, such as three beans, a spindle whorl, a shaft straightener, a bone awl, and pieces of charcoal—fewer than 120 artifacts total, and none exhibit worthy.

As would be the case in the coming weeks, the expedition passed through a canyon with archaeological sites at nearly every twist and bend in the stream. But they only stopped to describe a tiny fraction of them, passing others by without a mention. If Hill Creek is anything like Nine Mile Canyon—and its environmental characteristics are virtually identical, as are the architectural remains—then literally hundreds if not thousands of sites might be located along this stream and in the myriad side canyons entering from the east and west.

But more than eighty-five years after the Claflin-Emerson Expedition mounted their horses and rode west, we still don't know if that is the case. We don't know because no one has really looked. Reagan died a few years later and with him his interest in Hill Creek. James Gunnerson briefly visited in 1954, but his wasn't a comprehensive study.[91] Hill Creek, it seems, has been forgotten.

Contributing to this, the canyon is now all Ute tribal lands, and the tribe has not been eager to allow archaeological research there.

According to the state database of all archaeological sites, archaeologists have investigated only about one percent of the canyon drainage itself and documented only about fifteen prehistoric sites (most of the Claflin-Emerson sites have not been reidentified). Most of the recent archaeology has been focused on the mesa tops above Hill Creek, where archaeologists working in advance of oil and gas development have identified hundreds of sites. But the canyon itself remains largely unknown and the sites undocumented.

Hill Creek is still an important piece of the puzzle that is the Fremont Complex in this part of the world. It will be up to future generations of archaeologists, working hand in glove with the Ute tribe, to finish piecing that puzzle together.

5.1 Nordell's Fort in lower Nine Mile Canyon. Photo: Jerry D. Spangler.

5 Into the Thick of It

Nine Mile Canyon

How and why the Claflin-Emerson Expedition turned its focus toward Nine Mile Canyon is not altogether clear, or at least it was not written down in any of the expedition notes or records. Southern Utah cowboys might have regaled them with stories years earlier as they explored the ruins of Boulder Mountain, Waterpocket Fold, and Kaiparowits Plateau. It might have been a suggestion from another archaeologist who had visited the area. Or it might have been Dave Rust, their guide and photographer on the earlier Claflin-Emerson expeditions, who was paid seventy-five dollars on May 18 for a "reconnaissance report" in preparation for the grand expedition later that year.[1]

Even that report, however, did not prepare the expedition for the number of archaeological sites they encountered in Nine Mile Canyon, especially the rock art sites.[2] The transcription and summary of the original field notes, prepared by Donald Scott in late 1931, referred to Nine Mile Canyon as "almost a continuous picture gallery."[3] Even Rust seemed surprised, offering three consecutive journal entries between July 31 and August 8 that refer to "ruins everywhere," "some excellent sites," and "ruins all around."[4]

The archaeological riches of Nine Mile Canyon were hardly a well-guarded secret in 1931, at least not to locals. Some of them, like their contemporaries across the West, made a practice of acquiring artifacts for personal collections. As early as the 1880s, William Brock, proprietor of a hotel and saloon in Nine Mile Canyon, at what would later become the Preston Nutter Ranch, had assembled quite a collection of ancient pots and baskets from the ancient Fremont ruins in the area. His collection fascinated travelers on the Nine Mile Road, at least during the years before he fled the canyon to escape retribution for killing a local man in a saloon brawl.[5]

University of Utah geologist Henry Montgomery had visited briefly in 1892, and his colorful account in *The Archaeologist*, a popular journal of the day, probably drew the attention of Donald Scott and others at the Peabody Museum.[6] And others had visited over the years—esteemed archaeologist Byron Cummings in 1906 and budding anthropologist J. Alden Mason in 1909—but they left no written accounts that might have piqued the interest of the Peabody Museum.[7]

Most likely, the initial seed of interest was planted by one of their own, Noel Morss, a member of the 1928 and 1929 Claflin-Emerson Expeditions. Earlier in 1931, he finished his now-classic monograph that, for all intents and purposes, defined the Fremont culture for generations to come. In 1929, Morss and local guide Clarence Mulford took a break from their investigations near Torrey in central Utah and drove north roughly a hundred miles to Nine Mile Canyon. Once there, Morss noted an abundance of masonry architecture but did not assign any great antiquity to it, attributing it instead to more recent Ute arrivals. But he did stop long enough to excavate a cave, where he recovered the burial of a child.[8]

Archaeologists, especially in the early days of the discipline, have always been disproportionately interested in human burials. This particular cave, called Rasmussen Cave after their wrangler and the property's owner, Oliver Rasmussen, would become a primary focus of the 1931 expedition in the days ahead, when another burial would be recovered (see chapter 8).

But first the Peabody Museum crew focused their attention on lower Nine Mile—a bleak moonscape of a place never before visited by any archaeologist and somewhat off the beaten path, even by Nine Mile Canyon standards. A rutted, two-track road snaked its way west-to-east into lower Nine Mile, linking three remote ranches: Oliver Rasmussen's place at the mouth of Dry Canyon, Neal Hanks's lower ranch two miles farther east at the mouth of Cottonwood Canyon, and Al Pace's ranch another four miles to the east at the mouth of Maxies Canyon. Over the next two weeks, the expedition would base camp at all three ranches, paying the cash-strapped ranchers thirty-five cents a day for pasturage for their horses, and, on occasion, thirty-five cents per person for an evening supper.[9]

Available correspondence does not explain why the expedition chose to bivouac at the three lower ranches. Preston Nutter, who had a keen interest in archaeology, would probably have welcomed them as academic royalty. Nutter was a cattle baron, one who enjoyed the company of prominent politicians and judges. He had acquired an impressive library of archaeology and military tomes and had his own prized collection of relics and curiosities, including Navajo rugs and Crimean swords.[10] His daughter Katherine had even studied archaeology under Byron Cummings years before at the University of Arizona. And his palatial ranch—at least it was by Nine Mile standards—near the mouth of Gate Canyon not only afforded easier vehicle access to the Uinta Basin via the old Gate Canyon freight road, the area had abundant archaeological sites.

If the Peabody Museum crew had instead chosen to investigate middle Nine Mile Canyon around the Nutter Ranch, they would have encountered spectacular sites that today bear exotic names such as Fortress in the Sky and Warrior Ridge. The Peabody Museum crew nonetheless eschewed the creature comforts Nutter might have provided, preferring to literally pitch their tents with Rasmussen, Hanks, and Pace.

To the Pace Ranch

On July 31, the expedition's route to Nine Mile would have taken them west up Sand Wash a couple miles before the trail splits, with one track veering to the northwest towards Myton and the other to the southwest up and out of Sand Wash onto the north rim of Nine Mile Canyon. Their route must have followed what is today known as the Wrinkle Road, squeezed between the Badland Cliffs on the north and precarious canyon drops on the south. Whether or not a rough two-track road existed in 1931 is unknown. It is certainly possible, given the amount of traffic on the Sand Wash Ferry in those years—mostly ranchers moving sheep back and forth. At the very least, there would have been a good livestock trail, albeit a barren one with minimal vegetation and little water.

About ten miles from the Sand Wash Ferry they arrived at the head of Bull Canyon, the first major side canyon that allowed any sort of egress to the bottom of Nine Mile Canyon. It is

5.2 Lower Nine Mile Canyon along the Wrinkle Road is largely devoid of water and vegetation. Photo: Jerry D. Spangler.

5.3 Wildflowers in lower Nine Mile Canyon. Photo: Jerry D. Spangler.

then a five-mile ride from the rim. One journal mentions a road in the bottom of Bull Canyon,[11] although the seldom-used route today involves driving mostly in the wash and can hardly be called a road. About a mile and a half from the mouth of Bull Canyon, the group stopped at a small, circular stone structure perched high on a pinnacle (PR4-1). They paused long enough for Dennison and Bowers to describe the site[12] and obtain several photographs.

At the mouth of Bull Canyon they turned west and proceeded about two miles to the Pace Ranch. John Albert Pace kept one house in Price where his wife, Ada, and seven children lived, while he lived and worked the last ranch in lower Nine Mile proper. Census records for 1930 indicate he was living alone in lower Nine Mile Canyon and at the same time in Price with Ada and their children.[13] It was not uncommon for Nine Mile ranchers to maintain two places, their working ranch and another place in town far from the brutal winters in the canyon. Local legend has it that Pace, despondent over the continuing effects of the Great Depression, committed suicide at the ranch in 1937 while attempting to stay there through one punitive winter.[14]

Working for Pace in the 1930s was Dave Nordell, one of the most colorful characters in the history of the canyon, a notorious prankster and an ardent

5.4 (*above*) A small architectural site (PR4-1) on a pinnacle in Bulls Canyon, the first of the Nine Mile Canyon sites to be visited by the expedition. It was visited on July 31. Courtesy of the Peabody Museum of Archaeology and Ethnology, Harvard University (PM No. 971-21-10/100162.1.61, File 99380256).

5.5 (*right*) Modern view of the same pinnacle in Bulls Canyon where PR4-1 is located. Photo: Jerry D. Spangler.

collector of ancient artifacts (we would call him a looter today). Nordell's name is not mentioned in the field journals, but he would have been especially qualified to guide the expedition to the many ruins around the Pace Ranch.

Because Donald Scott was still in Salt Lake City, Brew was ostensibly in charge of the survey at this point, although there are no journal references by or about Brew until August 3. The initial investigations here seem to be unsystematic in that sites in the area were not investigated in linear order up or down the canyon as was the case during their previous investigations.

Also inhibiting an accurate reconstruction of the sequence of events over the next few days is the fact that none of the entries during this time are dated. By Sunday, August 2, Bowers, Dennison, and Forbes had left on their two-week odyssey to explore Range Creek and Desolation Canyon. We know, therefore, that any Nine Mile entries by these three crew members occurred before August 2. Brew offers an August 3 date for PR4-11, which also suggests they had

5.6 Alfred Pace Ranch in lower Nine Mile Canyon as it appeared in 1931. They arrived here on July 31. Courtesy of the Peabody Museum of Archaeology and Ethnology, Harvard University (PM No. 971-21-10/100162.1.23, File 99380261).

visited and documented ten sites before that time. If July 31 was a travel day and camp set up, then all ten sites would have been visited on August 1.[15]

They appear to have been focused on sites one to two miles below the Pace Ranch. The first one they encountered, PR4-2, was an unassuming rock shelter with pictographs on the ceiling and a stone retaining wall across the front. Dennison promptly disappeared down a figurative rabbit hole with page after page of highly detailed descriptions of the copious rock art there, finally conceding, "Good God! This would keep me here for a day or two."[16] They excavated a bit near the back wall of the shelter and along the wall but found "nothing either momentous or revolutionary."[17]

In the same area, Forbes briefly described a coursed masonry wall fourteen feet long and three feet high (PR4-3).[18] This is consistent with the rock wall later documented at 42Dc666, although if it is the same site, then the team missed the numerous granaries just upslope from the wall. The crew probably continued east to a point just past the mouth of Bull Canyon where the floodplain becomes a marshy bog. South of this bog is a narrow, flat-topped ridge or peninsula-like feature that juts into the valley bottom. On top of this, about 150 feet above the valley floor, they found circular masonry house structures and walls constructed around the edges (PR4-5). They estimated there were nine

5.7 Rock art at PR4-2 (42Dc671) as observed in 1931 (compare to Figure 5.8). This site was probably visited on August 1. Courtesy of the Peabody Museum of Archaeology and Ethnology, Harvard University (PM No. 2004.24.10532, File 120760012).

5.8 Rock art at PR4-2 (42Dc671) as observed in 1991 (compare to Figure 5.7). Photo: Jerry D. Spangler.

5.9 Aerial view of Sunstone Village (PR4-5 and 42Dc699), one of the largest village sites in the Tavaputs Plateau region. The expedition probably described this site on August 1. Photo: Jerry D. Spangler.

to twelve rooms here,[19] although a 1990 documentation identified nineteen constructed features of various shapes and sizes.[20]

Today, this site is known as Sunstone Village, one of the largest "village" sites in Nine Mile Canyon. Village sites, or places where multiple families aggregated into larger social groups, are actually quite rare in this area. More common are isolated residences probably used by a single family during the annual process of planting, tending, and harvesting maize. Sometimes, two such residences sit close to one another, suggesting an extended family unit. But only a handful of sites anywhere in the canyon resemble Sunstone Village with its five or more residences clustered together.

Sunstone Village was the easternmost of the sites they described in lower Nine Mile Canyon, and the journals do not indicate that they explored any farther to the east. Most likely, they returned to the Pace Ranch. Here, they investigated a large butte or pinnacle feature opposite the ranch, to which they assigned the number PR4-4. It is now known as the Cookie Jar. They identified eight granaries on inaccessible cliff ledges, some about seventy-five feet up and others about a hundred feet up.[21] They apparently spent their time looking up and didn't notice the two open residences near the base of the pinnacle, nor could they see that the ancients had somehow managed to reach the top of the pinnacle where other structures were built. And they never mentioned the rock art on various cliff surfaces at all different levels.

About a half-mile east of the ranch they found a rock shelter with an adobe floor and a granary tucked in the back (PR4-6). The deposits were rich in residential refuse: corncobs, knotted corn leaves, cordages, bone, flint flakes, pinyon nuts, a bean, pieces of leather, and something they referred to as a "flint salt spoon."[22]

About forty-five yards away they discovered an "impenetrable granary" constructed in a natural crevice in the cliff face and hidden behind a crude stone-and-adobe wall (PR4-7).[23] And in the same area they observed but could not access a massive, two-story granary high on a formidable, sheer cliff face (PR4-8).[24] In a single day, they had investigated seven sites—two of them more complex than anything they had seen in Hill Creek—and they excavated in at least three of them. The density of sites would become even thicker in the days ahead.

5.10 View of "The Cookie Jar" (PR4-4 and 42Dc653), a pinnacle covered with rock art, granaries, and other structures. It was probably described on August 1. Photo: Jerry D. Spangler.

Splitting Up

On August 2, Bowers, Dennison, and Forbes, along with wrangler Oliver Rasmussen, mounted their horses and set out for Range Creek and the west bank of the Green River (see chapter 6). Donald Scott was still in Salt Lake City and would remain there until at least August 4. That left Brew and Kidder as the only on-site archaeologists, assisted by wranglers Dave Rust and Dafton Thompson, and perhaps by Al Pace, although none of the journals mentioned him.[25]

It is unclear what, if anything, this party accomplished on August 2 because there are no journal entries for that day. It was also a Sunday, and they simply might have taken the day off. On August 3, Brew and Kidder set out to explore a series of sites just west of the Pace Ranch. They assigned the name "The

5.11 View of massive, inaccessible granaries (PR4-7 and 42Dc664). These were probably described on August 1. Photo: Jerry D. Spangler.

5.12 Aerial view of Nordell's Fort (PR4-11 and 42Dc5). Note the double-coursed masonry walls. The expedition visited this site on August 3. Photo: Jerry D. Spangler.

Pinnacle" (PR4-11) to the first site they encountered, but it is now known locally as Nordell's Fort, a massive stone tower perched on a bedrock outcrop high on the south side of Nine Mile Canyon with a commanding view up and down the canyon. The interior measured more than twenty feet in diameter, and the double-coursed masonry walls extended almost eight feet high.

They excavated the floor to bedrock, only five inches below, and found charcoal and bone, but nothing else.[26] The craftsmanship of the stone masons at this site is truly remarkable, with each layer of stone carefully fitted together and chinked with smaller stones to create a smooth, solid surface. It remains the best-preserved prehistoric structure anywhere in the Tavaputs Plateau region.

Somewhere in the same area of Maxies Canyon they climbed atop a pinnacle and found a poorly constructed stone wall (PR4-12), and a little farther up canyon they observed a granary perched on an inaccessible ledge (PR4-13) near the mouth of North Franks Canyon. They paused long enough to collect potsherds from the slope below and take a photograph.[27] They again crossed to the south side of the canyon where Kidder described a series of four rooms on another pinnacle top inside South Franks Canyon (PR4-14).[28]

These pinnacle sites were similar to ones Brew and Kidder had observed in Hill Creek. But these were also somewhat different, certainly of better quality. As they observed,

> On high points and "jugs," as in Hill Creek, are structures locally called forts. However, although presenting considerable similarity...these walls are of much finer construction, being laid up of selected stone in careful courses. This variation may be due to the presence in Nine Mile Canyon of a better quality of rock for wall building. Despite this difference, the sites are essentially the same.[29]

Brew and Kidder then backtracked down canyon a mile or so to a bench area above a spring where they found a circular

5.13 View of an inaccessible granary (PR4-13 and 42Cb769) on a ledge as observed in 1931 (compare to Figure 5.14). It was visited on August 3 or 4. Courtesy of the Peabody Museum of Archaeology and Ethnology, Harvard University (PM No. 2004.24.10572, File 138450006).

5.14 Same granary as observed in 1991. Note the amount of structural deterioration that has occurred since 1931. Photo: Jerry D. Spangler.

masonry structure, a large depression, and another "fort" (PR4-15).[30] Scott added a notation to Brew's original notes for this site, indicating,

> One of the unusual features of this site and other open bench sites in Nine Mile Canyon is the small number of stones lying about. There are usually walls of two or three courses or often merely a ring of stones completely dismantled. But there are never sufficient stones around to have been part of a wall or more than a very few courses. No artifacts found whatsoever, except an odd shaped stone which probably was a sort of hammerstone.[31]

In other words, the Peabody Museum crew just did not see enough evidence that people had actually lived in these structures. And given the large number of granaries, they assumed that a large population had once lived here. Scott later wrote that "a search was begun" to find the residences. He continued,

> At first it was thought that the living sites would be found in the rather copious overhangs on or near the valley bottom. Test pits were sunk in many of these but beyond an occasional slender charcoal layer no evidence of habitation was found. Certainly there was no lengthy habitation of these caves.[32]

5.15 View of residential structure (PR4-15 and 42Dc618) as observed in 1931. It was investigated on August 3 or 4. This site was later excavated in 1989–1991. Courtesy of the Peabody Museum of Archaeology and Ethnology, Harvard University (PM No. 2004.24.10567, File 120790003).

The more they searched, the more they realized that PR4-15 was probably a "typical" residence in that almost every one of these benches—and there are lots of them—had "circular rooms with occasionally a rectangular one; sometimes a fort or a defense wall at the point of access; and often with granaries in the wall of the cliff between the top of the bench and the valley bottom."[33]

Much of site PR4-15 was later destroyed when a modern ranch house was constructed at this location. What remained was excavated in 1990 by the Brigham Young University field school. In contrast to the dearth of artifacts evident in 1931, the field school observed more than a thousand artifacts from the deposits below the surface walls. Charcoal from a hearth inside the masonry structure returned a radiocarbon date of 880 ±50 BP, with a calibrated midpoint of AD 1173.[34] It seems that Brew and Kidder simply did not dig deep enough here.

5.16 Alfred Kidder excavating inside a rock shelter (PR4-16) in lower Nine Mile. The photo was taken on August 5, at the same time Donald Scott said Kidder was in Argyle Canyon. Courtesy of the Peabody Museum of Archaeology and Ethnology, Harvard University (PM No. 2004.24.10568, File 120790004).

Kidder's Quest

One of the most puzzling twists in the expedition journals is Alfred Kidder's exploration of upper Nine Mile Canyon. Scott's report to the Secretary of the Interior, which is largely a transcription of original field notes, indicates Kidder and "a local man" were dispatched to investigate Argyle Canyon and upper Minnie Maud Canyon, and they were gone about a week.[35] The "Journal of Expenses" for the expedition says the Argyle trip lasted from August 2 to August 7, and that four dollars covered pasturage. They spent twenty-five cents for sugar and seventy-five cents for mutton.[36]

The problem lies in Kidder's field journal, which describes twenty-seven different sites in the upper canyons, all of which occur under an August 7 notation. Kidder most certainly wasn't in Argyle Canyon on August 2 or August 3, because he and Brew were describing sites just west of the Pace Ranch on those days.

There are no references whatsoever in Kidder's journal for August 4 to August 6—three days where we do not know for certain where he was or what he was doing. But Kidder probably remained with Brew on August 4 and August 5: One photograph taken on August 5 at PR4-16 depicts Kidder chest-deep in an excavation pit.

It is certainly possible that the August 5 date for PR4-16 is wrong and that Kidder rode to upper Nine Mile on August 4 (at an average of three miles an hour it would have taken most of the day to get there), and he spent the next two days poking around, maybe even enjoying the seventy-five-cent mutton dinner billed to the expedition. Another scenario here is that Kidder and

5.17 One of the Argyle Canyon rock art sites visited by Kidder on August 7 (42Dc3922). Photo: Dan Bauer.

5.18 Another of the Argyle Canyon rock art sites visited by Kidder on August 7 (42Dc60). Photo: Dan Bauer.

the "local man" remained with Brew until at least August 5, and then on August 6 or 7 drove by automobile to upper Nine Mile. In other words, Kidder was up and back in only one or two days.[37] Of course, that does not explain the expense for pasturage for the horses.

All of the sites Kidder described in his journal are next to roads that existed at that time, and most site descriptions are a single line of text and, in the case of the rock art, simple sketches that could have been jotted in a matter of a few minutes at each site.

The "local man" is not identified in any of the museum records, but it was probably Neal Hanks. Hanks had a "lower" ranch at the mouth of Cottonwood Canyon, which later became a base camp during the expedition's excavations at Devil's Playground. And he had an "upper" ranch very near the mouth of Argyle Canyon; some of the sites mentioned in Kidder's journal were on Hanks's ranch.

Kidder's field notes state that he started his August 7 descriptions in Argyle Canyon. He identified several rock art sites, a granary (PR3-1), and two masonry structures (PR3-2 and PR3-3). He then described a few rock art sites at the mouth of Argyle Canyon and crossed to the south side of Nine Mile to the mouth of Sheep Canyon. Here his attention again focused on several rock art panels, including the famous red-and-white pictographs there that continue to fascinate

5.19 Kidder visited and photographed the famous Sheep Canyon Pictograph Panel in upper Nine Mile Canyon (42Cb657) but did not notice the large village site in the same area. It was visited on August 7. Courtesy of the Peabody Museum of Archaeology and Ethnology, Harvard University (PM No. 971-21-10/100162.1.290, File 99380252).

5.20 Kidder visited this granary site (PR3-4 and 42DC3916) at the mouth of Trail Canyon on his return to the expedition base camp on August 7. Courtesy of the Peabody Museum of Archaeology and Ethnology, Harvard University (PM No. 971-21-10/100162.1.96, File 99380323).

5.21 This large granary site (PR3-5 and 42DC2755) was the last to have been described by Kidder during his foray into upper Nine Mile. Kidder visited the site late on August 7. Photo: Jerry D. Spangler.

rock art enthusiasts to this day. He apparently did not see or simply ignored Valley Village, the cluster of Fremont residences at the mouth of Sheep Canyon that would be excavated five years later by the University of Utah's John Gillin, a Harvard graduate with close ties to the Peabody Museum.

He then proceeded west, apparently on his way back to the expedition base camp. He stopped long enough to describe and photograph granaries at the mouth of Trail Canyon (PR3-4), and at the Frank Alger Ranch where he described a large masonry granary (PR3-5). These latter granaries, although inaccessible to Kidder, had been "gotten into" by someone who had lowered himself into the granaries from above. They were "partly destroyed."[38] By August 8, Kidder was back with the main expedition helping with excavations at Rasmussen Cave.

Moving Toward Desbrough

Whether Kidder was gone six days or four days or even a single day, it seems that all of the descriptions in lower Nine Mile fell to Brew by August 5 (there are no entries at all for August 4). Brew continued to investigate sites near the Pace Ranch, stopping to excavate a rock shelter (PR4-16) where they found a charcoal layer at eight inches deep, a single flint flake, two animal bones, and fire-scarred rock.[39]

5.22 This open residential site (PR4-17 and 42Cb770) was largely dismissed in 1931 as "inferior," but later excavations revealed several residences, a burial, and radiocarbon dates consistent with Fremont farmers at about AD 1175. Photo: Jerry D. Spangler.

Curiously, Brew describes the next site (PR4-17) only as "south side, jutting ledge, 1/8 m. past South Franks."[40] The later transcription of the field notes adds details that it was an open residential site similar to PR4-15, but "inferior."[41] It turns out this site was anything but inferior. In 1989, the Brigham Young University Field School excavated four structures at this site, called Franks Place, identifying a wealth of artifacts and a human burial in the floor of the main residence where the deceased might have suffered a violent death. They reached a much clearer understanding of how these residences were constructed. The radiocarbon dates at this site were statistically identical to the one at PR4-15: about AD 1175.[42]

What Brew could not see from the surface evidence at this site or PR4-15 or the others located on benches in the area was that prehistoric builders first dug a circular pit about three feet deep. The pit walls were sometimes earthen and sometimes lined with stones. The floor was often composed of compacted soils, but on occasion wet clay was added to create a smooth surface. And above the pit edges, the Fremont stacked courses of flat stone slabs that were visible on the site surface to Brew and the others, sometimes just a few courses and other times up to three feet high. Brew's perception that there simply wasn't enough wall rubble derives, at least in part, from the fact that the floor was some distance below these walls. We now refer to these as semisubterranean pit houses. A good portion of the house was actually below ground.

The team photographed several rock art sites in this area, although Brew, unlike his colleagues, failed to provide any written description or sketches of them. Through comparison of the original 1931 photographs, we have identified five different rock art sites photographed in lower Nine Mile Canyon: 42Dc631 near the mouth of North Maxies Canyon, 42Dc639 and 42Dc640 just west of the Pace Ranch, 42Cb767 at the mouth of North Franks Canyon, and 42Cb3208 just west of Franks Canyon.

5.23 One of many rock art sites photographed by Brew in 1931 but not described in the field notes. The site has not yet been formally documented. Photo: Jerry D. Spangler.

5.24 One of many rock art sites (42Cb3208) photographed by Brew in 1931 but not described in the field notes. Photo: Jerry D. Spangler.

Brew then moved his crew another mile or so west to the mouth of Desbrough Canyon, at that time referred to as the upper Pace Ranch. On the east side of the canyon mouth they found a "triple cell" granary (PR4-18),[43] and another two hundred feet inside Desbrough was another "tripartite" granary (PR4-19),[44] neither of which was described in detail. And yet another series of granaries—at least four of them—they found opposite the mouth of the canyon on the south side (PR4-20).[45] In other words, at least ten individual granaries tucked in shelters and on cliff ledges within about 165 yards of each other, suggesting a large prehistoric population in this area.

For some reason, Brew did not investigate the north side of the canyon around the mouth of Desbrough beyond the granaries already noted. If he had, he would have seen a massive stone wall more than a hundred feet long and twenty feet high in places. If he had climbed to the wall, he would have found residences at nearly every level up to the wall and on the butte behind the wall. In fact, this area of Nine Mile Canyon features dozens of archaeological sites large and small, perhaps more so than any other area of lower Nine Mile they had previously investigated. They just did not recognize it, or perhaps they ran out of time to give the area due diligence.

After photographing three rock art sites next to the road without a word of description,

5.25 This rock art site near the mouth of Argyle Canyon is located on what used to be the Neal Hanks upper ranch. Hanks probably guided Kidder in this region on August 7. Photo: Dan Bauer.

Brew called it a day and returned to their base camp at the Pace Ranch. Donald Scott might have returned from Salt Lake City that day or early the next. On the following morning, August 6, the crew packed their gear and supplies and moved the base camp to the Neal Hanks Ranch just above the mouth of Devils Canyon, about four miles up canyon from the Pace Ranch.

Archaeologists did not return to investigate this area of lower Nine Mile Canyon for almost sixty years. As noted earlier, from 1989 to 1991 Brigham Young University sponsored a field school here.[46] They identified many of the Claflin-Emerson sites at that time, based on James Gunnerson's brief (and sometimes inaccurate) site summaries.[47] But the field school in those days did not have access to the Claflin-Emerson field notes or the photographs, and several of the 1931 sites remain undiscovered and undocumented to this day. By pure happenstance, the field school base-camped at the exact location as the Claflin-Emerson Expedition base camp, at what was once Al Pace's ranch.

The multitude of sites at the mouth of Desbrough Canyon has yet to be formally documented nearly ninety years after Brew's initial descriptions here.

6.1 Scenic view of Range Creek Canyon. Photo: Dan Miller.

6

Unnoticed Treasures

The Expedition to Range Creek Canyon

SUNDAY MORNING, August 2, must have been frenetic as Bill Bowers, Waldo Forbes, and Jim Dennison readied their horses for the great hundred-mile trek into the unknown—the West Tavaputs Plateau. The area was so rugged and inaccessible that it had scarcely been mapped by government surveyors, and the maps the Harvard boys carried with them were generally useless. Streams and canyons were plotted in the wrong place. The few cow trails did not, as they would soon discover, always lead to their desired destination, and their guide would prove underqualified for the task ahead. This part of the expedition was the most arduous and remarkable of all.

The paniers were undoubtedly double- and triple-checked. Once these young men rode out of the Pace Ranch in lower Nine Mile Canyon, they were on their own for the next two weeks, far from resupply and even farther from any help should the need arise. The first priority was Range Creek, a remote place with no roads and only two lonely cabins inhabited by cowboys. Beyond that, they would find no people whatsoever, only a wilderness inhabited by black bears, cougars, and rattlesnakes. It was the kind of adventure that young men relish when they are too young to recognize the severity of the challenge ahead.

The expedition knew next to nothing about the land deep in the heart of the West Tavaputs. They had certainly talked to cowboys, and they had Oliver Rasmussen, a veteran of the country for at least the past decade or so. They had heard about the ruins of Range Creek, and also of a distant drainage called Flat Canyon loaded with rock art and granaries. They had heard enough that Donald Scott wanted to investigate the reports.

Yet Scott must not have been impressed upon their return. The two-week adventure, where his students saw things no archaeologist had seen before, received short shrift in the subsequent expedition summary. The expedition report offers only two sentences: "This reconnaissance revealed a continuation of the same types of pictographs as found in the main canyon of Nine Mile. Very few of the open sites were encountered but a large number of stone and adobe granaries with pole roofs are to be found there."[1]

Not only does that summary fail to adequately represent what they observed in Range Creek, but it was flat-out wrong on many different levels. Actually scores of open residential sites, even small villages, perch on virtually every bench level and ridgeline in the canyon and in some instances on the canyon floodplain itself. There is no mention of the granaries built using a unique architectural technique, called cantilevering, where elaborate stone-and-adobe chambers were constructed on sheer cliff faces using wooden platforms wedged into niches and cracks to create a base for the granary. There is offered scarcely a word that these sites had far more artifacts than any site they had encountered in Nine Mile Canyon, or that many of these artifacts clearly had their origins in northern Arizona among Ancestral Puebloan peoples.

One can surmise that Scott—who was not along for the adventure—didn't appreciate what the observers noted in their journals. Or maybe Bowers, Dennison, and Forbes did not fully comprehend the importance of the sites they saw in Range Creek. What the journals say, though, is that they discovered and described twenty-nine sites in just four days, obtained a wealth of photographic images, and even conducted some excavations. Unfortunately, the observations

6.2 William Bowers (left) and Waldo Forbes (right) celebrate in Range Creek Canyon in 1931. © President and Fellows of Harvard College, Peabody Museum of Archaeology and Ethnology (PM No. 971-21-10/100162.1.26, File 99380245).

of these first archaeologists to visit Range Creek would remain largely forgotten and unappreciated for decades to come. It is now one of America's greatest archaeological treasures, thanks in large part to the preservation efforts of long-time Range Creek rancher Waldo Wilcox and his parents before him, Ray "Budge" and Pearl McPherson Wilcox.

The Wilcox Legacy

Most who knew him would agree Waldo Wilcox was a crusty cowboy of the Old West tradition. Strongly opinionated and often politically incorrect, Waldo, who died July 5, 2017, at age eighty-seven, lived the better part of five decades at his remote ranch in Range Creek where amenities were scarce and the few visitors came only when invited. Only two roads snaked into his ranch, one at the upper end of Range Creek Canyon and the other at the lower end of the canyon, and Waldo had both blocked with iron gates chained with heavy padlocks. Legend has it that he would run off trespassers with a shotgun he always carried in his pickup truck. When asked about those stories, Waldo just smiled, neither denying them nor attesting to their veracity.

Waldo would have been content to live out the rest of his life at his beloved Range Creek Ranch. But old age had limited his ability to care for the sprawling ranch, and his grown children were not interested in the ranch or their father's somewhat hermit lifestyle. Thus, in 2002, he decided the time had come to sell the ranch that had been in his family since the 1950s. The Trust for Public Lands initially ponied up the money to buy the ranch—deemed to be exceptional big-game habitat—and then they sold it to the state of Utah, which had also eyed the area for its big game hunting potential.

As a condition of the 2002 sale, archaeologists were invited to spend a few days looking around the canyon to determine what kinds of archaeological sites might be impacted by increased public access. The canyon had long been rumored to be rich in archaeological treasures, but few had ever seen it in person. Archaeologists had briefly visited the canyon in the 1930s and again in the 1950s, producing two short, unremarkable, and largely unnoticed articles.[2]

The rumors of unspoiled archaeological treasures spread, fueled in large part by the discovery in the 1950s of twelve perfectly intact, unusually ornate clay figurines, each with painted designs and clay applique depicting noses and eyes. Named for Clarence Pilling who owned a Range Creek ranch at the time, the clay artifacts remain to this day the most remarkable figurines ever found

6.3 One of the figurines recovered from Range Creek Canyon, now on display at the Prehistoric Museum in Price, Utah. Photo: Jerry D. Spangler.

north of the Colorado River. And they were reportedly worth a mint to private collectors.[3]

In 2002, archaeologists with Uinta Research, the Utah Rock Art Research Association, and the University of Utah were certainly aware of the legends and lore surrounding Range Creek, and they jumped at the chance to visit it. They were left speechless by what they actually saw. In a matter of only four days they had discovered and documented nearly fifty sites ranging from elaborate rock art panels to ancient farming villages to granaries large and small on nearly every cliff face. Everywhere they looked they found something new. And they had only looked at a tiny portion—less than one percent—of the canyon.[4]

Even more unbelievable was that, with only a few exceptions, the sites were in pristine condition—no looters' holes, no graffiti, no vandalism. To archaeologists accustomed to the widespread pillaging of ancient sites, to find an entire undisturbed human ecosystem where the past could be carefully studied layer upon layer was nothing short of a Holy Grail. Understandably, within a year the scientific treasure trove made international headlines. Hundreds of articles were written, many focused on Waldo's life-long efforts to save the canyon from looters.[5]

When William Bowers, James Dennison, and Waldo Forbes rode into the canyon in the summer of 1931, however, they had no inkling of just how important this place would become to science. There are scant references in their journals to the astoundingly high site densities here, often approaching fifty sites per square mile, nor did they discuss their thoughts or impressions of a place brimming with traces of the past at every bend in the canyon, perhaps more so than any canyon they had thus far investigated.

A Contested Land

They also had no idea they were initiating scientific work in an area that would one day become world famous as the "most pristine archaeological area in the lower forty-eight states."[6] They may, however, have learned from their guide, Rasmussen, that Range Creek had been fought over in court for a number of years (and would be for some years to come). For such a small, out-of-the-way canyon, it was the site of probably as much litigation as any ranching canyon in Utah's history. What they saw was a canyon whose beauty was self-evident, but whose range, as settler Joseph E. Wing later wrote, had been "denuded of its grass."[7] But their focus was neither on grass nor litigation. They were looking for Fremont ruins and rock art, of which there are considerable examples. When they later camped at John Darioli's ranch, Rasmussen may have told them a little about the tangled history of ranching in Range Creek. It is a tale with more plot turns than a Dickens novel.

Range Creek (originally called Ranch Creek) was, like other grazing lands around Desolation Canyon, one of the last places in Utah, or the West, to be homesteaded. In 1884, Augustus "Gus" Ferron, a deputy US surveyor, took his crew into the area and mapped it. The next year, he returned with four other men and formed the Range Valley Cattle Company. All four stakeholders that Ferron recruited were non-Mormon, well-educated, and prominent in business or professional life. They were Benjamin Van Dusen, Dr. James Dart, George Tracy, and John Scott. The group hired Clarence Allen to manage the ranch. He and his wife, Corinna Tuckerman Allen, a prominent women's rights activist, later joined the partners in business.[8]

In 1886 one of Van Dusen's nephews, twenty-four-year-old Joseph E. Wing, traveled from Mechanicsburg, Ohio, to work on the ranch. One could say he was Range Creek's poet. Much of what we know of the first twenty-five years of ranching life there derives from Wing's letters to his family and from articles he wrote years later. His writings show both the challenges and pleasures of ranching in an isolated canyon in eastern Utah. Three decades after he first went there, he would write nostalgically about living in Range Creek, saying that he "loved every hill and every mesa and every canyon... loved the horses that he rode and the great herd of cattle in his charge and his comrades, rough as bears and loving as brothers."[9] Wing fancied the area so much he filed on 160 acres of Range Creek land near the mouth of Turtle Canyon shortly after he arrived there. His filing later got caught up in a legal controversy between cattle baron Preston Nutter and John Niles and then between Nutter and John Darioli, the man at whose ranch the Claflin-Emerson group stayed.

The legal complications on these different sections of land in Range Creek (Nutter bought out the Range Valley Cattle Company in 1902) are too intricate to explain here. Suffice it to say that Nutter lost his suit; he died in 1936

6.4 A scenic view of one of John Darioli's later cabins in the heart of Nutter's Range Creek Ranch. Photo: Dan Miller.

at age eighty-one after he was thrown from a horse, five years after the Claflin-Emerson group came through.[10] Nutter's descendants later recovered the property, however, and sold it to Henning Olsen and his son Lloyd. The Olsens' struggle to make it in Range Creek ended when Lloyd shot himself in 1944 in a stone house Darioli built.[11]

Henning Olsen then sold to Bert and Clarence Pilling, the latter gaining notoriety as the discoverer of the aforementioned Pilling Figurines. These eleven expertly sculpted clay figurines date to about AD 1000–1100, or late in the Fremont period. Not wanting to live in the house where Lloyd killed himself, they built a log home nearby. They struggled as well and sold out several years later to Irwin Gerber, a Carbon County commissioner and a rancher. He owned land on the West Tavaputs Plateau as well as Rock Creek Ranch, where the Claflin-Emerson group headed after Range Creek. Gerber lost a lawsuit over access to his property and eventually sold the ranch to Budge Wilcox in 1950. As discussed in chapter 2, Wilcox had been forced to sell his Cradle M Ranch on Florence Creek to the Bureau of Indian Affairs a decade earlier.[12] Following Budge's death in 1981, his son Waldo took over the Range Creek property while his son Don ran the Wilcox land on the plateau.

Due to the nature of the canyon, Waldo could gate it at the top and bottom and completely control access. He had inherited from his grandfather, Jim McPherson, an ethic of leaving artifacts, structures, and rock art as is. Thus, after he sold the ranch in 2002, Range Creek became famous as one of the most untouched, unspoiled archaeological areas in the United States. Wilcox himself became a folk hero.

Cottonwood to Gooseberry

The Claflin-Emerson foray into Range Creek Canyon was but the first leg of an overland adventure into some of the most rugged terrain anywhere in North America. Range Creek was also the easiest leg. Cattle baron Preston Nutter, who had a headquarters ranch in Nine Mile Canyon, also had a satellite ranch at Cherry Meadows in middle Range Creek, and his cowboys had forged (or improved) different trails to move the large cattle herds between the two ranches. A year or two before the Claflin-Emerson Expedition arrived here, Nutter had improved the Cottonwood Canyon trail into a primitive road, which led to the top of the plateau but no farther.

Getting from Nine Mile Canyon to Range Creek involved dramatic climbs in elevations and precarious switchback descents of nearly five thousand feet in only a few miles. But there was a well-established trail the entire way, and their guide, the quirky cowman Oliver Rasmussen, probably knew it well.

Rasmussen had come to the West Tavaputs about two decades before by way of Sunnyside, a small mining community at the foot of the Book Cliffs. He arrived with friends and business partners Mental Taylor, Bill Gwithers, and Cecil Rouse, each of whom bought up ranches from old-timers willing to sell. Rasmussen ended up with a small spread—less than a hundred acres—at the mouth of Daddy Canyon. They all ran cattle—everyone in the area ran cattle—but their real interest seems to have been mining for various petroleum products, such as paraffin wax and asphalt road base.

At fifty-two years old, Oliver was older by far than the Harvard boys (and about the same age as Donald Scott). He was born in 1879 in San Pete County, the third son of Danish parents Rastus and Hannah Rasmussen, who had converted to Mormonism and made the overseas trek to join the saints in Utah. By 1900, Rastus, Hannah, and Oliver, by then twenty years old, were living in Sunnyside.[13]

Oliver does not show up on the 1910, 1920, or 1930 US Censuses, although he had moved to Nine Mile Canyon by at least 1918 when he dutifully registered for the World War I draft (he lied and said he was two years older than he actually was).[14] Oliver was not well suited to living the strict tenets of his Mormon faith, and he seems to have preferred the lonely life of a bachelor cowboy.

6.5 Oliver Rasmussen on the left with Nine Mile Canyon residents. Photo courtesy of Norma Dalton.

Nine Mile Canyon historian Norma Dalton remembers Oliver as an affable, wiry fellow, quiet and reserved without the usual cowboy braggadocio. He also had a bad tobacco habit. Dalton said, "He always had tobacco juice dripping from his face. He chewed tobacco and smoked both, probably at the same time." And his oral hygiene apparently left a lot to be desired. Dalton recalls her father always carried a jug of wine to share with his canyon neighbors, and most residents were "clean drinkers." But if Oliver took a swig, her father would quickly cork the jug and give it back to him. It seems no one wanted to follow after Oliver's mouth had been on the wine jug.[15]

Oliver had been an expedition guide and wrangler from the first day out of Green River, probably recruited by Dave Rust. There is no indication he knew the East Tavaputs Plateau country—Florence, Chandler, Hill, and Willow Canyons—but he was familiar with the West Tavaputs. He had been running cows here for more than a decade. He certainly knew Range Creek because all cowboys in this country knew Range Creek. As we discuss in chapter 7, he seems not to have known Desolation Canyon much at all.

There is no paper trail as to why the expedition chose Rasmussen over someone more familiar with the region, especially Desolation Canyon. The reason might well have been rooted in the fact that Scott wanted to excavate the cave on Rasmussen's small ranch. In other words, Scott got permission to dig and Rasmussen got a two-month job at decent pay, a rarity during the Great Depression.

The Range Creek expedition, composed of three younger members of the expedition—Bowers, Dennison, and Forbes—departed from their Nine Mile Canyon base camp at the Pace Ranch on August 2, aided only by Rasmussen and an unspecified number of pack animals. Beginning at 5,300 feet elevation, they began ascending Cottonwood Canyon, following Nutter's primitive road—actually more of a wide cow trail—stopping briefly about four or five miles up to photograph "several indistinct figures" before continuing to the top of the plateau near Bruin Point.[16]

Cottonwood Canyon is the largest drainage to Nine Mile Canyon, trending north from the high, forested plateau to the bottom of Nine Mile Canyon, a distance of about twelve miles. This route is longer, although not nearly as steep as other drainages. The canyon is dry today, but water flows in it during exceptionally wet years, and Bowers mentions they had access to water along the way. Bruin Point is the highest point on the West Tavaputs Plateau at 10,131 feet, or about 4,800 feet higher than their Nine Mile base camp, and it is a natural divide with some drainages flowing south toward Range Creek and others north toward Nine Mile.

Of Cottonwood Canyon, Bowers wrote, "Water is good, but we are told [it is found] in very variable quantities. Canyon strata and formations are well suited to house granaries, etc. as far as we went, but the canyon becomes so narrow [there is] little level floor."[17] The cooler high elevations of the high plateau must have been a delightful respite from the searing August heat of the canyon bottom, and photographs taken here depict a crew in high spirits waving their hats and grinning. This area is characterized by a sagebrush steppe interspersed with patches of quaking aspens, firs, and pines, as well as plenty of grass for the livestock. Temperatures here are a good twenty to thirty degrees cooler than in the canyon bottoms.

Once on the summit, the crew traveled south along the upper rim of Range Creek about three more miles until they reached Willow Springs, a fresh-water oasis at the head of Rock Creek, a permanent water source flowing east toward the Green River. Nutter's cowboys had built a cabin here, and the crew camped on the plateau, probably at the Willow Springs cabin before they began the descent down Gooseberry Canyon the following day, August 3. Gooseberry is a short, steep drainage to Range Creek, descending in three miles from about 9,600 feet elevation at its headwaters to 6,900 feet elevation—almost 1,000 vertical feet per mile in rocky, unstable terrain.

They arrived at the mouth of Gooseberry about midday, greeted by an absence of archaeological sites. Bowers wrote of their entrance into Range Creek,

> Above this, no strata or formations are suited, just sloping wooded niches. The water is good and constant, a small brook to at least 5 miles below Gooseberry. The valley bottom becomes wide and flat 2 miles above Gooseberry, and there are (suitable) formations 1.5 miles above Gooseberry, but still nothing was noted. Rock is mostly big, lumpy, strong, thick stratum sandstone.[18]

This reference implies the crew explored up canyon from the mouth of Gooseberry about a mile and a half before turning around and descending Range Creek. They encountered their first site about two miles below the

6.6 Preston Nutter cowboy cabin at Willow Spring where the overland crew spent the night before descending into Range Creek Canyon. Preston Nutter Corporation Collection, Special Collections, Marriott Library, University of Utah.

6.7 This unassuming rock art site is the first Range Creek site encountered by the expedition. Photo: Jerry D. Spangler.

mouth of Gooseberry at a quarter past one in the afternoon: a small petroglyph panel opposite the mouth of Little Horse Canyon.[19] A short distance away, they stopped at a rock shelter with red-and-gold pictographs on the interior and pecked figures outside the shelter.[20]

Locomotive Rock

The exploring party had continued only another mile, presumably following the existing cow trail, when they encountered a large sheltered area next to the valley floor and a granary tucked in a niche above (PR12-1). Forbes wrote, "The only remains are the parts of the wall next to the cliff at each side.... The only trace of woodwork is a stick [twenty-four by one and a half inches] in vertical position next to and outside of the south wall."[21] This stick remains standing to this day. The crew then focused their attention on the shelter itself, excavating a pit of unspecified size. He went on to say, "There are traces of charcoal down to [thirty inches] where there is an abundance of it."[22]

From this location, the crew scanned their surroundings, and they could not help but notice a large natural cave about eighty feet above and seemingly inaccessible, at least from their vantage point. The cliff face below the large alcove was sheer with no hand and toe holds. But they were beckoned by vivid images on the interior painted in a palette of reds, whites, yellows, and blacks. To reach the site, they needed to backtrack about a half-mile up canyon, ascend the north wall to a point level with the alcove, and then crawl along a precariously narrow ledge, all while packing delicate camera gear. The ascent must not have been as memorable as it was for later archaeologists. Bowers only mentioned they made it "with some rock climbing,"[23] obtaining seven photographic images of one of the most spectacular pictograph panels anywhere in the region.

Forbes's daily log indicates they traveled 13.5 miles that day, but in reality they had traveled only 8 miles—2 miles along the canyon rim, 3 miles in the treacherous descent of Gooseberry, and 3 miles down Range Creek to Donna's Alcove (PR12-1).[24] Forbes might be afforded some benefit of the doubt if one factors in the countless switchbacks getting down Gooseberry and a three-mile round-trip into upper Range Creek above the mouth of Gooseberry.

The next day, on August 4, the crew started early, but they had scarcely begun when they discovered two granaries constructed on a wooden platform above a complex panel of petroglyphs and pictographs.[25] They collected some potsherds and flint fragments, then quickly continued down canyon another

6.8 Bill Bowers documents the rock art inside an alcove above the expedition's first camp in Range Creek. Courtesy of the Peabody Museum of Archaeology and Ethnology, Harvard University (PM No. 2004.24.10537, File 120770002).

6.9 Modern view of the same rock art panel. Photo: Dan Miller.

half-mile before stopping to conduct excavations at an undisturbed rock shelter on the south side of the canyon. They found a greasewood digging stick, but not much else.[26]

At this point, they were still within eyesight of their evening camp the night before. Returning to the canyon bottom, they came to an area now known as The Cove, where they noticed three side-by-side granaries on "a good horizontal ledge" about twenty-five feet above the valley floor, arriving at 9:45 a.m. They could not reach the structures, but instead climbed a tree opposite them to take photographs and offer five pages of detailed descriptions.[27] They had scarcely gone another couple hundred yards before they noticed a crevice with a wooden platform on the inside.[28] Had they explored a bit, they would have found prehistoric houses on the benches above both of these sites and on the prominent topographic feature that dominates this area, called Locomotive Rock.

Having traveled down canyon less than a mile, they spurred their horses southeast another mile or so until they came to the mouth of Nelson Canyon, the first major drainage on the west side of the canyon. On the north side opposite the mouth, they found a red-and-white pictograph of a classic Fremont anthropomorph,[29] and on the east side a jaw-dropping, spectacular triple granary, now referred to as Nelson House. Nelson

House is not actually a house but rather large storage chambers that sit on a sheltered ledge about 130 feet above the bottom of the canyon. It was constructed using stone and adobe that matches perfectly the surrounding cliffs, giving it a camouflaged effect. The granaries are not accessible today without specialized climbing gear, but there must have been a ledge there in 1931 because the crew offered detailed measurements and descriptions, as well as an abundance of photographs. Dennison was especially impressed, calling Nelson House "very complete, very exceptional granaries, and traces of a fourth, smaller one."[30] He goes on to offer five pages of descriptions and sketches in what must have been an effort requiring two or three hours.

They went another hundred yards or so when their attention was diverted to two large complexes of petroglyphs. They stopped long enough to make brief descriptions and sketches.[31] The crew had barely resumed their investigations when they came to a large structure constructed on a bedrock outcrop. Judging from the amount of rubble, it must have had substantial walls at one point, or, as Bowers wrote, "A very much broken down wall of rounded rocks."[32]

At this point, the crew was only about two miles from their camp the night before. They had identified and described nine granaries, one open residence, and four different clusters of rock

6.10 A 1931 view of PR12-2 (42Em2835). Courtesy of the Peabody Museum of Archaeology and Ethnology, Harvard University (PM No. 971-21-10/100162.1.10, File 99380234).

6.11 A modern view of the same rock art images at PR12-2. Photo: Dan Miller.

6.12 (*above*) A crew member climbs to a wooden platform in a crevice (PR12-5). It is probably Waldo Forbes because he was almost always shirtless. Courtesy of the Peabody Museum of Archaeology and Ethnology, Harvard University (PM No. 971-21-10/100162.1.27, File 99380241).

6.13 (*right*) Rock art near the mouth of Nelson Canyon. It was sketched in detail in the 1931 notes. Photo: Jerry D. Spangler.

art, and still they found time to excavate in a rock shelter. All were next to or visible from the existing cow trail, and all but one of them were on the west side of the canyon. The unusually high density of sites must have been obvious to them. They must have questioned what might be found on the north side of the canyon—numerous granaries are visible there even from great distances. What is not so obvious is why the crew chose to suspend their investigations in upper Range Creek at this point.

Monumental Miscalculation

It might have been late in the day, and the Crimson Cowboys were eager to get to a scheduled camp at the John Darioli Ranch another twelve miles downstream just above the mouth of Turtle Canyon. Or we can take Bowers's words at face value: "Below site PR12-7 [the large structure on bedrock] formation of

wall becomes unsuited for granaries in protected positions. That is, walls are rather crumbly. This continues on [to a point just] north of John Darioli's where there begins a sort of secondary canyon."[33]

It is also possible the local cowboys intentionally misled the crew. Bowers wrote, "Below Nutter's first ranch [at Cherry Meadows] for some distance there are low gravelly mesas on each side. There would be good [indecipherable] for village type structures, but I was told by one of Nutter's men that he knew the area very well indeed and that there was nothing at all... so I did not explore the region."[34]

In other words, the next ten miles or so of canyon topography did not appear suitable, and a local cowboy had confirmed their suspicions, so they ignored it entirely. And in so doing, the crew skipped the heart of prehistoric occupations in Range Creek. The cowboy's statement that there was "nothing at all" was a bald-faced lie. And Bowers's own assessment of the potential here could not have been more wrong.

6.14 (*left*) A 1931 lateral view of the large granary (PR12-6) at the mouth of Nelson Canyon. It was accessible in 1931, but not today without specialized climbing gear. Courtesy of the Peabody Museum of Archaeology and Ethnology, Harvard University (PM No. 971-21-10/100162.1.33, File 99380237).

6.15 (*above*) A modern view of the same PR12-6 granary (now known as 42Em741). Photo: Dan Miller.

As they rode southeast to the Darioli Ranch, they passed scores of spectacular granaries, some that now have names like Granary Row and Cow Canyon Granary. They traveled next to and sometimes through the middle of open residential sites that now bear names like Burnout Village, Lighthouse Complex, and Big Village, the Media Site, Three Bears, and Mojo. Finally, they missed or ignored rock art sites the entire length of their horseback ride.

These are not small, obscure sites easily missed by all but experienced observers. These are large and impressive sites with standing walls of coursed masonry, often with abundant lithic materials and potsherds. Today, the University of Utah Field Station has documented more than three hundred of them in this stretch of the canyon alone. Had the Harvard boys spent more time here, they might have chosen to forego the next leg of the exploration along the Green River and spend the entire two weeks in Range Creek.

The Darioli Base Camp

Nonetheless, they apparently intended to camp at a small ranch owned at the time by John Darioli. The ranch featured a simple, one-room cabin built some four decades before by the easterner-turned-wilderness-rancher Joe Wing. It is not clear why they chose to stay there. At that time Darioli was embroiled in a contentious lawsuit with Preston Nutter, and by some accounts he constantly feared that Nutter's henchmen intended him violence.[35] It was almost as if the Harvard boys were going out of their way to avoid Nutter.

6.16 A view of the crew camped at John Darioli's cabin on August 6. Courtesy of the Peabody Museum of Archaeology and Ethnology, Harvard University (PM No. 971-21-10/100162.1.20, File 99380243).

The Crimson Cowboys spent the next two nights camped at Darioli's, using it as a base from which to explore the lower reaches of Range Creek. Based on the sheer number of sites they described in two days, they must have been overwhelmed, as is evidenced by the confusing nature of their field notes. Sites are out of order, as if they went in later and added numbers to the sites they visited that day, perhaps to lend order to sites that were investigated in no particular order. For example, Dennison's first journal entry at this time is a remarkably detailed description of PR12-20, a two-chambered granary. The crew had to construct a ladder to reach it. But this entry occurs in his journal two pages before his description of PR12-15. Site PR12-18 comes before PR12-16, and so on.

If the journal entries are an accurate reflection of the order in which sites were investigated, it appears the first order of business on August 5, 1931, was to ride to the mouth of Range Creek, a distance of about five miles. Then they turned around and ascended Range Creek, investigating sites as they went. The lower reaches of Range Creek are remarkably different than the rest of the canyon. The canyon walls, colored in a swirl of red and brown sandstone, are less than a quarter-mile apart, but with an abundance of ledges, shelters, and hidey-holes.

As noted above, the first site they encountered that day was PR12-20, the remarkably well-preserved double-chambered granary. Dennison indicated it was one mile from the mouth of the canyon, but in reality it was closer to two miles. While investigating the double granary on a second cliff ledge, they also found another granary in a shelter on the first level.[36]

6.17 The crew constructed a one-pole ladder to gain access to the granaries at PR12-20 (42Em761). Courtesy of the Peabody Museum of Archaeology and Ethnology, Harvard University (PM No. 971-21-10/100162.1.44, File 99380239).

Continuing upstream only a couple hundred yards, they then found PR12-19, three masonry residences constructed against the base of a cliff and protected by a slight overhang. Bowers wrote, "We excavated a little in the house debris and under the wall at the door but found it very sterile, only one potsherd, corncobs, two pieces of red ochre, bark.... This site would be fair for excavation I think, but not rich enough to justify staying longer this trip."[37] Unfortunately, looters

6.18 (*left*) A 1931 view across the top of the two-chambered granary at PR12-20 (42Em761). Courtesy of the Peabody Museum of Archaeology and Ethnology, Harvard University (PM No. 971-21-10/100162.1.43, File 99380240).

6.19 (*above*) Modern view of the PR12-20 granaries. These are not accessible today. Photo: Jerry D. Spangler.

later discovered the site, which today is mostly a series of deep craters. Modern archaeologists have little left here to study.

The crew continued their ascent, investigating three sites in close proximity to one another. Two were rock shelters with walls constructed across the front, and the other was a rock shelter with building rubble, but not much else. Their descriptions were brief, and they did not bother to take photographs.[38]

The crew then entered an area of lower Range Creek called "The Narrows" where the canyon walls are but a stone's throw apart. Bowers wrote of this area, "Below John Darioli's ranch the valley bottom is only about one-fourth to one-third mile wide at most, sometimes only 150 yards and not especially fertile soil, more sandy than otherwise."[39]

They paused here long enough to describe a D-shaped residential structure inside a rock shelter and a "pie-shaped" granary on a small ledge.[40] The journals at this point do not have dates attached to the specific sites investigated. Based on the order that sites were described, the crew probably called it a day after they documented the "pie-shaped" granary and returned to the Darioli Ranch. They

6.20 Modern view of the PR12-14 granary (42Em755). The 1931 crew got into this granary, although access today is extremely difficult. Photo: Jerry D. Spangler.

had traveled ten miles on horseback, investigating four granaries, four sheltered residences, and three rock shelters with remains of walls.

The following day, August 6, they spent exploring within a mile or two of the ranch itself, located just upstream from the mouth of Turtle Canyon. Although they never traveled far, there was plenty to keep them busy. On a bench adjacent to and south of the ranch, they discovered a circular stone residence (PR12-8), and a short distance downstream they investigated a rock shelter with rock art and artifacts (PR12-9), and opposite that two more residences on a bench area above the creek (PR12-10).[41]

They also visited three rock art sites in the same area. Dennison offered brief descriptions, and in a few instances he took photographs. He was particularly impressed by one human figure painted red that was at least six feet high.[42] His sketches, although crude, have allowed for positive identification of all of the rock art sites they described in lower Range Creek.

They stopped to document what they called a "fort"—a large oval masonry structure thirteen to sixteen feet in size on a bench area with walls almost three

6.21 Modern view of the stone residential structure described in the notes as PR12-12 (42Em754). Photo: Jerry D. Spangler.

6.22 Modern view of the colorful pictographs at PR12-11 (42Em2881). Photo: Dan Miller.

feet high.[43] The structure is actually a typical open residential structure common throughout the canyon in areas the crew had earlier ignored. Directly opposite this site, on the south side of the canyon, they described a granary with an abundance of long wooden poles.[44] And the crew was especially impressed with a granary site they called PR12-11, not so much the two collapsed granaries there as the row of polychrome Fremont figures painted in combinations of red, white, and green.[45]

By the end of the day, they had described three granaries, five clusters of rock art, a rock shelter, and three open residential sites. In four days, they had visited and described and sometimes photographed twenty-nine sites, and they had barely touched the tip of the iceberg. They had ignored more of the canyon than they had actually investigated. And they never saw what would astound archaeologists eighty years later.

Postscript

Today, the University of Utah Range Creek Field Station has documented more than five hundred sites here representing a nearly two-thousand-year span of human history. These were early farmers of corn, squash, and probably beans, although only a single bean has been recovered here. In many respects, they were classic Fremont Complex peoples who constructed pit houses on small

6.23 A 1931 view of the rock art in lower Range Creek Canyon. Courtesy of the Peabody Museum of Archaeology and Ethnology, Harvard University (PM No. 2004.24.10538, File 120770003).

6.24 Modern view of the same pictographs. The site is now known as 42Em2883. Photo: James M. Aton.

6.25 Range Creek rock art panel. Photo: Dan Miller.

rises above the floodplain, used plain-gray pottery vessels tempered with basalt or calcite, and painted and pecked distinctive rock art images dominated by trapezoidal human figures, wider at the shoulders and narrower at the waist.

In other respects, they were unique. They also erected towers and fortresses on inaccessible outcrops, sometimes a thousand feet or more above the floodplain. They built granaries, sometimes massive in size, on sheer cliff faces where they could be monitored and protected. And they must have had contact with distant peoples hundreds of miles away, as evidenced by the abundant black-on-white, redware, and polychrome pottery.

Although Scott's unpublished official summary of the Range Creek observations asserted there were "very few" open residential sites, in reality such sites are ubiquitous. At least ninety-three open residential sites have been documented there as of this writing, and another sixteen sites have residential structures in sheltered settings. Quite simply, Range Creek appears to have been packed with prehistoric farmers, and population densities there might have been greater than at any other area of the Tavaputs Plateau.

Based on a suite of radiocarbon dates obtained by University of Utah researchers, the first farmers probably arrived here about AD 400, but they were few in number. Then between AD 850 and 1200 populations seem to have exploded. Of the thirty-three radiocarbon dates, twenty-nine fit into this narrow window of human history. Why did this happen?

New generations of researchers will undoubtedly answer those questions. The University of Utah now owns the Wilcox Ranch and protects the canyon for its scientific research qualities. Each year, more and more graduate students probe the many mysteries of Range Creek to better understand how the ancients thrived in the arid climate. The Wilcox ranch never became the big-game hunters' paradise that some had hoped for in 2002. Instead it evolved into something far more important.

7.1 The Green River is always laden with sand, and the water is not recommended for human consumption. Photo: Dan Bauer.

Wildest Desolation

Exploring the Green River's West Bank

7

As Bill Bowers, Waldo Forbes, Jim Dennison, and their guide, Oliver Rasmussen, turned their horses toward the unknown canyons along the west bank of the Green River, they were venturing into a wild land where no archaeologists had gone before. It was a land visited by only a handful of hard-bitten misfits and miscreants, otherwise labeled as cowboys and, in days long past, outlaws. The daunting wilderness here is a natural fortress of sheer cliffs, box canyons, and intense heat.

Their 104-mile route would take them 46 miles along the western bank of the Green River, a fine source of water for the horses but laden with so much sand as to make it highly unpleasant for humans. As W. H. Bradley of the US Geological Survey wrote, "Water from the Green River is drunk by a few people who live near it but I do not recommend it."[1] Dave Rust, the expedition guide who had managed the pretrip planning, disagreed with Bradley, however, writing to Scott, "The Green is good drinking water, and corn should flourish on the floor of the canyon, near the banks of the river."[2]

7.2 Wildflowers in Desolation Canyon. Photo: Dan Bauer.

The most important person on this leg of the expedition was undoubtedly Oliver Rasmussen, their cowboy guide, who probably knew where the few scattered freshwater springs were tucked in the side canyons. The location of fresh water would dictate the course of their foray along the Green River.

It is unclear from the field notes and correspondence why the expedition wanted to explore this formidable country or what they expected to find here. It is possible that local cowboys had regaled Scott with stories of unspoiled cliff ruins that teased the expedition leader with the prospect of a

7.3 Scenic view of the heart of Desolation Canyon. Photo: Dan Bauer.

grand discovery. Or maybe it was simply because the land was still unexplored—a last frontier of sorts for archaeological discovery. Rust was enthusiastic about the region's potential, selling Scott on the idea that "such a region is [a] likely place of habitation for our prehistoric brethren."[3]

It is most probable that Scott had no real appreciation of what he was asking of his crew or just how remarkable it was that they accomplished this feat with no injury to life or limb. Even the most weathered cowboys today would take pause at such a journey. It would require the most sure-footed horses accustomed to narrow trails on canyon ledges where one slip could mean death to horse and rider. The rocky, unstable trails were, in many places, cut into steep slopes of sixty to eighty degrees, where frequent rock slides remove all traces of the trail itself, mandating that riders dismount and painstakingly lead their horses through boulder fields so as to avoid injury to the horses' legs. Cowboys who use the trails to this day say it can take hours to travel a mile or two, picking one's way around the rock slides.

The West Tavaputs Plateau is one of the last great wilderness areas in the Lower 48, composed of hundreds of square miles of untamed canyon country. More than a dozen major canyon tributaries flow east from the high plateau to the Green River, and there are dozens more minor, unnamed canyons. The highest spot on the plateau is Bruin Point, a bony outcrop 10,131 feet above sea level. The lowest point the expedition would encounter was along the Green River at 4,200 feet, at the mouth of Three Fords Canyon. In other words, they experienced an elevation change of nearly 6,000 feet in only about ten miles as the crow flies.

The canyon escarpments are often sheer, rising in ascending levels to hundreds of feet above the narrow floodplains. Almost all are devoid of permanent, clear water. Even today, despite the rash of natural gas development on the high plateau, these narrow canyons have defied attempts to build roads here or otherwise develop the land. Only one permanent ranch was ever established here, at Rock Creek. This area remains as wild and ferocious a landscape today as it did in 1869 and 1871 when John Wesley Powell and his erstwhile band of explorers first floated the Green River.[4] In 1969, to celebrate the centennial anniversary of the first Powell expedition, the Secretary of the Interior designated this stretch of the Green River the Desolation Canyon National Historic Landmark, in large part because of its untamed character.[5]

7.4 It is not known if the 1931 expedition drank from the Green River, but there are not many freshwater springs. Photo: Dan Bauer.

To our knowledge, the Peabody Museum horseback odyssey has never since been duplicated by archaeologists. Seventy-five years passed before archaeologists returned here to study the ancients—not on horseback but rather aboard rubber rafts laden with modern amenities: coolers chock-full of ice, solar showers, guitars for evening entertainment, fresh-ground coffee, and plenty of adult beverages. In terms of difficulty, the modern research projects share little in common with the 1931 expedition.

With Rasmussen leading the way, Bowers, Forbes, and Dennison departed the Darioli cabin in Range Creek on August 7, 1931, presumably later in the day because their evening camp on one of three islands at the mouth of Three Fords Canyon[6] was only about five miles from the Darioli cabin. They followed an old cowboy trail east into an unnamed Range Creek tributary about two miles up and onto Last Chance Bench. Since the early 1900s, this trail had been the primary lifeline to a remote ranch at Rock Creek and a route used to trail cattle from that ranch to railheads at Woodside. Only a few scattered remnants of the trail exist today. Once on the bench, the group continued east along the bench another mile to the head of Three Fords Canyon where the trail splits, one fork following the south rim of Three Fords and the other snaking along the north rim. Either trail would have worked, but likely they chose the southern trail because it was the easiest and most direct access to the Green River. Bowers indicated they "saw no traces [of prehistoric archaeology] on the way."[7]

Setting Course for Rock Creek

The following morning the crew set out north along the west bank of the Green River on what would be a twenty-one-mile ride to Three Canyon, seeing nothing because "most ledges and shelters, however, are very high off valley, at least 75–100 feet for most, at the top of talus slopes."[8] The trail would have been easy going the first two miles. The first impediment came at the mouth of Rain Canyon where the trail hugs tightly against the face of sheer cliffs rising from the river's edge. At about three miles, they would have seen the Jim McPherson–Budge Wilcox Cradle M Ranch on the opposite bank—a reminder of their second night's camp out of Green River. The miles melted away with no mention of the many tributary canyons they had passed: Rain Canyon, Big Canyon, Bull Canyon, Joe Hutch Canyon, Trail Canyon, and Wire Fence Canyon. But they did mention Bear Canyon—a puzzling reference since there is no Bear Canyon along the Green River listed on any of today's maps for Desolation Canyon.

The first discovery of August 8, assigned the number PR12-21, occurred inside Bear Canyon. Dennison's field notes indicate they discovered the remains of a two-chambered granary on a ledge about three-eighths of a mile inside the canyon. One of the rooms was in far better shape than the other, and several logs from the room construction lay about the ledge, along with fibers used to lash the roof matrix and a round capstone that once acted as a lid to the chamber.[9]

Our initial attempts to relocate this site were unsuccessful, due to the absence of any map references to a Bear Canyon in the area and the suite of possible canyons to which they might have been referring. We subsequently provided BLM river rangers with copies of the 1931 field notes and sent them out to find the elusive site. During the course of their river patrols, they investigated all of the tributary canyons between the mouth of Three Fords Canyon and the August 8 camp at the mouth of Three Canyon. They eventually discovered the site in 2008 exactly as described, tucked on the south wall of Trail Canyon, about ten miles from the expedition's camp at Three Fords. In other words, "Bear Canyon" is actually Trail Canyon.

In retrospect, the fact the crew would explore Trail Canyon and not the other canyons along the way was obvious. About two miles up Trail Canyon a spring of fresh water gushes out where they could have replenished their drinking water supplies. It is the source of a flowing creek for a short distance before the water disappears underground; at the mouth of Trail Canyon, the creek is bone dry. But Oliver Rasmussen would have known about the spring—all cowboys in the region knew about the spring. The granary site was probably discovered by happenstance as the crew quickly ascended the canyon bottom to fill their canteens. They never noticed the remains of ancient house structures nearby.

After returning to the river, the crew continued north along the west bank a short distance when Dennison reportedly saw, according to Bowers's journal, "what appeared to be a rock wall, no adobe, large rocks, location not remembered. He was riding behind the rest of the outfit who did not see the wall." A little later, opposite the mouth of Chandler Canyon, Dennison reported seeing a circular structure on top of a small pinnacle about seventy-five feet above the river, but he "did not look at this with glasses so he thinks there may be some doubt as to its existence." Immediately after this entry is a reference to a "low rock wall at mouth of cave, 20 feet off bottom of valley, irregular masonry, no adobe."[10] None of these three sites warranted a site number, and someone later added a handwritten note to Bowers's journal that Bowers was highly suspicious as to whether these sites existed or not. Subsequent investigations in this area have not identified any.

Within two miles of leaving Trail Canyon, the crew arrived at Lion Hollow, a minor and unimposing canyon tributary like so many others they had passed. But here, the trail led them past a large rock shelter at the edge of the floodplain, which they dubbed PR12-22. They noted six groups of red and yellow pictographs, and a stone that had been worn by abrasion. The roof of the shelter was scarred with smoke stains, but they attributed this to modern cowboy camps because there were "tin cans scattered about."[11]

The crew apparently did not excavate the deposits below the rock art panels, staying only long enough to jot a few notes, make a sketch, and take a photograph. Unfortunately, vandals later destroyed the site, leaving behind massive

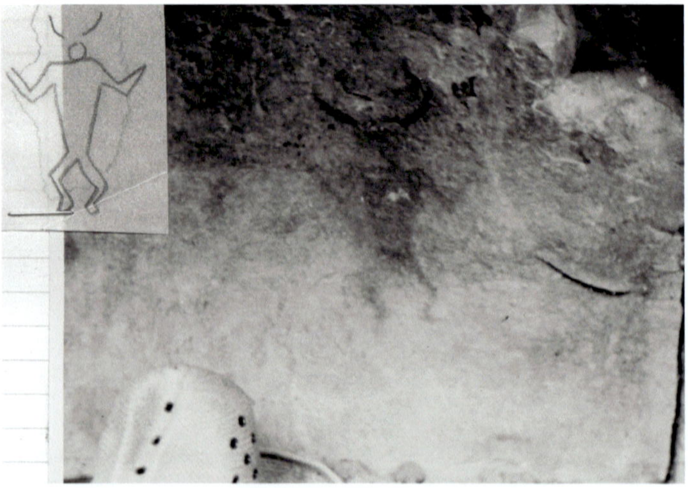

7.5 A view of one rock art image at PR12-22 at Lion Hollow. This image was taken on August 7. Courtesy of the Peabody Museum of Archaeology and Ethnology, Harvard University (PM No. 971-21-10/100162.1.15, File 99380235).

7.6 Close-up view of the same rock art image taken in 2016. Photo: Dan Bauer.

craters up to four feet deep and rimmed by piles of back dirt still littered today with artifacts that looters had ignored as worthless and unsaleable. The scientific value of this site, once immeasurable, is now almost entirely destroyed. Only the pictographs in bright red, yellow, and orange remain undisturbed.

At Lion Hollow, the pack trail veers away from the river briefly, ascending the cliffs behind the rock shelter about eight hundred to a thousand feet and then over a ridgeline into Three Canyon. Once at the mouth of Three Canyon, they rode up the canyon about a mile and a quarter "until valley bottom became narrow, less than 200 feet. Saw several suitable ledges, shelters, etc. but no traces."[12] At some point here they rode past a large, perfectly intact granary without noticing it.

They camped that night at the mouth of Three Canyon after at least twenty-one miles in the saddle, having encountered only two sites. They did not mention the petroglyphs at the mouth of Three Canyon, nor the many cowboy inscriptions. Some were nearly fifty years old, suggesting this was a favored camp spot long before the Crimson Cowboys arrived. We have since discovered and documented more than twenty sites—mostly granaries, rock shelters, and rock art sites—along the expedition route between Lion Hollow and the Three Canyon camp.

The next day the crew again headed north toward the remote ranch at the mouth of Rock Creek, following the trail as it hugged the edge of the river (often with scarcely any wiggle room between cliff face and river's edge). The journals refer to the ranch, located only five river miles to the north, as both the Downard Ranch and the Seamount Ranch.

The Downard reference is to two cousins, Manuel and Ernest Downard, local cowboys who had become intimately familiar with the rugged terrain as wranglers for Jim McPherson and Preston Nutter. In fact, Rust had earlier recommended to Scott that he hire the cousins as their guides for the West Tavaputs Plateau,[13] but Scott went with Rasmussen instead. The two cowboys had purchased the ranch about six years before from the Seamount brothers: Bill, Dan, Ed, and Alph.

Exploring Rock Creek

About a quarter-mile before reaching the ranch, the expedition stopped to visit a well-preserved two-chambered granary tucked in a small side canyon on a ledge thirty feet high on the cliff face (PR8-1). They accessed it by climbing a pole leaned against the cliff. This allowed Bowers to obtain detailed descriptions and measurements of the walls and a distinct lateral doorway. They collected a corncob from the site, took a photograph, and continued on their way. The granary, today referred to as Calf-and-a-Half Granary, is not visible from

7.7 View of Calf-and-a-Half Granary south of Rock Creek. The expedition visited this site on August 8. Photo: Dan Bauer.

the main pack trail. In all likelihood, Rasmussen knew about this granary and guided them there.

The Rock Creek area of the Green River is an oasis of sorts, with its broad floodplains and clear water. Fremont farmers had settled here at least a thousand years ago, and Anglo ranchers had found it no less enticing. First used as a cattle-grazing area by Shadrach "Shed" Lunt around 1887, Rock Creek has some of the best bottomland along the river. Lunt may have built a cabin there, but he only used the area seasonally. Born in Birmingham, England, in 1851, he and his extended family converted to the Mormon faith, eventually settling in Nephi, Utah. From there he and his brother were the first to range their cattle herds into Nine Mile Canyon in 1877. Summering his cattle on the West Tavaputs Plateau led to his discovery of Desolation Canyon and Rock Creek. Lunt's Horse Pasture, north of Rock Creek and Steer Ridge, still bears his name. Sometime around 1905, Lunt sold his interest in Rock Creek to the Seamount brothers.[14]

The four brothers came into the area just after the turn of the century, probably at the urging of their brother-in-law, Jim McPherson.[15] All four were involved in Rock Creek, but Bill and Dan took the lead in working and living there. The brothers built a beautiful, carved sandstone house and outbuilding. Like their brother-in-law, they had the help of a mason from Provo named "Frenchy." According to the Seamount daughters, Ed learned to cut rock and supervised the chiseling and building.[16] The brothers also built the other structures at the ranch, planted fruit trees, and dug the long irrigation ditch that heads around the bend up the canyon. Their immaculate gardens, pastures, and orchards drew praise from all who saw them.

7.8 The Rock Creek Ranch, once a masterpiece of cut-stone frontier architecture, now lies in ruins. Photo: Dan Bauer.

Bill had the best mind for business and, with his wife, Jean McIntire Seamount, spent the most time at Rock Creek. They were married on April 14, 1914, and honeymooned at the ranch. They owned a gramophone and a set of records. They especially loved the music of Fritz Kreisler, a famous Austrian-born violinist. Bill played the violin, and numerous visitors to the ranch commented on being both shocked and delighted to hear duets from Bill and his sometime employee, Tom Creek (or Crick), who accompanied him on mandolin.[17]

In 1925, however, the Seamounts lost their ranch because of a March blizzard on the plateau. They had taken their herd up a little too early, and the snowstorm killed virtually all their cattle.[18] The Seamounts sold out to first cousins Manuel and Ernest Downard. They had enormous debts and spent years paying them off. According to their children, the brothers viewed the Rock Creek days as the highlight of their lives.[19]

Ernest Downard had been in the Price area for some time. His father, William, helped settle the town in 1880. Manuel's father, John, lived in Spring City, Utah, but ran cattle with his brother William. Both cousins grew up ranching, working as young men for various cattlemen like Jim McPherson. Ernest was thirty-one and Manuel thirty when they bought Rock Creek.[20] Although they owned the ranch when the Claflin-Emerson contingent came through, the Harvard boys arrived there to find no one at home. The brothers were probably with their cattle on the West Tavaputs.

The Downards ran the Rock Creek ranch until 1946 when Irwin Gerber, of Range Creek, bought it from them. Gerber's son Lloyd described the ranch as somewhat neglected because of the war. He noted, however, that it had ninety irrigated acres; five or six cubic feet per second of water flowing in the irrigation ditch running out of Rock Creek; and apple, plum, peach, cherry, and apricot trees.[21]

Gerber held the land until his unsuccessful lawsuit over in Range Creek and then sold out to his attorney, Therald (T.N.) Jensen of Price, in 1953. Jensen was the first person to actually file on the land in 1962 as a Desert Land Act property; like the smart attorney he was (he also had a PhD in philosophy from the University of Chicago), he put the land in his wife Bonnie's name. The ranch burned four years later in 1966 and has since been used primarily for pasturing Jensen family horses and cattle.[22] T.N.'s son Butch and his wife, Jeanie (Don Wilcox's daughter), have owned the ranch since the 1970s, with Butch's siblings. Recently his siblings sold their share to Hunt Oil of Dallas, Texas, the largest landowner on the West Tavaputs Plateau today.

The Rock Creek ranch has been a favorite stop for river runners since the 1960s. Unfortunately, some of those river runners did not respect private property. Many of the ranch artifacts, especially those in the shop, have disappeared.

The ranch that the Claflin-Emerson Expedition saw, however, was a wonderfully functioning cattle operation in the middle of one of the most remote and rugged canyons in the West. It must have seemed like a miracle to those Ivy League boys. Oliver Rasmussen, no doubt, told them plenty of stories about the former and current owners because Rasmussen had worked with them all.

The crew continued on another quarter-mile to the mouth of Rock Creek—the only permanent freshwater creek on the West Tavaputs Plateau between Nine Mile Canyon forty-two miles to the north and Range Creek twenty-two river miles to the south.[23] Sixty years before, John Wesley Powell's crew, led by Powell's brother-in-law Almon Harris Thompson, had also camped here, staying long enough to make some maps and collect an arrowhead (Powell was not on the expedition at that time). They referred to the creek as Nine Mile Creek, not to be confused with the stream of the same name today farther to the north.[24]

At the mouth of the canyon, the Peabody Museum crew stopped long enough for Dennison to sketch and briefly describe a series of rock art panels,

7.9 This rock art site was the first encountered as the expedition began its explorations into Rock Creek on August 8. Photo: James M. Aton.

some pecked and others painted in red and orange. Interestingly, they paid no heed to the small rock shelter just below the images filled with charcoal, burned bone, corncobs, a mano, and a metate. This shelter later produced some of the most interesting archaeological data yet reported from the region. A radiocarbon date from a corncob indicated it was grown in the AD 1500s. Archaeologists have traditionally believed that maize agriculture disappeared in this region by about AD 1250. But an AD 1500s radiocarbon date suggests the possibility that some maize farmers persisted in isolated niches like Rock Creek long after others had given up farming. Of course, the sample might have been contaminated and the results simply wrong. But this possibility is minimized by a second, almost identical AD 1500s radiocarbon date from a granary about a quarter-mile away.[25]

The crew then began moving west up Rock Creek. They followed a well-worn trail, now called the Van Dusen Trail but first pioneered by the Seamount brothers, up the bottom of Rock Creek Canyon. Cattlemen used it to move livestock back and forth from the ranch at Rock Creek to their summer range on the high plateau. The Harvard crew had gone only about a quarter-mile when they came upon another two-chambered mud-and-stone granary (PR8-2) much like the ones previously encountered. Although access was somewhat difficult, Dennison managed to get into the structure, and he excavated the interior deposits to a depth of five inches where he reported the presence of thirteen potsherds and organic materials from the collapsed roof. They photographed the site and continued west.[26]

They passed other sites without mention, including a small village site with the stone foundations of circular houses, suggesting the group was moving fast and with a specific destination in mind. It might well have been a famous petroglyph site that lures hundreds of river runners today and was probably known to Oliver Rasmussen. About two miles from the mouth, Rock Creek splits into two major forks, and just below the confluence is an impressive rock art panel with more than a hundred images of bizarre human shapes, bighorn sheep, and abstract compositions. Bowers offered a brief description of the site,[27] and they photographed the site in panoramic fashion to capture its size and complexity.

There is no indication they rode farther than the "forks." If they had, they would have certainly discovered more and more cliff granaries and rock art panels. Instead, they returned to camp at the Rock Creek Ranch. There was plenty of clean water nearby, and with the Downards gone to parts unknown, they

7.10 A view of the rock art site at the "forks" in Rock Creek Canyon as seen in 1931. This site was visited on August 8. Courtesy of the Peabody Museum of Archaeology and Ethnology, Harvard University (PM No. 971-21-10/100162.1.17, File 99380236).

7.11 Same view as observed in 2016. Photo: Dan Bauer.

might even have helped themselves to ripening fruit in the orchard next to the main ranch house. In all, it had been an easy day, only nine miles on horseback. And even though the sites were few in number, compared to what they had just experienced in Range Creek, a pattern was emerging: stone-and-mud granaries with wooden pole roofs situated on cliff ledges and clusters of prehistoric rock art images on the cliff faces.

The cool shade at the ranch and cold mountain creek water must have seemed a paradise in the scorching August heat when temperatures commonly climb well into the triple digits. To this point the expedition had gone as expected and without incident. But things were about to get a whole lot more complicated.

Chasing the Will-o'-the-Wisp

The goal for the next day, August 10, was to "ride to Flat Canyon to investigate three structures and one group of petroglyphs reported there."[28] It was only ten river miles to the mouth of Flat Canyon, but the trail in between did not follow the river; rather it twisted and turned up the sides of canyon walls that reached skyward hundreds of feet. The section between the Rock Creek Ranch and the mouth of Steer Ridge is today called the Son-of-a-Bitch Trail, an aptly named labyrinth of ups and downs and rock slides that still provokes cursing by all who attempt it. It is only two river miles from the Rock Creek Ranch to the mouth of Steer Ridge Canyon, but Bowers estimated it was four or five miles by horseback on the SOB Trail. It took them the entire day to travel those five miles before camping the night at the mouth of Steer. They never mentioned the granaries and petroglyph panels there.

Determined to reach Flat Canyon, the following morning, on August 11, the crew proceeded another four or five miles to the north, working their way along the Green River, up and over obstacles. It was not much of a trail, and

7.12 A 1931 view into Desolation Canyon taken from a trail high above the Green River. Courtesy of the Peabody Museum of Archaeology and Ethnology, Harvard University (PM No. 971-21-10/100162.1.448, File 99380247).

once they were within about two miles of Flat Canyon, the trail disappeared entirely. There was simply no way around or over the cliffs to the mouth of Flat Canyon. They were forced to backtrack to the mouth of Steer Ridge Canyon. Wrote Bowers, "Inspected a couple of small unnamed canyons on way, about 6–7 miles above Downards. Bottoms are very rough. No water. Formations formidable. Nothing found."[29]

There are only two minor side canyons between Steer Ridge and Flat Canyon, and most certainly the "unnamed canyons" to which Bowers referred are those in an area of Desolation Canyon referred to by locals as Long Bottom, a broad flat of stabilized dunes covered in Indian rice grass where two short side canyons enter from the west. River runners know it by the more ominous-sounding Fretwater Falls, an incongruous name considering there are no falls here and the rapids are far from death-defying.

That the crew found nothing, however, is puzzling. Subsequent archaeological investigations have identified the rough outlines of ancient structures on the flats, circular residences at the base of the talus slope, and a massive stone

7.13 The expedition failed to reach its goal of exploring Flat Canyon. If they had made it there, they would have observed dozens of granaries like this one. Photo: Dan Miller.

structure on a ledge above the flats that has a commanding view of the river. By Desolation Canyon standards, the area was a virtual beehive of prehistoric activity. But somehow the Harvard boys missed it altogether. Weary and disappointed, they again camped at the mouth of Steer Ridge Canyon, having pushed their horses about ten miles over the nastiest terrain yet encountered without discovering a single site to show for their troubles.

The aborted attempt to reach Flat Canyon illustrates the possibility that their guide, Oliver Rasmussen, was not as intimately familiar with the region as a seasoned "guide" should have been. Quite simply, there is no trail from the mouth of Steer Ridge to the mouth of Flat Canyon. Access into Flat Canyon has always involved a circuitous route up Steer Ridge Canyon to the high plateau and then down a switchback pack trail into middle Flat Canyon. Rasmussen should have known that.

In 2006, before we had access to the original Claflin-Emerson Expedition field journals, we repeated Oliver's mistake. The Colorado Plateau Archaeological Alliance dispatched an overland horseback crew from the Rock Creek Ranch with the ultimate objective of reaching Flat Canyon. We had discussed the route with local ranchers, who assured us it was possible but difficult. Our crew successfully negotiated the Son-of-a-Bitch trail to Steer Ridge, but beyond that the trail—if it ever had been a trail—had been entirely obscured by rock slides. After only a couple miles of leading their horses through treacherous topography, the CPAA crew also abandoned their efforts to reach Flat Canyon, returning to Steer Ridge—an adventure made even more colorful in the retellings by the onset of a freak early September snowstorm.

The Peabody Museum crew never met their objective of exploring Flat Canyon. If they had, the might have been awestruck at the sheer density of prehistoric sites there: dozens and dozens of masonry granaries, the largest petroglyph panel anywhere in Desolation Canyon, and even a complex of prehistoric residences perched on an outcrop overlooking the broad Flat Canyon floodplain. It has the highest concentration of prehistoric sites on the West Tavaputs Plateau outside of Range Creek and Nine Mile Canyon. Archaeologists are still grappling with why this is the case. Yes, the lower part of the canyon is broad and flat, and prehistoric corn farmers could have diverted the creek onto the flats. But the creek, which runs clear and cold in the upper, narrow reaches of the canyon, disappears underground by the time it reaches the broader canyon flats suitable for farming. Yet the sheer number of granaries in the dry, lower section suggests that prehistoric farming was highly successful. Were climates wetter a thousand years ago, allowing farmers to grow their crops by managing consistent rainfall? Or were hydrological patterns different then, allowing the creek to flow constantly all the way to the Green River and thereby enabling farmers to use irrigation?

At the end of a hard ten miles in the saddle, The Crimson Cowboys found themselves back where they had started the day, only two miles from Rock Creek and, with more detours still in front of them, they had another fifty-five miles to ride.

Skirting the Edges

The difficulty in traversing the Son-of-a-Bitch Trail and their subsequent failure to reach Flat Canyon had cost them considerable time and energy. But they were not trapped, nor were they lost. They were simply uncertain how best to complete their objective to investigate sites along the west bank of the Green River. And clean water was probably in short supply: There is no fresh water anywhere along this segment of Desolation Canyon, and it had been two full days since they had left behind the clear waters of Rock Creek.

On August 12, the crew decided to leave the Green River behind and ride to the high plateau above where there was a reliable water source, Johnson Spring, at the top of Steer Ridge Canyon. As local legends go, early cattleman Shadrach "Shed" Lunt had in the late 1870s or early 1880s used dynamite to blast a horse path from the top of Steer Ridge to the grassy flats at the mouth of the canyon.[30]

On August 12, Bowers wrote that they left the Green River and made the five-mile, nearly four-thousand-foot ascent out of Steer Ridge Canyon to "Cecil's homestead."[31] This refers to Cecil Rouse, a small cattle operator with a one-room summer cabin at the head of Steer Ridge Canyon. Onetime cattleman Lloyd Gerber, who later bought out the Downard brothers, remembered the Rouse Cabin thusly:

> A log cabin greeted us as the canyon opened up on top. It sat near a spring just above where a round, sandstone ledge looked down the canyon. The one-room cabin had no floor or furniture and was used to camp in when they worked on the lower end of Steer Ridge. We rode on up the ridge and stayed the night at a one-room homestead cabin that Cecil Rouse built. It sat in a brushy draw with an occasional clump of

> scraggly quaking aspens growing here and there. The ridge was several miles wide on the bottom end and lacked the heavy stands of quakies that we had seen elsewhere on the top. It was a good range with lots of grass and brush.[32]

At this point, uncertainty seems to have permeated the spirit of the overland expedition. It appears Oliver Rasmussen might not have known this country very well at all. The journals hint that no one knew how to get the crew to Flat Canyon or even back to the Green River except the way they had come. The group decided to split up to explore different possibilities. By late in the day, Rasmussen had failed to return, and Bowers went searching for him. By then, it was too late in the day to return to their camp at the mouth of Steer Ridge Canyon, so the Harvard boys helped themselves to Rouse's cabin. Bowers wrote, "Tried to cross over to Cedar Ridge but got left behind trying to find Oliver. Spent night and rejoined Oliver next day about noon. Too late to go to the river again. Porty [probably his horse] needs rest anyway, sleeping out without beds at this altitude, 7000. Rather fatiguing."[33] The actual elevation was closer to eight thousand feet at this point.

7.14 Pictographs in Jack Canyon. Photo: Dan Bauer.

It appears the crew spent the entire day scouting out the top of the plateau, looking for ways down one of the side canyons back to the Green River. About a mile south from Johnson Spring, a cow trail leads from Cedar Ridge into the middle of Flat Canyon, but they either didn't find it or they decided to give up on their initial objective to explore the Flat Canyon ruins. Instead, they chose a well-known cow trail about six miles to the northwest that begins at the headwaters of Jack Canyon. Shadrach Lunt and his brother Alford also pioneered this trail in the 1880s as a way to get their cattle to the broad, grassy flats near the mouth of Jack Canyon—an area that bears the name Lunt Horse Pasture to this day. Nothing in the notes indicates why they decided such, but it seems likely that Jack Canyon was not part of their original itinerary.

The following morning, on August 13, the crew saddled up and began riding northwest about six miles across relatively flat terrain at eight thousand feet elevation, first across Steer Ridge and then Bishop Ridge to the head of Jack Canyon. Rasmussen, who had gone missing the day before, met up with them about midday. At the head of Jack Canyon, the crew was only a short, half-day ride to the bottom of Nine Mile Canyon where Scott, Brew, and Kidder were at that same time excavating Rasmussen Cave, had they chosen to call it quits. Instead, they descended Jack Canyon towards the canyon mouth another ten miles distant.

In its upper reaches, Jack Canyon is narrow and rocky with massive boulder fields across what little floodplain is evident, making for tricky riding with weary horses. Although a creek flows here much of the year, it is chalky white in color, laden with minerals probably suitable for the horses but unpalatable to the crew members. About halfway down, two major forks join together, and the main canyon becomes wider and flatter (conditions better suited to prehistoric agriculture), although the creek at this point dives underground. This area also features more than a dozen large alcoves that would have been ideal for prehistoric habitations.

7.15 Red handprints at PR8-4. This site was originally visited on August 13. Photo: Dan Bauer.

At about five miles from the head of the canyon, the group came across a small group of petroglyphs and a few pictographs—the first archaeological site the group had encountered since leaving Rock Creek three days before.[34] Another hundred yards beyond that, they discovered a rock shelter with traces of a rock wall; the back wall of the shelter displayed painted circles in red and white, four red hand prints, and a few scattered petroglyphs of human and animal figures (PR8-4).[35] The shelter offered good potential for excavation, and the crew intended to return later for that purpose, but they apparently decided against it once they realized the shelter was five hard miles from their camp at the mouth of the canyon. Looters later destroyed the scientific potential of the deposits, but the rock art images remain intact.[36]

7.16 Rock art panel at the lower forks in Jack Canyon. This site was visited on August 13. Photo: Dan Bauer.

The Harvard boys then continued their descent, traveling another two miles to a major fork in the canyon, called the lower forks. Here they described two different petroglyph sites, one on the south side of the canyon that was sketched by Bowers,[37] and the other on the north side that was described by Dennison only as "20 feet above creek bed. Pecked on brown sandstone. At fork in the canyon. Some only line pecked. Others filled in."[38] They apparently did not notice the D-shaped house foundation at the base of the cliff next to the rock art on the south side of the canyon.

Below the forks, the canyon resumed the parched character of the other canyons they had already traveled. Jack Canyon broadened somewhat, and the floodplain became less steep, although it was still covered by massive rock slides, called debris flows. These result from flash flooding of the small side canyons and draws. Outside of the large alcoves, which were not investigated, few places along lower Jack Canyon would seem to be enticing to prehistoric humans. The crew did not mention any sites along this stretch.

The Colorado Plateau Archaeological Alliance briefly investigated this lower part of Jack Canyon in 2007 and found very little in the way of archaeological sites and nothing in the way of granaries or rock art. In some respects,

Jack Canyon and Flat Canyon are similar: They both have flowing water in the upper reaches, and in both instances the creek goes underground about two miles above the canyon mouth. At Flat Canyon, an abundance of granaries perch along the now-dry lower canyon. But in lower Jack Canyon, nothing (yet) suggests that ancient farmers worked these floodplains.

Upon reaching the mouth of the canyon, the crew then rode south another mile to Lunt's Horse Pasture, a small side canyon that drains directly into the Green River. At its mouth sits an isolated, seventy-five-foot-high, mushroom-shaped pinnacle, at the base of which is another petroglyph panel. Dennison offered another minimalist description, writing only "mostly irregular pecked lines scrawling about 1–1.5 [inches] thick, several circles. Two or three dogs or sheep."[39] A 1931 photograph of the site allowed us to positively identify it.

7.17 Rock art panel in Lunt's Horse Pasture. It was visited late in the day on August 13. Photo: Dan Bauer.

The crew camped for the night at the mouth of Jack Canyon in a dense grove of tall cottonwood and box elder trees that most certainly offered some respite from the stifling heat. To modern river runners, the camp is one of the very best in Desolation Canyon. In all, they had traveled at least eighteen miles, most of it in boulder fields and rock slides; they had explored and described four rock art sites and one rock shelter; and they had returned to their overarching objective to explore sites along the Green River.

End of the Trail

If the crew had not realized it before, they would soon discover that the landscape had changed. It was still the same formidable wilderness of canyons and cliffs, but unimaginably it had become even more barren, more desolate. There was a ribbon of willows, box elders, and a canopy of thorny greasewood along the Green River, but gone were patches of pinyons, junipers, and sagebrush clinging to the steep slopes above. John Wesley Powell once wrote that even the juniper trees here looked like "ugly clumps, like war clubs beset with spines."[40] In fact, hardly any vegetation of any kind grows on the slopes and crags and cliffs here, just seared rock in myriad shades of brown weathered into Gothic images and shapes. And there were no reliable freshwater springs,[41] nor would there be for the remainder of their journey.

As they departed on the morning of August 14, they were determined to resume their explorations along the west bank of the Green River. But there are no formal pack trails in this area. The cowboys in these parts moved their animals east–west up and down the many side canyons, using the sheer cliffs as natural corrals to inhibit wandering cattle. No one moved their cows up and down the river. From the mouth of Jack Creek, the crew was "bushwhacking" along the edge of the river, in places choked with nasty greasewood that can shred clothing and horse flesh alike.

They proceeded north, hugging a narrow passage along the bank of the river, somehow managing to make it around two areas where the river pinches up against the cliff wall. They passed Lighthouse Rock, made famous fifty years before by a photograph taken by the 1871 Powell Expedition. And within three miles of their Jack Canyon camp, they arrived at a relatively expansive flat area a mile long and up to a quarter-mile wide. This unnamed area opposite Peters Point features three small side canyons, also unnamed, that drain into the Green River. On the south end of this flat they encountered a strange circular stone tower constructed on a bedrock surface (ET5-1). It was only seven feet in diameter with dry-laid stone walls three and a half feet high. Their excavations of the shallow interior deposits revealed nothing.[42]

7.18 This small tower site (ET5-1) was visited on August 14. Forbes (*right*) is wearing a trench coat, which suggests it had been raining. Courtesy of the Peabody Museum of Archaeology and Ethnology, Harvard University (PM No. 971-21-10/100162.1.385, File 99380317).

On the north end of the flats they discovered a series of three stone-and-adobe granaries tucked on a cliff ledge and remnants of a house foundation ten to twelve feet in diameter on a narrow ridge just below (ET5-2). They could not reach any of the three granaries.[43] They apparently never noticed a fourth, massive granary several hundred feet above the house foundation perched precariously on a ledge, nor did they mention the petroglyph sites scattered

7.19 One of the granaries at ET5-2. This site was visited on August 14. Courtesy of the Peabody Museum of Archaeology and Ethnology, Harvard University (PM No. 971-21-10/100162.1.214, File 99380262).

7.20 Same granary as observed in 2016. Photo: Dan Bauer.

along the cliff faces between the lower tower and the upper granaries. Photographs of both sites taken at that time allowed us to positively identify them.

Riding next to the Green River would have become increasingly precarious as the cliff walls conjoin the edge of the river almost continuously for the next four miles, unless they managed somehow to ford the river to the broad flats on the other side, called Stampede Flats. The journals do not mention such an attempt, and to do so would have been foolhardy because the river is deeper and swifter than it appears.

Later that day, they rode into the mouth of Rock House Canyon, ten river miles from the Jack Canyon camp. Here, Dennison described and photographed a petroglyph panel at the mouth: "Numerous deer, goats, and other animals. 2 or 3 men, one with bow and arrow. A scrawling line on two more around the corner of wall."[44] It was Dennison's last entry for Desolation Canyon.

At this point, we feel compelled to discuss one of the unresolved mysteries of their Desolation Canyon adventure. It involves site PR8-3, a rather remarkable stone, mud, and pole granary with a circular capstone and a number of pictographs on the cliff wall. Both the edited version of the notes, transcribed by Donald Scott after they had returned to Cambridge, and James Gunnerson's later monograph indicate this site is located a half-mile inside Rock House Canyon.[45] After expending hundreds of man-hours searching for it, we have concluded that both Scott and Gunnerson are mistaken and that the site is actually located in Rock Creek Canyon (we have yet to find it there, either, but we have not searched Rock Creek as extensively).

The description of PR8-3 is found in the journal of Waldo Forbes, whose Desolation Canyon journal is otherwise sparse. The entry begins with the tag "PR-8-3 (Rock H) Granary and Pictographs."[46] It is easy to see how the "Rock H" might be later interpreted as Rock House Canyon. But a closer review of Forbes's earlier entries, beginning in Range Creek, indicates he assigned alphabet monikers to each site, such as Range A, Range B, etc. In other words, the "Rock H" could just as easily be interpreted to be the eighth site they had visited. As discussed above, the expedition only described six sites near the mouth of Rock Creek Canyon. But it was the eighth site discovered since they left Range Creek. In other words, Rock H refers to Site H, or the eighth site discovered since leaving the Darioli Ranch.

We have concluded that the site is actually in Rock Creek which is also supported by the PR8-3 site number Forbes assigned to it. As detailed in Scott's report, "The [site] number is composed of three elements: the letter or letters indicating the name of the topographical sheet; a number indicating in which of the sixteen divisions of the map the site lies, counting from the top left-hand corner; and a third number which is the actual numerical indicator of the site."[47] In this case, the number PR8-3 would be found on the Price River topographical map, second row in the far right of four subsections on that row, and it would be the third site encountered in that subsection. Rock Creek and Jack Canyon are located in this subsection (as is Flat Canyon, but we know they never made it there). The mouth of Rock House Canyon is actually located on the East Tavaputs topographic map, and if the site were actually located there, it should have carried a number with an ET5 prefix. We also know they encountered PR8-3 before reaching PR8-4, which is located about five miles up Jack Creek and two full days before they reached Rock House Canyon.

Site numbering problems notwithstanding, it is unclear how far the expedition traveled on August 14 because all of the journals abruptly go silent at this time. Possibly they camped at the mouth of Rock House Canyon. After all, ten miles on horseback along the river without the benefit of trails would have been arduous and slow going. But a camp here would have meant the end of a second day without palatable water—the last springs had been on the plateau above Jack Creek. There are obscure hints in Dave Rust's journal, one dated August 10–13 where he states, "We look for Bowers-Oliver party but they don't come," and another dated August 14–15 when he states, "Waiting for Bowers party."[48] This implies the Desolation crew did not arrive at the main Nine Mile camp until sometime on August 15, after Rust's journal entry.

It is also possible they were exhausted, way overdue, and anxious to get back to Nine Mile Canyon, so they simply pushed on. It would have been four miles more to ascend to the head of Rock House Canyon to the ridgeline separating that canyon from Nine Mile Canyon, another six miles to descend South Frank's Canyon to the bottom of Nine Mile, and another six miles back up Nine Mile to the main camp at Rasmussen's cabin at the mouth of Dry Canyon. If they returned on August 14, it would have been an unimaginable twenty-six-mile, bone-jarring ride. They had certainly proved themselves tough enough.

Their arrival at the main camp, however, did not even warrant a mention in any of the journals. In fact, the entire Range Creek–Desolation Canyon foray seems to have been casually dismissed. The editor of the journals, Donald Scott, devotes only a single paragraph to the remarkable odyssey, lumping the Range Creek and Desolation Canyon observations into a mere two sentences: "This reconnaissance revealed a continuation of the same types of pictographs as found in the main canyon of Nine Mile. Very few of the open sites were encountered but a large number of stone and adobe granaries with pole roofs are to be found here."[49]

Perhaps the later chronicles would have been more effusive had Bowers, Dennison, and Forbes spent more time exploring the rich archaeology of Rock Creek or if they had actually made it to Flat Canyon where they would have found spectacular granaries and rock art panels. Archaeologists have now documented more than 275 archaeological sites in Desolation Canyon and its tributaries, including all but one of the 16 sites mentioned in the 1931 field journals.

The Harvard boys got it monumentally wrong when they concluded that Range Creek had plenty of granaries but not much in the way of residential sites. But that assessment appears to be valid for Desolation Canyon. There are at least forty-three sites with granaries found along the Green River and in the side canyons, but only seventeen sites with open residential structures, almost all of these tucked up in side canyons instead of along the river corridor. And there appears to be a higher use of rock shelters as temporary residences.

In other words, ongoing research here is painting a picture of prehistoric farmers working the river floodplains during the spring, summer, and fall, using rock shelters as temporary homes. They built multiple granaries near their fields to store their harvest. But once the cold weather arrived, they retreated to more permanent residences two or three miles up in the side canyons where fresh water and firewood were plentiful. Forays to recover their stored maize probably occurred throughout the winter. By early May, they would have again scattered to the distant fields to begin again the planting and tending of fields, some along the river corridor and others along the side canyons with suitable floodplains.

7.21 Desolation Canyon rock art. Photo: Dan Bauer.

These ancients—we call them the Fremont Complex today—were probably country cousins to the families living in Nine Mile Canyon and Range Creek, although uniquely adapted to the isolated environments of Desolation Canyon. They used the same plain-gray pottery, the same style of arrow points, and constructed their homes and granaries in the same manner. Their rock art tradition shares many of the same motifs and styles as those found in more densely populated Nine Mile Canyon and Range Creek. If aggregated communities lived here, they were probably small winter hamlets with only a few families, a few clustered in Rock Creek and a few more in Flat Canyon. And some of these ancient farmers might have survived in this isolated refuge for two or three centuries after their more distant relatives had given up on farming in the wake of crushing droughts in the mid-1200s AD and the violence that ensues from food shortages.

The first archaeologists here—Bowers, Dennison, and Forbes—had no way of knowing this during their 104-mile odyssey. But they have the distinction of being the first to explore the scientific potential of this remarkable landscape. And they did it on horseback, a feat likely never to be duplicated.

8.1 Scenic view of Nine Mile Canyon near the mouth of the Cottonwood Canyon tributary. Photo: Dan Bauer.

Dirty Shovels

Devil's Playground and Rasmussen Cave

8

WHILE BOWERS, Forbes, and Dennison were on their epic adventure to Range Creek and Desolation Canyon, the rest of the crew inched their way westward up Nine Mile Canyon. The sheer number of sites in lower Nine Mile Canyon is daunting by any measure. In some areas, the number approaches nearly a hundred per square mile—far more than the remaining skeleton crew of Alfred Kidder and J.O. Brew could hope to visit in the short time allotted to Nine Mile Canyon. Brew, who was in charge of the Nine Mile crew in Scott's absence, seems to have preferred a slow, methodical approach to the investigations.

By the evening of August 5, the expedition had explored roughly four miles of lower Nine Mile Canyon, about two miles below the Pace Ranch and two miles above. Over the six days since they had arrived at the Pace Ranch, they had discovered and described eighteen archaeological sites, or three sites per day on average. They had photographed at least seven other rock art sites, but Brew did not share the same passion for describing the rock art as Bowers, Dennison, and Forbes, all long gone on their Range Creek–Desolation odyssey.

The main party—Brew, Kidder, guide Dave Rust, and wrangler Dafton Thompson—had not covered that much territory, and they still had miles to go before their ultimate objective: Rasmussen Cave. Donald Scott had probably returned from Salt Lake City by the evening of August 5 or the morning of August 6—just in time to help the crew move the base camp about four miles upcanyon to the Neal Hanks Ranch, situated near the mouth of Devils Canyon. And his return seemed to have sparked a renewed urgency to investigate more and investigate faster.

Over the next several days, they documented sixteen more sites, conducted important excavations at Devil's Playground (PR4-25) and Rasmussen Cave (PR4-31), and obtained a wealth of photographs of various sites and rock art that have proven invaluable to later researchers. The Rasmussen Cave excavations in particular would greatly influence archaeologists' understanding of the Tavaputs Plateau for generations to come.

8.2 Nine Mile Canyon resident. Photo: Dan Bauer.

Treasure Hunters and Pinnacles

August 6 began with a return to the mouth of Desbrough Canyon. Brew searched the south side of Nine Mile Canyon opposite the mouth of Desbrough to find the residences that must have been associated with the ten granaries discovered the day before. But he found little. He noted a single rubble mound on the bench above the four granaries described earlier at PR4-20. This was probably a residence, as was another circular room farther upslope (PR4-21).[1] And on a pinnacle top another three hundred feet above perched another circular structure (PR4-22) that warranted only a single line of description: "a fort on a prominence."[2] Ten granaries and only three unassuming residences certainly did not constitute the metropolis they might have expected.

For some reason, Brew did not investigate the north side of Nine Mile Canyon in this area. If he had, he would have seen a massive stone wall more than a hundred feet long and twenty feet high in places. If he had climbed to the wall, he would have found residences at nearly every level up to the wall and on the butte behind the wall. In fact, this area of Nine Mile Canyon has dozens of archaeological sites big and small, perhaps more than any other area of lower Nine Mile they had previously investigated. They just did not recognize it, or perhaps they ran out of time to give the area due diligence.

They moved west another half-mile to Pinnacle Canyon, a major south-to-north tributary to Nine Mile Canyon. On the bench area above the mouth they found a small rubble mound, probably a collapsed open residential structure, although little remained of it, and farther upslope they investigated a rock shelter with a coursed stone wall perpendicular to the shelter opening (PR4-23).[3] They spent some time exploring around the mouth of Pinnacle Canyon, photographing (but not describing) six different rock art sites, including a spectacular panel at the east edge of the mouth with hundreds of individual images. The photos also depict a historic inscription "F.E. Grames," a reference to Frederic Grames, who was among the first group of white settlers to arrive in Price in 1878.[4]

Also present here, but not depicted in the photos, is the inscription "Rhoades 1879." This refers to either Thomas Rhoades or his son Caleb, both of whom generated considerable public interest in the latter half of the nineteenth century with claims that Ute chief Wakara had shown the elder Rhoades deposits of lost Spanish gold, ostensibly hidden in the Uinta Mountains. Thousands of pages have been written over the years on the Lost Rhoades Mine. We only mention this here because of a strange notation in Rust's 1931 journal that between August 10 and August 13, "Nels, Snyder, and Thisset come to hunt the lost Rhoades Mine."[5] The presence of treasure hunters in Nine Mile Canyon did not, however, warrant a mention in the other Claflin-Emerson journals.

8.3 A 1931 view of rock art and the Frederic Grames inscription at the mouth of Pinnacle Canyon. Courtesy of the Peabody Museum of Archaeology and Ethnology, Harvard University (PM No. 971-21-10/100162.1.66, File 99380257).

8.4 A comparative view of the same site taken in 2015. Grames was among the original white settlers of Price in 1878. Photo: Jerry D. Spangler.

Devil of a Time

The expedition then moved another half-mile west to the mouth of Devils Canyon, passing by, without noticing, one of the largest masonry cliff granaries anywhere in the canyon. At Devils Canyon, they described yet another inaccessible granary at the east edge of the canyon mouth (PR4-24)[6] and photographed a rock art panel nearby.

At the west edge of the mouth of Devils Canyon stands an imposing butte with sheer drops on the Nine Mile Canyon side of about three hundred feet. Access to the butte involves walking into Devils Canyon, ascending a steep talus slope, and then backtracking to a less-imposing cliff where the ancients had carved hand-and-toe holds to reach the top. At the top of this prehistoric ladder, a stone wall with a small doorway guarded passage to the top of the butte. This butte is now known as Devil's Playground.

8.5 This rock art site just inside the mouth of Devils Canyon was photographed in 1931 but was not mentioned in the field notes. Photo: Jerry D. Spangler.

8.6 A view of the defensive wall that blocks access to the top of the butte now known as Devil's Playground. Photo: Jerry D. Spangler.

As Scott later summarized:

> Here is a veritable prehistoric apartment house.... Directly above this is a defense wall with a doorway, and a series of narrow ledges upon which are, as discovered by excavation, unquestionable living sites. Above these ledges, which are on the west end of the butte, are granaries. The trail to the top, however, swings around the northern end of the butte towards the east, and here are wider ledges upon which are the typical, round, low-walled rooms. On top of the butte on two different levels are groups of two or three of these rooms. The true summit is a large boulder perched on the ledge dividing the last two levels and overhanging, to a certain extent, part of one of the rooms of each group. Under each overhang is a storage cist of upright slabs. And on top of the boulder crowning the whole is a perfectly round fort.[7]

The site (PR4-25) was most certainly visited on August 6 because Kidder is photographed there. He would be in upper Nine Mile the following day and might have missed the excavations here, described in Brew's journal. In fact, most of the major structures here were excavated, and a large assemblage of potsherds, corncobs, corn husks, adobe fragments, worked wood and bone, and a piece of squash rind were recovered.[8]

8.7 John O. Brew investigates a granary tucked on a ledge at Devil's Playground. Courtesy of the Peabody Museum of Archaeology and Ethnology, Harvard University (PM No. 971-21-10/100162.1.82, File 99380258).

Scott speculated that even more structures dotted the slope and saddle below the butte,[9] and indeed he was correct. In 2013, the Colorado Plateau Archaeological Alliance investigated this site, documenting thirty-five separate features—open residences, sheltered residences, granaries, rock art panels, rock walls, etc.—not only on the butte, but on the surrounding saddle. In fact, the ruins at Devil's Playground continue uninterrupted to the west for nearly a quarter-mile.[10] This site is now listed on the National Register of Historic Places.

As much time as they spent at this site, no one noticed, or at least they never mentioned, a prominent butte on the east side of Devils Canyon and a little higher than Devil's Playground. The entire top of that butte is also covered in prehistoric structures, some with stacked stone walls clearly visible from Devil's Playground. The two sites are strikingly similar. Both feature the same open residential structures, most on top of the butte but at least one at the base of the butte. Plus, both have defensive walls around the edges that inhibit access to the top.

Given the amount of excavation that occurred here, the remaining crew of Brew, Scott,

8.8 (*above*) An unknown crew member (probably Brew) stands next to a small tower structure that crowns a knob at the top of the butte. Note the holes drilled into the bedrock surface next to the structure wall. Courtesy of the Peabody Museum of Archaeology and Ethnology, Harvard University (PM No. 971-21-10/100162.1.85, File 99380259).

8.9 (*left*) A 2015 close-up view of the same bedrock holes. These were probably part of a brush superstructure. Photo: Jerry D. Spangler.

Rust, and Thompson—at that time camped at Hanks's ranch a half-mile up-canyon—probably worked on this site throughout August 7. They took time to photograph two rock art sites near the ranch, but again they did not describe them.[11] They also noted "three granaries" on the south canyon wall about 250 feet high and opposite their camp (PR4-26),[12] but they apparently never actually went to look at them. If they had, they would have found an entire series of open residential sites along the only route to the granaries, and one large, fort-like structure guarding access to the ledge where the granaries sit.

It is easy to imagine Brew and Scott sitting around camp at the end of the long, hard day of shoveling at Devil's Playground, enjoying a relaxing evening meal, when someone spots the granaries in the distance. "You go take a look." "No, you go look." "No you." So Brew pulls out his journal and writes what he can see from a quarter-mile away. Good enough!

Their new base camp was clearly at the Hanks Ranch because a photograph taken at that time depicts a large camp tent pitched under a large cottonwood

8.10 A 1931 view of the Claflin-Emerson Expedition camped at the Neal Hanks Ranch. The cottonwood tree still stands today. Courtesy of the Peabody Museum of Archaeology and Ethnology, Harvard University (PM No. 971-21-10/100162.1.22, File 99380242).

tree next to the ranch house. The cottonwood tree still stands, appearing not much different than it did in 1931. The Hanks cabin, meanwhile, has collapsed into ruins.

Neal Hanks was a long-time stalwart of Nine Mile Canyon, and by most accounts was a gregarious man who made friends easily. One historian even called him the most beloved of all ranchers in the canyon.[13] Hanks and his best friend, Hank Stewart, were among the earliest settlers of Argyle Canyon in the early 1900s. Stewart married a local girl named Minerva Van Wagoner, and from time to time Neal ate supper with the couple and their three children. Sometime after 1910, Stewart divorced Minerva, preferring an unburdened life of river running and ferry operating with his new fifteen-year-old bride. Hanks then married Minerva and raised Stewart's children as his own. Hanks and Stewart remained close friends through all the family drama.[14]

It is not known from the journals whether or not Minerva was present at the lower ranch at the time the expedition camped there. She was renowned as a delightful hostess and wonderful cook, and if the crew had taken supper there, someone would probably have mentioned it. According to Rust's journal, the crew camped at the Hanks Ranch eight nights from August 6 through August 13, with no work being done on Sunday, August 9, a time to "loiter some and shave. Bathed last night."[15] We could find no entry in the "Journal of Expenses" that Hanks was ever paid the standard thirty-five cents a day for pasturage.

Neal Hanks's lower ranch at the east edge of the mouth of Cottonwood Canyon, the largest tributary in lower Nine Mile Canyon, certainly offered prehistoric residents access to prime hunting terrain on the high plateau to the south. The density of prehistoric sites here is perhaps the highest anywhere in Nine Mile Canyon. More than a dozen impressive sites sit within a five-minute walk of the expedition base camp.[16]

One of these is now called Sekani Village. It features a remarkable sheltered residence with a lateral doorway, at least two open residences, numerous other unknown structures, and several granaries located nearby. Brew was probably referring to this site when he wrote, "surface site directly above Hanks ranch. Granary above that, also granary around the corner" (PR4-32).[17] The problem with this entry is that it is the last one in Brew's journal for Nine Mile, made after the crew had moved the base camp to Rasmussen Cave. Either Brew backtracked two miles to Hanks's ranch after finishing the Rasmussen Cave excavations to jot two simple lines of description and collect a few potsherds and flint

8.11 View of a large masonry structure with a lateral doorway just above the Neal Hanks Ranch, part of a complex of features now known as Sekani Village. Photo: Jerry D. Spangler.

chips, or he had visited the site earlier during an evening jaunt and later decided to add the site description to his journal from memory.

The crew spent August 7 excavating at Devil's Playground. The next morning, they steered their horses west. They had ridden only about a half-mile when they came to a series of five circular open rooms and a platform granary in a crack in the cliff face (PR4-27),[18] located directly opposite the mouth of Cottonwood Canyon. They excavated a cist and perhaps other structures, collecting forty artifacts from the cist and the site surface, mostly gray potsherds. They might have remained here the entire day before returning to their base camp.

Rust's journal indicates they explored Cottonwood Canyon and Dry Canyon (Rust referred to it as Box Elder Canyon, but Scott called it Dry Canyon, its name today) from August 10 to 13, but this same entry states they had already begun digging in Rasmussen Cave by August 12, when "I struck burial in Oliver's camp, #31 site which turned out to be very interesting basket-maker."[19]

Only three sites are mentioned in the tributary canyons—one in Cottonwood Canyon and two in Dry Canyon—even though there are dozens of sites in both canyons readily visible from the trail in the canyon bottoms. The crew probably visited them on August 10, and by August 11 they had at long last turned their attention to the much-anticipated Rasmussen Cave.

Dry Canyon is a major south-to-north tributary canyon that natural gas companies use to access well heads on the upper plateau. They rode several miles up canyon and then described two sites on the way back down. Near a spring, they stopped to excavate in a promising rock shelter (PR4-28), recovering matting, twine, corncobs, twigs tied into knots, a squash rind, and lumps of salt.[20] Scott was unimpressed, noting the "finds were still very meager."[21]

About a mile from the mouth of Dry Canyon they observed two granaries on a ledge only about eight feet above the bottom of the canyon (PR4-29). One featured typical stone-and-adobe construction, and the other was constructed mostly of adobe bricks, called turtlebacks.[22] They then rode to the mouth of Dry Canyon, turned east for another mile, and then up Cottonwood Canyon a mile and a half to another large, promising rock shelter (PR4-30).[23] Excavations at several points in the shelter revealed only a thin ash layer two inches thick at a depth of twenty-four inches and a single mano. Scott observed, "It does not seem to have been used for any long period of time."[24] They collected the mano, nonetheless.

On their way to and from PR4-30 they would have ridden past the most famous rock art panel in the entire canyon with not even a

8.12 (*above*) A 1931 view of a granary and wooden platform at 42Dc903. Courtesy of the Peabody Museum of Archaeology and Ethnology, Harvard University (PM No. 971-21-10/100162.1.99, File 99380324).

8.13 (*left*) A 2017 view of the same granary and wooden platform. Photo: Dan Bauer.

8.14 A 2016 view of the rock shelter at 42Cb2068 that was excavated in 1931. The shelter deposits have been severely looted. Photo: Jerry D. Spangler.

8.15 This site is known today as the Great Hunt, perhaps the most famous rock art site in all of Nine Mile Canyon. It is not mentioned in the 1931 field journals, even though the trail passed next to the site. Photo: Jerry D. Spangler.

mention or a photograph. The Great Hunt Panel has been featured in scores of books, magazines, and other media over the years since, and today the panel is a major attraction to thousands of canyon visitors from around the world. There are two different images of the Great Hunt Panel in the Peabody Museum collection, but one is dated in the 1950s and the other contains catalog numbers inconsistent with the Claflin-Emerson Expedition.

Rasmussen Cave

Rasmussen Cave had been an expedition priority since day one of the adventure. Their colleague, Noel Morss, had dug a small area of the shelter in 1929 and had recovered a burial. What more might be found with a more thorough investigation? For the most part, the expedition so far did not have much in the way of spectacular artifacts, mostly just some potsherds, stone flakes, and corncobs.

Excavations probably began on August 11. Rust's meager journal tells us that they commuted back and forth to the base camp at Hanks's ranch, about two miles each way. On August 14, they finally packed and moved to Rasmussen's place for the final two nights.

8.16 A view of Rasmussen Cave as the crew pauses for a photograph. © President and Fellows of Harvard College, Peabody Museum of Archaeology and Ethnology (PM No. 2005.1.110.1.121, File 99380230).

Rasmussen Cave is located on the north side of Nine Mile Canyon nearly opposite the mouth of Dry Canyon and only a hundred yards or so west of the mouth of Daddy Canyon, named for early canyon settler Andrew Jackson "Daddy" Russell. Oliver Rasmussen owned the cave itself and the adjacent pasturelands, although it was a small spread, not nearly big enough for much livestock. His small, one-room cabin crouched on the south side of the canyon next to a spring.

According to local historian Norma Dalton, Harrison Russell first homesteaded this parcel in the early 1900s. Sometime in the 1910s or 1920s, he was approached by men who claimed to be miners wanting to buy the homestead. He said it wasn't for sale, but the men said it was for sale and they told him just how much they would pay for it. He could accept their terms or die. He sold. Local legend has it the "miners" were frontmen for Preston Nutter, who was trying to wrest control of all private lands between his headquarters at Gate Canyon and his satellite ranch about fifteen miles away at the mouth of Nine Mile Canyon.[25] It is not entirely clear how Rasmussen came to acquire the property.

The cave itself is quite large by Nine Mile standards, nearly thirty yards wide and seven yards deep. The back walls display dozens of vivid pictographs in red, white, and black, as well as pecked figures. A nearly life-sized elk painted in red dominates the catalog of images, but there are other unusual elements here, including animals that appear to be dancing on their hind legs. The boulders at the east end of the cave are covered in petroglyphs and bedrock metates. Unlike the other shelters they had so far investigated, this one had all the trappings of an extended occupation.

At this point it should be mentioned that the descriptions in Kidder's and Brew's field journals are rather sparse as they relate to the excavations, often little more than a list of artifacts recovered. But Scott's later summary of the excavation includes considerably more detail, suggesting that he kept a journal or made notes from which he drew details not found in the other journals. As previously noted, we have looked and looked for Scott's journal with no luck.

After months of anticipation, it is hard to imagine what must have passed through their minds when they finally saw Rasmussen Cave. Instead of a pristine cave ripe for excavation, Scott lamented that "it had been gophered by a large number of local enthusiasts, and the total number of burials removed, according to various reports, runs between three and eight."[26]

Looters had beaten them to the site, ravaging the site only a few weeks before. Digging on private property is not illegal if you have the permission of the landowner. It is not known whether Rasmussen, the owner, granted such permission before heading off to Green River to join the Claflin-Emerson Expedition. If he did, it would have been a monumental betrayal of trust—he knew that Donald Scott and company intended to dig there and granted them permission to do so.

The looting was reported in two separate journal articles later in 1931. Frank Beckwith, a newspaper publisher from Delta, Utah, and a thoughtful photo-documentarian of Utah rock art, mentioned in the journal *El Palacio* that two weeks before he arrived in Nine Mile Canyon a "party had dug in a cave at the Rasmussen property, and found a tiny mummy which was resting upon a coarsely woven mat of cedar bark." He also described other artifacts from Rasmussen Cave recovered by the amateurs, including a woven bag, two moccasins, a corncob on a broken metate, two woven baskets (one with an arrow foreshaft inside), a needle, and fragments of cloth. "A most wonderful find" was a necklace eleven feet long, consisting of 2,750 cut-to-size, bored, and polished stones of a shiny black, varied with a thin, shelllike white bone.[27]

Albert Reagan, writing in late 1931 and again in 1933, identified the diggers as Lee Snyder[28] and E. S. Noe, both of nearby Myton. Reagan augmented the list of artifacts removed from Rasmussen Cave to include two human scalps, black obsidian, a snowshoe frame, knife blades eight inches long, a possible dog skeleton "the size of a Norway rat," a piece of sandstone that had been used as a paint palette, and two additional human skeletons.[29] Reagan indicated the collection was exhibited at rodeos throughout the Pacific Northwest until the owners divided it in half. The necklace? Also cut in half.

These looters might have had help from someone who knew what he was doing. In two richly detailed reports in the journal *The Masterkey*, Alfred E. Gaumer—we don't know who he was or if he represented a research institution—wrote that he conducted excavations at a cave site in August 1934. Among the items he mentions were a "puppy" associated with the burial of a child and, at the head of another burial,

> a string of beads composed of slate and white bone, with a single bead of red stone. Irregularly strung, the beads lay in eight coils, with the original sinew string in place, and measuring 11 feet in length. There were 2,771 beads altogether, representing an incredible amount of work and lapidarian skill, and a fine example of ancient pre-Pueblo Art.[30]

Gaumer leads the reader to believe the cave is located in Desolation Canyon along the Green River. But what are the chances that two virtually identical necklaces, both eleven feet long and both with almost the same number of beads, would be recovered from the same general area at roughly the same time? And how much more unlikely is it that both sites would have contained the remains of a very small dog associated with the burial of a child?

8.17 A 1929 view of a green elk-like figure at the mouth of Daddy Canyon. Courtesy of the Peabody Museum of Archaeology and Ethnology, Harvard University (PM No. 971-21-10/100162.1.252, File 99380218).

8.18 A 2016 view of the same green elk-like figure. Photo: Dan Bauer.

Suspiciously, Gaumer never once mentioned he had been in Nine Mile Canyon, even though the canyon was well known at the time of his reports. And he was clearly there. The 1937 article contains one photograph of a rock art site purportedly near Desbrough Canyon east of Rasmussen Cave but is actually of a rock art site near Gate Canyon west of Rasmussen Cave.[31]

A careful reading of the Gaumer report strongly suggests, although not provable, that Gaumer actually participated in the June 1931 excavations of Rasmussen Cave, and he was assisted in that endeavor by at least two local men from Myton. The 1937 report, as well as a supplemental report in 1939, might have been Gaumer's belated attempts to apologize and atone for the fact the expedition devolved into nothing more than a scavenger hunt for exotic artifacts. But rather than accept personal ownership of the egregious lapse in judgment, he obscured the location of the cave sites, and he modified the year he dug there to make it appear that it occurred after the "discovery" had already been published in reports by both Reagan and Beckwith.[32]

To Sterile Ground

As Scott surveyed the damage in front of him, he speculated that "the frantic search for mummies" might only have damaged the surface of the site "in scattered places," and below these pits there might be noteworthy, undisturbed deposits.[33] James Gunnerson, who later reexamined the excavation materials as part of his Harvard dissertation, seemed less certain, noting that the top thirty-one inches of the deposits had been repeatedly disturbed by looters, "making the stratigraphic position of artifacts recovered meaningless."[34]

Scott decided to excavate below the looters' pits as far as sterile soil. The cave excavations occurred in two phases, one on the west side of the cave and the other in the central portion (the east end was covered by large boulders from an ancient ceiling collapse).

The crew began digging into the less-disturbed west side of the shelter below the big red elk figure, and the "first" finds reported were four clay figurine fragments and one three-colored figurine, a stone knife, and corn still on the cob. They identified a wall of upright slabs, probably part of a room, although Scott was not convinced, referring to it as a "so-called room." At eighteen to twenty-five inches deep, they found an olla, or at least what was once a big water jug. It had been broken, and the large pieces carefully stacked in layers one fragment inside the other. At thirty-five inches deep, they hit a bedrock floor.[35]

8.19 An unknown crew member excavates below the boulders at the east side of Rasmussen Cave. Courtesy of the Peabody Museum of Archaeology and Ethnology, Harvard University (PM No. 971-21-10/100162.1.141, File 99380260).

The excavations then shifted to the "refuse pit" just outside and east of the wall. In modern archaeological parlance, a refuse pit is a midden, or a place where the ancients discarded household waste. What humans throw away can tell archaeologists a lot about the people who lived there: what they ate, what kinds of animals they hunted, the tools they used, how food was processed, etc. The Peabody Museum excavators probably focused on the midden for an entirely different reason: Middens are composed of looser, softer soils that, in prehistoric times, were preferred burial locations.

Excavators shoveled into this area to a depth of a little more than three feet, encountering hundreds of artifacts: five metates, animal bone fragments, knotted cords, withes, flint flakes, squash rind, a piece of cedar-bark rope, and lots and lots of maize remains. In one area of the pit, at a depth of thirty-five inches, they found a cache of one hundred fifty corncobs, two of which had sticks inserted in the ends and another with a hole where a stick had once been inserted. In another, they found six ears of corn with the kernels still in place.[36] In other words, they found the byproducts of daily life but nothing remarkable that warranted elaboration.

8.20 A large number of clay blobs flattened on one side were recovered in Rasmussen Cave. The crew indicated they observed no evidence they had been thrown against the walls or ceiling, but such marks are clearly evident. Photo: Jerry D. Spangler.

They shifted their next pit eastward into the center of the refuse pit next to the large boulders at the east end of the shelter. As Scott noted, this was the same area previously disturbed by looters and "at least two and in all probability more burials have been taken." The midden here was deeper, almost two yards deep, and the amount of discarded refuse was substantially greater. They carefully cataloged their finds: four manos, pieces of coiled basketry, an owl-like figurine, a reed mat, an arrow point, a fragment of wood with designs burned onto it, sharpened sticks, corncobs, squash rinds, cedar bark, human feces, a chunk of Gilsonite, and on and on.[37]

At this point, Scott made two interesting observations. They had encountered numerous clay "blobs," flat on one side, suggesting "they may have been stuck on the wall or thrown against the ceiling of the cave. Both walls and roof were inspected for marks which would substantiate this but none were found."[38] Actually, during a recent visit to the cave, we identified dozens of distinct marks where it appears that wet clay objects had been thrown against the ceiling. We can't see how the Peabody Museum crew missed them.

Scott's second point is also intriguing: "A strange and significant fact in connection with these refuse heaps is that although pottery was found in the living floors toward the west end of the cave, no potsherds whatsoever were encountered in the refuse heaps," although there were large numbers of figurine fragments and clay blobs.[39]

The presence—or absence—of potsherds is an important temporal indicator. Ceramic technology appeared in this part of the prehistoric world about AD 600, maybe as much as a hundred years earlier in some areas. By and large, these ceramic vessels were plain gray in nature, some tempered with a dark, crushed rock (possibly basalt) and some tempered with crushed limestone or calcite. This plain-gray pottery style remained largely unchanged for six hundred years or more. By about AD 1050 or 1100, however, corrugated pottery and grayware with painted designs were added to the grayware tradition. All three of these pottery styles seem to have disappeared in the Tavaputs Plateau region by AD 1250 or 1300 at the latest.

The presence of ceramics is considered by archaeologists to be a hallmark of the Formative period when groups were more sedentary, practiced agriculture, and often aggregated into larger social units. Ceramics were a technological advancement that allowed people to cook their foods for longer periods of time, especially beans that require considerable boiling time to become digestible. In short, any site with potsherds could be attributed to this period of time. And many of the open residences and granaries they had investigated thus far had these potsherds on the surface.

The east side of Rasmussen Cave had lots of maize remains and some squash rinds, but no pottery. Might this be evidence that prehistoric farmers were here before the advent of ceramics? One possible answer to that question was found in clefts below the large boulders at the east end of the shelter. Cleft A was a natural cavity created by the joining of three boulders. Looters had ravaged this area, digging through three to six feet of midden. As Scott related, "However, the diggers had stopped in time so that when we had cleared but a few centimeters [an inch or so] of refuse away a skeleton was uncovered...in a flexed position."[40]

Although they had exposed the lower portion of the body, the upper portion was still covered by six feet of refuse. It had to be carefully removed layer by layer to determine what, if anything, was associated with the burial and what represented human trash that had simply accumulated since the burial. The catalog of artifacts was largely the same as elsewhere in the cave: burned and unburned clay, clay blobs, figurines, basket fragments, a corncob with a stick, a reed mat, a knotted twig, an antler fragment possibly used to flake stone tools, cords of animal fur, a fragment of mountain sheep horn, bark, and squash rinds.

But once they reached the level of the upper torso, the catalog of artifacts was suddenly much, much different. An animal tooth grooved to be worn as a necklace and three spear foreshafts, two with the points still attached, were discovered in the face area; a bone awl and atlatl foreshafts were observed in the abdomen area; four spear points (atlatl dart points) and a knife were found in the lower back area; two leather moccasins were located "strangely enough" covering the face, a third had been placed beneath the head, along with a "large mass of buckskin," and broken spear shafts and an atlatl were identified below the body and paralleling the spine. The body rested on compacted earthen floor and was then covered with grass and "straw" that had become intermixed with corncobs, cordage, and animal fur.[41]

Gunnerson's subsequent reanalysis offered a few more details of the burial not found in the writings of Kidder, Brew, and Scott. He noted the bundle of buckskin under the head was actually buckskin leggings. And the third moccasin under the head was a pouch containing red pigment, a serrated bone artifact, a hafted blade, four wooden spear foreshafts, and a piece of worked horn (probably from a bighorn sheep).

The artifact assemblage was so different from the other artifacts that Gunnerson observed,

8.21 A 1929 view of rock art found in a second, smaller shelter just east of Rasmussen Cave. Courtesy of the Peabody Museum of Archaeology and Ethnology, Harvard University (PM No. 971-21-10/100162.1.246, File 99380217).

8.22 Close-up view of the "dancing" animals at the same site as observed in 2016. Photo: Dan Bauer.

> There is little evidence to associate the individual with the occupation of the shelter, which he obviously predated. The artifacts buried with this man closely resemble what would be expected in a Basketmaker II burial except for the hide moccasins and leggings.... Since no habitation sites reported from Nine Mile Canyon or adjacent areas appear to have the same cultural affiliation as the burial, it is possible that the individual died and was buried far from home. Nothing associated with him would be out of place for a man to have been carrying on a hunting or exploring trip.[42]

Gunnerson might be correct that the deceased was a traveler far from home and that the overlying refuse dominated by maize remains came from later Fremont farmers. Then again, it might be completely wrong. In the decades since his reanalysis of the burial, scores of archaeologists working throughout the Southwest have repeatedly demonstrated that Basketmaker II peoples were highly dependent on maize agriculture, perhaps as early as 1000 BC. They would not adopt ceramic technologies for another 1,500 years, but unfired clay objects were fairly common.

But were Basketmaker-like farmers actually present this far north in northeastern Utah at this time? The answer to that is an unequivocal maybe. In the Steinaker Reservoir area near Vernal, investigations by Brigham Young University convincingly demonstrated that maize-growing groups had become well entrenched by AD 250, at least three hundred years before the advent of ceramics. And rock art in the same area bears a striking resemblance to rock art images in the Basketmaker heartland in the San Juan River country. This raises the possibility that the origins of what we call the Fremont Complex may lie in Basketmaker II times, perhaps stimulated by migrant farmers into northern Utah.[43]

More and more evidence from sites north of the Colorado River demonstrates that ancestral Fremont groups were farming corn as early as 150 BC in the Richfield area, and Ancestral Puebloans as early as 1000 BC in the Kanab area.[44] It is certainly possible that maize farming spread to northeastern Utah much earlier than traditionally thought.

Another interesting indicator at Rasmussen Cave is the presence of atlatls and dart points. These were certainly the preferred hunting implements for thousands of years of hunting and gathering on the northern Colorado Plateau.

The bow and arrow did not appear in this part of the world until about AD 100, and it did not replace the atlatl until several centuries later. In other words, the atlatl would not have been out of place among the first farmers in northeastern Utah.

If the Rasmussen Cave burial is reexamined within the context of what archaeologists know now, it is just as possible the burial represents an early maize farming community in Nine Mile Canyon with similarities to Basketmaker II farming adaptations elsewhere, and it was ancestral to Fremont farming that would later come to dominate human adaptations to Nine Mile Canyon. Scott was, in 1931, puzzled by the absence of ceramics in the refuse heaps associated with the burial. Today, archaeologists would ask a different question: Were people farming here centuries before the full-fledged Fremont presence manifest in the open residences, cliff granaries, and defensive retreats to pinnacles and buttes?

Archaeologist David Yoder has been reexamining the Rasmussen Cave collection and, with the help of four recent radiocarbon dates, he has come up with interesting findings, although they also raise even more questions. Human bone from a child burial recovered by Morss in 1929 produced a radiocarbon date between AD 125 and 250—just before or at the beginning of maize farming in the region. Maize remains from the west, undisturbed end of the cave were dated to AD 900 to 1025, or the height of the Fremont occupation of Nine Mile Canyon. In fact, most radiocarbon dates from Nine Mile Canyon fall within the range of AD 900 to 1100.[45]

But what about the Basketmaker-like burial that so intrigued the expedition? Yoder's results are puzzling to say the least. A cord used to wrap the leather leggings found under the head returned a radiocarbon date between AD 420 and 520, which would be consistent with early maize farmers in the region just before the advent of grayware ceramics. But a radiocarbon date from a human bone returned a date of AD 750 to 850, or about three hundred years later than the cord. This date is consistent with later Fremont farmers, although it is somewhat earlier than most Fremont farming dates in the canyon.[46]

What does that mean? Yoder offers several explanations. One is that one of the two radiocarbon dates is simply wrong (materials can get contaminated during museum storage). Another possibility is that the artifacts Scott and Brew thought were associated with the burial were actually not part of the burial. Rather, a deceased Fremont farmer just happened to be buried over the top of artifacts left behind by earlier occupants, and the burial and Basketmaker-like artifacts are unrelated.

Or maybe the leather cord used to bind the leggings—Yoder dated the cord that wrapped the leggings, not the leggings themselves—had been floating around the cave for some time, and the owner of the leggings recycled the loose cord and it is actually unrelated to the leather bundle and burial. Or maybe the leather sample he dated was not the one Yoder thought it was.

8.23 Close-up view of a wooden platform used to create a level surface for a granary. Photo: Dan Bauer.

Whatever the explanation (Yoder prefers the idea the burial and the artifacts around it are unrelated to one another), two of the radiocarbon dates—the child burial and the rawhide strap—represent the two oldest dates yet reported from Nine Mile Canyon. And both dates suggest that people were here at a time when foragers throughout the region began to add maize farming to their subsistence.

Almost nine decades after "Basketmaker" was disinterred and carted away to the Peabody Museum, he continues to generate more questions than answers.

End of the Trail

Scott and his colleagues rooted around in Rasmussen Cave for five days through at least August 15. Much of that time was probably spent cataloging and packaging artifacts to be shipped to the Peabody Museum. And they had been watching and waiting for the return of Bowers's crew, by then long overdue from their Desolation Canyon explorations. When Bowers and company arrived sometime on August 15, no one wrote anything about it in their journals.

After eighteen days and more than one hundred fifty combined miles on horseback, the grand exploration of the West Tavaputs Plateau was concluded. But not the expedition itself. There was still less adventurous work to be done in the Uinta Basin.

On August 16, the reunited crew loaded into a car and a truck and set out for Roosevelt on the bumpy freight road through Gate Canyon. No one says whether Oliver Rasmussen and Daf Thompson accompanied them, but probably not. They had to account for their horses and pack animals that were no longer needed. On August 15, Thompson was paid $150, including $35 for the use of two horses and $105 for thirty-five days of guide service. He also got a $10 bonus. Rasmussen was paid $180 for thirty-five days of service, including $70 for the use of four horses and $105 for guide service. Scott also chipped in a $5 bonus.[47]

Locals say Rasmussen, who was in his early fifties at the time of the expedition, lived out the remainder of his life at his small ranch at Dry Canyon; he died there in 1947 at age sixty-eight and was buried in Emery County.[48]

Dafton Thompson, who was twenty-two years old in 1931,[49] disappeared from the official record.

Archaeologists returned to Nine Mile Canyon periodically in the years that followed, but the lower part of the canyon—the area investigated by the Claflin-Emerson Expedition—was largely ignored for more than fifty years until the late

1980s and early 1990s. Archaeological interest here has blossomed even more in recent years, the result of natural gas discoveries and federal mandates that require archaeological surveys *before* development. To date, nearly two thousand archaeological sites have been documented, more than half of which are rock art localities. The canyon's moniker, "World's Longest Art Gallery," seems justified.

Why is there so much rock art here? That question apparently escaped the attention of the Claflin-Emerson participants, who seemed content to merely photograph certain panels and on occasion write a line of two of text in their journals. But they did provide the earliest overview of the prehistoric residents in the Tavaputs Plateau. They were farmers who built stone houses on the benches above the floodplain and constructed elaborate granaries in the cliff faces to store their foods. They were masons who erected massive stone towers on pinnacles and buttes with commanding views of the canyon. The towers were unlike anything the crew had observed in the regions farther to the south.

And in that regard, what the Claflin-Emerson Expedition saw in 1931 remains valid to this day. But we know they saw only a tiny fraction of what is here, describing maybe two percent of the sites now documented in the canyon. And what archaeologists know now paints a much more complex picture of the ancients.

For one, an overwhelming prevalence of rock art sites exceeds anything reported elsewhere in the state of Utah and maybe even in the United States. More than eighty percent of all documented sites have rock art elements, and more than seventy percent are exclusively rock art sites.

The number of rock art sites tends to overshadow the fact that the ancients were also living here. Prehistoric residences take a wide variety of forms, including stacked masonry one- and two-room surface structures, semisubterranean pit houses, D-shaped houses built next to a cliff face, and occasionally casual structures inside rock shelters. With few exceptions, all are small (usually less than ten feet in diameter) and would have been suitable for a single family. No single preferred house style predominates.

There is no significant difference in the ratio of site types—rock art, storage, and residential—by increased elevation above the valley floor. In total, there may be fewer sites at higher elevations, but the types of sites and their ratio are virtually the same as at lower elevations. Evidence of longer-term occupations is indeed rare. Artifacts of any kind are rare. If the handful of sites with substantial artifacts are excluded, each site typically averages less than one artifact per site.

Although sites are numerous, they are generally small. Most rock art sites average fewer than ten images, most granaries occur as a single unit and are less than ten cubic feet in size, and residences are scattered up and down the canyon with very little evidence of aggregation into villages.

Yet patterns are beginning to emerge as to the nature and distribution of rock art sites. They generally cluster in relatively close proximity to suspected residential sites, but not necessarily with storage sites. Certain motifs, such as the horned snake and the dot matrix, are universal, occurring in abundance throughout the canyon. Others, such as the combatants, long-legged shorebirds, and strange linear human figures with upside-down trapezoidal bodies, occur in only small geographic areas of the canyon, usually within a half-mile of each other. Classic Fremont human figures are actually quite rare.

As we try to understand the totality of Nine Mile Canyon, we recognize that these observations, based on small areas within the canyon, offer only a glimpse of the whole. Most of the canyon remains uninvestigated and the sites undocumented. We do not know yet if settlement patterns are different from one area of the canyon to another, or whether those patterns changed over time. It may be several more decades before the prehistory of Nine Mile Canyon is largely understood.

Archaeologists are still struggling with fundamental questions about how the ancients thrived in this unusually harsh desert environment. They do not yet understand how human behavior changed over time, the role of the local environment in those changes, and when those changes might have occurred. The most encouraging sign is that the region has been the focus of intense ongoing scholarly research for the past decade, and this research is likely to continue for another two decades. Cumulatively, the amount of research being conducted now and into the future will make the area one of the most thoroughly investigated regions anywhere in the state and potentially one of the best understood.

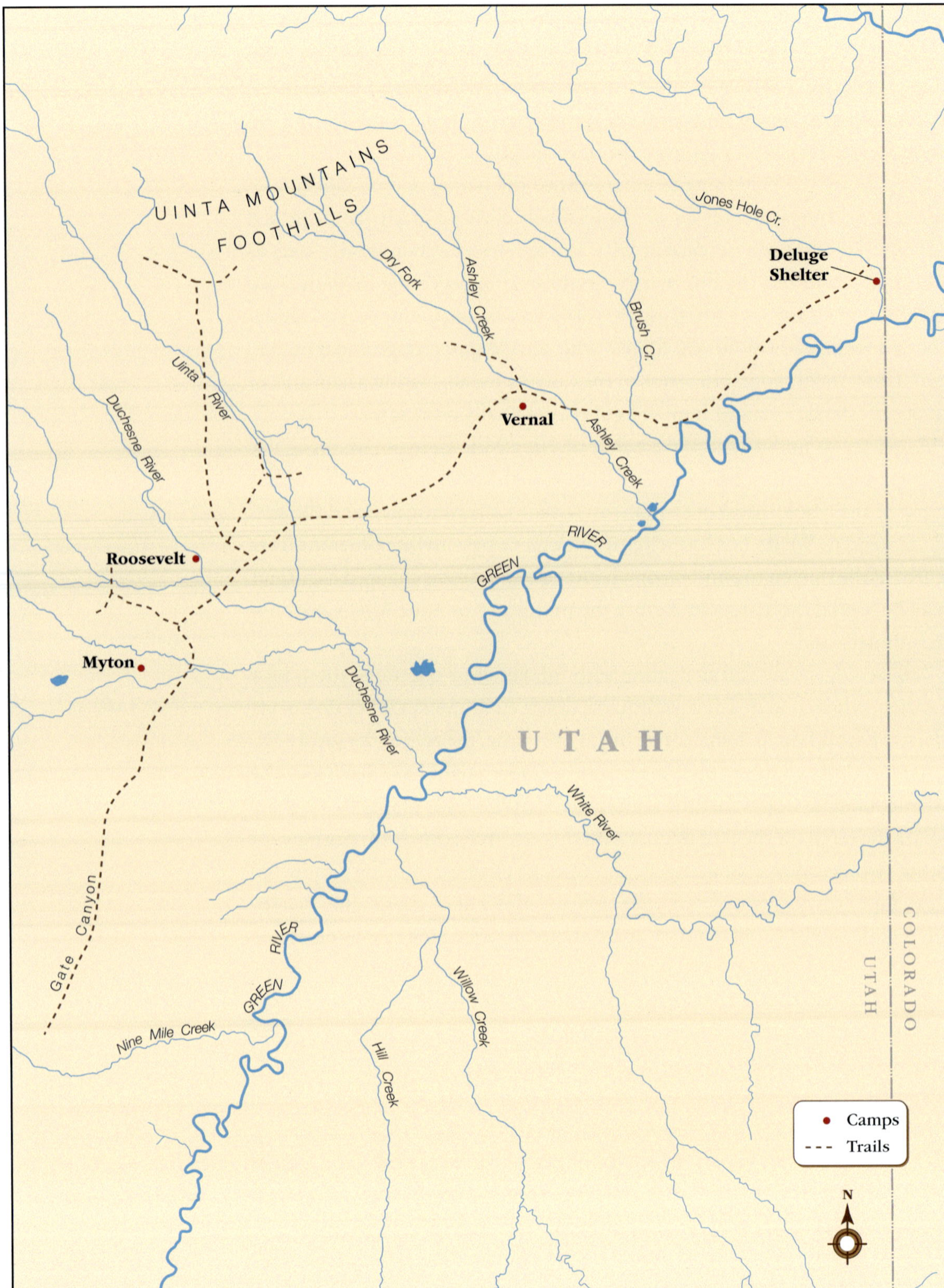

9.1 Map of the expedition route through the Uinta Basin.

Out with a Whimper

The Uinta Basin Investigations

9

The saddle-weary Crimson Cowboys had just completed the unthinkable: a roughly four-hundred-mile horseback odyssey through the wildest canyon country imaginable. Conducted on a scale never before attempted by archaeologists, the adventure might have been over, but there was work still to be done and seventeen days left to do it. The expedition was nonetheless lean on exhibit-quality artifacts, and we assume expedition leader Donald Scott was determined to bring to the Peabody something worthy of their benefactors' investment in the expedition.

Akin to conquistadors convinced that El Dorado lay just beyond the horizon, Scott turned his focus northward to the Uinta Basin, where locals had reported fantastic archaeological sites awaiting their shovels. And if they were skeptical of tall tales from locals, none other than Julian Steward of the University of Utah—a highly respected friend and peer of the Peabody Museum—also spoke highly of the region's potential for significant discoveries. Scott must have been optimistic as their vehicles rumbled and rattled into Roosevelt on August 16, 1931.

Donald Scott and Dave Rust had visited the Uinta Basin three weeks before to procure supplies, and Scott had spent several days exploring the countryside in the company of local guides. They showed him the remarkable rock art sites now hailed as some of the best in the world, the deep alcoves of Ashley–Dry Fork that had yielded mummies, and the faint outline of open ruins outside of Roosevelt and at Brush Creek. He knew exactly where he would investigate.

But unlike the Tavaputs Plateau, which was largely unknown except to a few cowboys, the Uinta Basin was civilized. Towns, roads, schools, and churches dotted the basin. And there were plenty of people, some of whom had a keen interest in collecting the pre-Columbian curiosities left behind by the ancients

9.2 Scenic view of the Ashley–Dry Fork area. Photo: Dan Bauer.

who had lived here a millennium ago. By the time Scott arrived, however, these same people had already ravaged many if not most of the high-potential sites here, searching for pots, baskets, and burials. Undeterred, Scott believed that careful excavation might reveal evidence—and artifacts—the untrained looters had missed. That had certainly been the case at Rasmussen Cave.

On August 16, the Harvard crew, along with Rust, loaded into a pickup truck and car in Nine Mile Canyon for the ride north to the Uinta Basin. They stopped briefly at a site on the Preston Nutter Ranch to photograph some rock art, then turned north onto the Gate Canyon Road. Fresh from their Desolation Canyon horseback odyssey, Waldo Forbes, James Dennison, and William Bowers probably felt the jostle in their bones as the pickup truck bounced along the rutted ranch road that wends its way through Gate Canyon towards the Uinta Basin some forty miles to the north.

From 1886 to the early twentieth century, the two-track road through Gate Canyon had been a bustling freight route that connected the Uinta Basin (and its rich Gilsonite deposits) to the Denver & Rio Grande railhead in Price. The U.S. Army maintained the road in those days, but it had fallen into disrepair after the state built a new highway to the west, now US 191 through Indian

Canyon. Moreover, the Gilsonite interests built a railroad to the mines that proved far more efficient than a wagon route that could turn into a muddy quagmire at the slightest brush with inclement weather.

As the Peabody crew made the seven-mile ascent up Gate Canyon to the rim of Nine Mile Canyon, they passed scores of axle-grease signatures left by the freighters in the 1880s and 1890s and by homesteaders bound for the Uinta Basin in the last great American land rush of 1906. Once on the summit, they saw the basin stretched before them—a vast bowl rimmed on the north by the Uinta Mountains and the west by the Wasatch Plateau. The Green River meandered lazily off to the east. It was a far cry from the canyon gorges and impassable cliffs of the Tavaputs.

The geology of the Uinta Basin is different than what they had become accustomed to in the previous two months. The Jurassic sandstones here, laden with fossils big and small, are more conducive to large, deep sandstone alcoves ideal for human habitation. And the dry climate ensures that most perishable artifacts would be preserved. Throughout the Tavaputs Plateau, they had been preoccupied with excavating rock shelters for signs of prehistoric life, though finding relatively little. If Scott had observed these Uinta Basin alcoves before the 1931 expedition, he might have reconsidered the

9.3 Rock art panel in Ashley–Dry Fork Canyon. Photo: Dan Bauer.

9.4 The expedition stopped to photograph this rock art site near the mouth of Gate Canyon as they traveled from their base camp at Rasmussen Cave to the Uinta Basin. Photo: Dan Bauer.

9.5 Dave Rust's son, Nelson, hired a flatbed truck and helped the crew in the Uinta Basin. Courtesy of the Peabody Museum of Archaeology and Ethnology, Harvard University (PM No. 971-21-10/ 100162.1.996, File 122390255).

9.6 The Jurassic Sandstone formations in the Uinta Basin are quite different from the sandstones found on the Tavaputs Plateau. Photo: Dan Bauer.

overland expedition in favor of the more impressive Uinta Basin shelters. Or he might not have waited four years into the expedition to visit them.

The Uinta Basin was always part of the 1931 Claflin-Emerson Expedition itinerary, but Scott's interest here was clearly piqued by his short visits to various sites in the area, and by the words and deeds of three individuals in particular: local schoolteacher Walter Atwood, photographer Leo Thorne, and Albert Reagan, a competitor for museum artifacts who had a year's head start on the Harvard crew.

South Myton Bench

Their gear and supplies loaded into a pickup truck and a car, the expedition first drove to Roosevelt. The small town must have seemed like a thriving metropolis compared to their past stops at isolated ranches. Their expense log reveals they enjoyed the luxury of fresh produce and prepared meals. They rented rooms at least one evening, probably a welcome respite from sleeping on the ground and the first chance in weeks to bathe in anything but dirty creek water.

They even splurged, paying eighty cents to visit the local movie theater.[1] They do not say which movie they watched. Maybe in keeping with the spirit of their Western adventure, they took in *Cimarron*, the first Western to win an Oscar for Best Picture, a film based on an Edna Ferber novel that was being serialized in the *Roosevelt Standard* at that same time. More likely, it was *Sin Takes a Holiday*, a romantic comedy starring Basil Rathbone, Constance Bennett, and Kenneth MacKenna, at least according to Utopia Theatre ads in that same newspaper on August 16, 17, and 18.[2]

Their first order of business on August 17 was to investigate a cluster of sites about five miles outside of Roosevelt on what is called the South Myton Bench, a prominent terrace about seventy-five to a hundred feet above the valley floor. Atwood had taken Scott to this area in late July, and he accompanied the Peabody Museum crew there again. This time he carried the official title "archaeological scout" and earned a stipend of $1.25 an hour for nearly seven days of service.[3] A fellow named Ivan Atwood—probably a relation—was camp cook and manager.

Born in 1886, Walter Edward Atwood was a high school teacher at Union High School in Roosevelt, Utah, when the Claflin-Emerson Expedition came to the basin. It is not clear how he got connected with the Harvard team, but it is likely he did so through a friendship and common interest in prehistory with

Leo Thorne and Albert B. Reagan. Atwood had the archaeology bug and was by 1931 digging near Roosevelt on the Ute reservation; he had a tribal permit.[4] The spring after the expedition returned from the field, Donald Scott wrote Atwood, thanking him for all he did to help him while they were working south of Roosevelt.[5]

Atwood's journey to the Uinta Basin began south of Salt Lake City near Sandy. His father was a farmer, and Walter was the oldest of six children in their Mormon family.[6] He was drafted into the U.S. Army in 1917 and sent to Neufchâteau, France, where the American Expeditionary Forces were billeted.[7] He was injured in the war and listed in the 1920 census as a "disabled soldier," living in Salt Lake City and working there at Royal Laundry and for the railroad. He attended Utah State University and graduated in 1924 with a bachelor's degree in animal husbandry. Atwood married Nellie Ione Snow in 1918, and they had four daughters.[8]

By 1927 he was back in Crescent (near Sandy, Utah) working as a high school teacher. And by 1930 he was teaching in Roosevelt.[9] He probably taught animal husbandry or vocational education. He was also the advisor to the local F.F.A. club, known as the Toyackers (a Ute word reported to mean "okay"). In 1933 Atwood helped his charges raise money for a trip to the Chicago World's Fair, an undertaking almost unheard of in a small, poverty-stricken place like

9.7 A 1931 view of the South Myton Bench where seven sites were excavated. Courtesy of the Peabody Museum of Archaeology and Ethnology, Harvard University (PM No. 971-21-10/100162.1.403, File 99380211).

the Uinta Basin. For most, it was the most memorable event of their lives.[10] Atwood stayed in the Uinta Basin until 1941 when he took a job at Central Union High School in Fresno, California. He taught vocational education there and was again the sponsor of the F.F.A. Club. He died in Fresno almost forty years later in 1985, at age 98.[11]

Of Atwood's sites on the South Myton Bench, Scott wrote, "Numbers of very large boulders are to be found at the base of the slope. In the shelter of these boulders and in overhangs formed by them are very crude habitation sites. In a few instances, low walls of upright slabs were found, but mostly the sites are without walls, the boulders having afforded, apparently, enough protection."[12] The crew spent four days excavating seven sites here (U16-1 to U16-7), recovering a few nondescript potsherds and finely worked arrow points. But they found little in the way of substantial human occupation.

But there was a lot of detritus from the manufacturing of stone tools, enough so that it warranted closer analysis and organization. Scott noted two distinct types of stone artifacts: (1) very finely crafted small points with notches, "some very beautiful indeed," and (2) crudely flaked, heavy implements "resembling Early Palaeoliths [*sic*]" scattered on the valley floor along with an abundance of cobbles of all sizes and shapes. He said, "These crude flints seemed to be beyond reasonable doubt the product of human workmanship."[13]

We surmise that the Harvard boys had stumbled on a prehistoric quarry where cobbles of chert, chalcedony, and quartzite had eroded from the South Myton Bench to the valley floor. In prehistoric times, groups might have traveled to this locale to procure raw materials for their stone tools, breaking the cobbles to identify those of highest quality. The best stone was then reduced even more into a crude biface—archaeologists sometimes call them "blanks" or "preforms"—for easier transport to their homes where they were further reduced into points, drills, etc. These were the crude "Palaeoliths" to which Scott referred. The nearby shelters were merely convenient camp spots used briefly by many and all over a long period of time during their mining of the cobbles.

Atwood also took Donald Scott to visit a man with a large arrowhead collection. With Atwood's assistance, Scott sorted the collection into seven types. He later asked Atwood if the teacher would ask if the man would sell one representative point from each group for two to three dollars apiece, "in the interests of science."[14] We do not know if he ever did this, but the Peabody Museum has projectile points from the Uinta Basin all neatly arranged in collections.

Scott clearly thought highly of Atwood because his post-expedition letter promised him copies of Noel Morss's groundbreaking paper which defined the Fremont culture, as well as an Alfred Kidder–Samuel Guernsey paper on the Basketmakers of northern Arizona. He also told Atwood about Henry Roberts' projected report on the 1931 expedition (which was never completed) and that the teacher would "get one of the first copies." He even offered to find him a copy of Alfred V. Kidder's out-of-print *Introduction to Southwestern Archaeology* (1924). In his correspondence with Atwood, Scott went on to discuss other issues relating to the Peabody's research.[15] Clearly, Scott admired Atwood's intellect and valued his contributions to the expedition's success.

Rock Creek and Other Diversions

By August 21, they had moved their camp to Rock Creek about four miles west of Talmadge. They investigated several promising alcoves with no results (they had been scoured clean by water runoff). They then turned their attention to an open area "loaded with potsherds and burned bone," but their excavations here (U11-1) revealed nothing more than arrow points, a stone bead, and yet more bluish-gray potsherds. The only hint of architecture of any kind was an alignment of stones that might or might not have been human made.[16]

9.8 A 1931 view of a "rock wall" at U11-1 in the Uinta Mountains foothills. Courtesy of the Peabody Museum of Archaeology and Ethnology, Harvard University (PM No. 971-21-10/100162.1.389, File 99380208).

They spent perhaps a week at the Talmadge Camp not doing much in terms of archaeology but having fun nonetheless. According to Rust's journal, there were plenty of other diversions going on at this time. On August 20, Scott drove to Green River, Utah, by way of Price to pick up Henry Roberts, who had traveled to Utah by train. They secured rooms at the Midland Hotel, the same establishment where the crew had taken rooms at the start of the expedition,[17] and then set out to rejoin the others in the Uinta Basin. Scott and Roberts spent the next week motoring around to visit various sites in the area, but we have found no record

9.9 The Claflin-Emerson Expedition crew enjoying a high-elevation fishing trip in 1931 in the Chain Lakes area of the Uinta Mountains. Courtesy of the Peabody Museum of Archaeology and Ethnology, Harvard University (PM No. 971-21-10/100162.1.872, File 122390131).

of what they saw or what they thought of it. It was undoubtedly to familiarize Roberts with the local archaeology in anticipation of his pending monograph of the Claflin-Emerson Expedition.

In the meantime, the crew also took time off to go fishing in the High Uintas. With the help of local guide Burt Burgess and eleven saddle animals, Scott, Rust, Roberts, and the students all set out to climb Mount Emmons, a 13,440-foot-high peak once thought to be Utah's highest. Photographs depict the crew in a jovial mood. Scott paid Burgess $2.25 for fishing tackle, but there is no entry from expedition accounts saying he ever paid for the pack animals and guide services.[18]

After a week of diversions, it was time to get back to work. On August 28 (or August 30),[19] Forbes loaded Roberts into the expedition car and drove him to Craig, Colorado, to catch a train to Denver. The remaining crew moved their camp to Roosevelt to investigate three sites on tribal lands just outside of Fort Duchesne, a sister city bordering Roosevelt on the east. One of the sites had

9.10 The expedition excavating a series of structures (A9-1) on a bench above the Uintah River. Courtesy of the Peabody Museum of Archaeology and Ethnology, Harvard University (PM No. 971-21-10/100162.1.406, File 99380212).

9.11 Crew members investigate a second site (A9-2) above the Uintah River in 1931. Courtesy of the Peabody Museum of Archaeology and Ethnology, Harvard University (PM No. 971-21-10/100162.1.408, File 99380213).

been excavated earlier, and the outline of stone walls was clearly visible. Their own excavations indicated, as Scott noted, "that the roof and probably a large part, if not all of the walls were of wood and adobe construction, the burning of which was responsible for the bricklike consistency of the adobe."[20]

At these three sites (A9-1 to A9-3), the crew noted the presence of symmetrical holes carved into the bedrock sandstone, some only an inch or two in diameter and others up to sixteen inches in diameter. Some of these were "unmistakably" storage pits, while others appeared to be post holes, the poles themselves and superstructure long since eroded away.[21] Such holes are actually common in the Uinta Basin, especially in the Cub Creek drainage where they are even larger and deeper, but they are quite rare outside of the basin.[22]

Ashley–Dry Fork

By Sunday, August 30, the expedition had moved its base camp to the confluence of Ashley Canyon and Dry Fork about nine miles above Vernal, where Leo Thorne joined them. Thorne knew this country better than anyone, and Scott embraced his wealth of knowledge while ignoring the methods by which Thorne had acquired it. The sites the Harvard boys investigated here had already been dug, at least partially and probably by Thorne. Not all of this was illegal; some of the sites were on private land. The expedition even paid five dollars to a Mrs. Shiner for allowing them to dig on her property.[23]

9.12 Leo Thorne. Photo courtesy of the Uintah County Regional History Center.

Leo Cuthbert Thorne was born in Nebraska in 1883, but his grandfather, James, was one of the first white settlers of the Vernal area in 1876. Leo's parents moved to the Dry Fork Canyon area northwest of Vernal when Leo was three. Not long after, he began hunting for arrowheads and points.[24] Collecting and searching for prehistoric artifacts became an obsession for Thorne until the end of his life. By the time the Claflin-Emerson Expedition arrived in the Uinta Basin, Thorne's reputation made consulting him a prerequisite for the Peabody team or any other archaeologist who might venture here.

Thorne's parents were farmers and ranchers, but Leo could not follow in their footsteps due to a back injury at age nineteen when his horse threw him.[25] He turned to photography, and in doing so became the man who compiled a remarkably complete visual history of the young town through the first half of the twentieth century.

Probably through Dave Rust, Donald Scott knew that Thorne would be a valuable guide in the Vernal area. And indeed he was. He led them to the sites on Ashley Creek and Dry Fork Canyon that they excavated in early September. They dug in "Elizabeth's Cave," named by Thorne after a mummy he removed shortly after his daughter Mary Law discovered it.[26] "Elizabeth Fremont" was on display in Thorne's studio for many years until it was finally repatriated under provisions of the Native American Graves Protection and Repatriation Act. Elizabeth was not the only mummy he had unearthed. A year later in 1932, the General Land Office (precursor to the Bureau of Land Management) took possession of another mummy that Thorne had excavated. Shortly thereafter, GLO division chief Archie D. Ryan admonished Thorne, saying, "There is absolutely no way whatsoever that an individual can receive a permit to collect prehistoric artifacts from the public domain."[27]

By today's standards, Thorne and probably Atwood were looters, digging through the caves for artifacts without thought to scientific technique and proper procedures. They considered themselves to be archaeologists, and in their own minds they were contributing to science through their local exhibits. But in the eye of the trained archaeologist, they were and still are considered a destructive bane to our nation's cultural heritage.

Thorne, Atwood, and many other "gophers," as Donald Scott called them, were violating the Antiquities Act of 1906 by collecting and excavating cultural artifacts from public lands. Nonetheless, Scott and the Peabody team knew that it was in their best interest to work with looters like Thorne. These men knew where many of the best sites were and were eager to help the Harvard scientists in their work. Thorne had considerable experience working alongside Albert Reagan as photographer and chief shovel-man. The Claflin-Emerson Expedition paid him forty dollars for his services.

For a few years after the expedition, Thorne maintained a lively correspondence with Donald Scott, sending him photographs of rock art as well as many artifacts that Thorne already possessed or had recently acquired. Scott seemed genuinely to appreciate everything Thorne sent him. He even told Thorne, "You are certainly an indefatigable archaeologist."[28] One can imagine Thorne beaming with pride, being acknowledged as a fellow researcher engaged in the pursuit of knowledge, by the director of the premier ethnographic institution in the country. Thorne continued to work with Albert B. Reagan as well.

Thorne pursued his twin passions—archaeology and photography—right up until the end of his life at age eighty-six. His photographic record of the Uinta Basin is a priceless resource for researchers, amounting to more than ten

9.13 This large alcove is located at the junction of Dry Fork and Ashley Fork near where the expedition camped. Photo: Dan Bauer.

thousand images; they are currently available online at the Regional History Center of the Uintah County Library in Vernal. Among these are hundreds of rock art photographs of exceptional quality for that day.[29] His artifact collection, which for many years was displayed in Thorne's photography studio on Main Street in Vernal, is now at the Uintah County Heritage Museum.

Thorne showed Scott and company around, but it was painfully obvious to the Harvard boys that they were too late. All of the cave sites that held such promise had already been looted. In fact, the only site where looting was not mentioned was A6-7, a granary constructed on a bedrock ledge where there were no deposits that could have been looted.

But not everything disappeared into looters' bags. At one site (A6-1), a slab-lined cist that had been "destroyed recently," they found intact baskets, basket fragments, a cane tube, and corncobs in the undisturbed deposits near the cist.[30] The baskets would make a fine addition to the Peabody collection.

But their good luck did not last. At another alcove (A6-2) they found two destroyed cists, along with grooves in a boulder for "ax sharpening," but not much else.[31] They moved on to another alcove near Red Mountain (A6-3) but were again greeted by looters' pits and discarded bits of corncobs and potsherds. A careful reexamination of the pit profiles and additional excavation revealed nothing but a little charcoal and knotted cord.[32] Another alcove nearby (A6-5), which they called Bandit Cave, revealed more of the same: looters' pits with nothing left behind but charcoal and cedar bark.[33]

9.14 A 1931 view of the basket recovered from A6-1. Courtesy of the Peabody Museum of Archaeology and Ethnology, Harvard University (PM No. 971-21-10/100162.1.365, File 99380207).

Brush Creek and Jones Hole

On September 1, the expedition turned its back on Ashley–Dry Fork—at one time rich in archaeological treasures, but now stripped clean—and began to move east and north towards the Ruple Ranch. The crew's energy level was obviously waning, as evidenced by the increasingly meager journal descriptions and the sloppy handwriting. Dave Rust and Jim Dennison motored ahead of the main party to make arrangements for the camp and inquire about horses for one last exploration into Jones Hole, located on the Utah-Colorado border deep in the heart of what is today Dinosaur National Monument.

The Ruple Ranch sat in an open area between Whirlpool and Split Mountain Canyons. On their way there they noted "some good pictographs" between Brush Creek and the ranch.[34] Rust clearly knew about the ranch and intended to acquire horses and meals from the owner, Henry "Hod" Ruple. The group still had one last site it wanted to check out in Jones Hole.

Ruple's parents, Hank and May, had come to Island Park in 1883 by way of Whiterocks on the Ute reservation. They had worked at Whiterocks for six years before they discovered the lush grasslands of Island Park and then migrated there to ranch. Hod was born a few years after they arrived in Island Park. The family ranched there until 1910 then sold out. Hod, though, repossessed the ranch five years later and lived there with his wife, Lilly, and two daughters, one of whom was Billie.[35]

9.15 The crew described these as sharpening grooves, but they appear to be bedrock metates. Courtesy of the Peabody Museum of Archaeology and Ethnology, Harvard University (PM No. 971-21-10/100162.1.397, File 99380210).

Though Hod later died of a burst appendix in 1937, he was hale and hearty in 1931, welcoming Rust and Dennison to the ranch and hosting them overnight.[36] During their conversation, Rust, a Stanford University man, noticed a University of California at Berkeley yearbook on the table, and asked about it. Hod and Lilly, no doubt with great pride, informed Rust that their daughter, Billie Ruple Untermann, had just earned her bachelor's degree in geology and was currently studying for her master's in the same, alongside her husband, G. Ernest Untermann Jr. The two had met when Untermann was a young geologist working in the area. He said he met Billie "swinging on the gate." The two quickly fell in love, and she joined Untermann in Berkeley where he was studying geology.[37]

During Rust's visit in 1931 he learned that Billie was then curator of the Geology Museum at Berkeley. She would receive her master's three years later, specializing in paleontology. This is not surprising, given the excitement in the area from the early twentieth century on about the dinosaur fossil excavations by Earl Douglass. In the 1940s Billie and Ernest came back to Vernal to work for the National Park Service in the newly expanded Dinosaur National

Monument. They published many scientific papers on the geology of the area. As Utah Geological and Mineralogical Survey director Arthur L. Crawford wrote, this seemed fitting because Billie had been pondering the landscape's origin since childhood. She found the answers in the classroom, and it made her want to drag her husband back "to the land of their romance, where together they could read the story of the rocks and interpret this fantastic history of a billion years for her neighbors, her townspeople, her state and for all the world."[38]

Besides their professional geology research and teaching, the Untermanns helped create the Utah Field House of Natural History.[39] They worked there for decades, he as director-curator and she as staff scientist. Both of them, Ernest especially, strongly supported the Echo Park Dam proposal. But environmentalists managed to stop it in 1955, a fight considered one of the great conservation battles of the twentieth century.[40]

The Untermanns may have stood on the wrong side of history in that instance, but Billie Ruple Untermann's life is an extraordinary story. Born in the most humble of circumstances on a frontier ranch, she rose to become a respected and well-published scientist. Having grown up surrounded by some of the most important paleontological resources in the world, she was inspired by them and returned to tell the region's story in her scientific studies. If Rust followed her career—and he probably did—he recognized a little of himself in Billie Ruple: a bright young person raised in poverty on a western ranch, yet succeeding in the highest of academic circles. None of the blue-blooded Claflin-Emerson members, however, except for maybe Brew, would have seen themselves in her story.

Nonetheless, the Ruple family had an abiding appreciation of science, and they probably welcomed the Harvard boys with open arms, although they only had two horses to spare. On September 2, Scott dispatched Rust and Dennison on horseback into Jones Hole on the upper Green River where locals had gushed about a cave there. Carrying with them a hand-drawn map provided by Hod Ruple, they rode eight miles into Jones Hole and eight miles back out the same day.[41]

The Jones Hole area is now a national fish hatchery, built in 1970 as part of the Colorado River Storage Project. The U.S. Fish and Wildlife Service raises sport fish there such as brown, cutthroat, and rainbow trout. In 1931, however, it was just another well-watered area that had attracted, in succession, Paleo-Indians, Archaic hunters and gatherers, Fremont farmers, Ute hunter-gatherers, and Anglo trappers and ranchers. It got its name, however, because of a colorful character named Charley Jones.

Jones, a trapper, buffalo hunter, and a bear of a man, had a child in 1882 with his wife, Mary Roena (Rene) Fairchild. She had moved to the Vernal area to live with her parents, John and Katherine Fairchild, after her husband, John Lindermann, abandoned her and their six children in Illinois. By the time she gave birth to Jones's child, she had had enough of his rough ways and moved back home with her parents. She claimed that Jones "needed an ox, not a wife."[42]

Three months later, Jones came to their home and pleaded with Rene to come home. When that did not work, he charged toward the Fairchild ranch house with steam coming out of his ears. Neighbors Hank and May Ruple, meanwhile, were out in the fields helping harvest the Fairchild crops. When Rene saw Jones coming, she made for the corncrib and locked the door behind her. Jones tried to break down the door but failed. One of the hired hands, Charlie Bangledork, heard the commotion and came running. Jones turned to Bangledork and cut him with a knife, inflicting a vicious wound that left Jones certain that he had killed the man. He then ran to the house, kidnapped the child, and rode off.[43]

Hank Ruple hopped on his horse and chased Jones, finally catching up to him at Paddy's Gap, north of Ashley Valley. Both men dismounted and had a heated argument. Finally, Ruple asked Jones why he had killed Bangledork and stolen Ruple's baby. When Jones looked at the baby wrapped in a red flannel blanket, he realized he had kidnapped someone else's child. He admitted defeat and rode off. Ruple returned with the baby and helped stop Bangledork's bleeding. The man somehow lived, but Jones did not know that.[44]

Jones fled, a murderer on the run, to a well-watered valley north of Red Creek, near the Utah-Colorado border. Six months later Ruple's brother-in-law, Abe Coon, was trailing cattle in the area and spied Jones, who was by then a good sixty pounds lighter. Coon caught up with Jones who at first tried to flee. When they finally talked, the mountain man learned about the fate of his child and that he was not a murderer after all. As Ellen Kiever writes, "Jones was incredulous...saying that he could [now] leave this God-forsaken hole and go back up to his family."[45] From that time on, the area became known as "Jones Hole."

Jones left for Arkansas but returned not long after. He made up with Rene and had two more children with her. One day he casually packed up and left to

9.16 A 1931 view of the red pictographs at Deluge Shelter in Jones Hole (A12-1). Courtesy of the Peabody Museum of Archaeology and Ethnology, Harvard University (PM No. 971-21-10/100162.1.366, File 99380215).

9.17 The same images as observed in 2017. Photo: Dan Bauer.

go hunt gold in Alaska. He left his wife and children a measly three dollars and fifty cents and never returned. Various rumors circulated that Jones had made enough money gold-mining to bathe in champagne and another that a bear had chewed off his arm.[46] Whatever his fate, the unsavory Jones has the honor of his name being affixed to this beautiful spot.

When Rust and Dennison arrived in "Charley Jones' Hole," they found the sought-for cave without problem and for two hours excavated there, uncovering remnants of an eroded structure of adobe and sticks, a hearth, and the usual detritus: corncobs, cut sticks, squash rinds, and a few potsherds extending more than a meter deep.[47] They also stopped to sketch and photograph rock art in the area (A12-2).[48] There simply wasn't time to investigate further. As Rust noted, "lunch on bank of a large stream and wish for fishing tackle."[49]

We don't know for certain which shelter in Jones Hole they excavated, but it was probably Deluge Shelter—the most obvious of the alcoves in the area. And we know for certain they at least visited Deluge Shelter because they took fifteen photographs of the rock art there. If it was, then Dennison and Rust had just scraped the surface of one of the most important archaeological sites in the West.

In 1966, Larry Leach, then a doctoral candidate at the University of Colorado, spent weeks at Deluge Shelter. He carefully uncovered fifteen layers of human occupation extending nearly twenty feet deep. At the bottom, he found points he attributed to the last Ice Age hunters in the region (Paleo-Indians). In the layers above that, he found sequential evidence of Early Archaic peoples, followed in order by Middle Archaic, Late Archaic, Fremont, and Ute groups, each identified by unique artifacts.

In some instances, the ancient inhabitants of Deluge Shelter shared an affinity with groups living on the Plains. At other times, they were more akin to those living in the Great Basin. But there was hardly a time when indigenous people did not call Deluge Shelter home.[50] In other words, the entire human prehistory of the region sits there, like a layer cake awaiting the knife of scientists.

If Dennison and Rust had had the time to dig deep enough, they might have gone racing back to retrieve Scott and the others—it was the unspoiled rock shelter they had sought to no avail for the past six weeks. Instead, they road back on the "Ruple Road" along Brush Creek, stopping to photograph and sketch even more rock art (A12-3)[51] and visit a granary in Spring Creek (A6-7).[52]

While Dennison and Rust were exploring Jones Hole—there were apparently not enough horses available for anyone else to go—the rest of the crew returned to Brush Creek. They stopped at two sites along the creek about thirteen miles east of Vernal, where Reagan had also been excavating sites. At A7-1, an excavation trench revealed a square room thirty feet to a side and surrounded by smaller rooms six to ten feet in diameter. Artifacts were rare: a few pieces of flint, a pot handle, a mano, and a metate.[53] Another site (A7-2) about a mile away was identical in site layout with a rectangular room and two small circular rooms nearby. Artifacts here were also scarce.[54] They didn't mention whether Reagan had previously dug these sites.

Albert B. Reagan

The third character in the Uinta Basin cast was Albert B. Reagan, a teacher at the Indian school in Ouray and a self-taught archaeologist. He was obviously a bright man—he earned a PhD in geology at Stanford—but he was also eccentric. And he was fanatical about archaeology and prolific in his writings about it. A 1934 entry in the *Encyclopedia of American Biography* credits him with 547 publications.[55]

Reagan's interest in archaeology may have stemmed from his first Indian Field Service posting, at age twenty-eight, to New Mexico, a land rich in archaeological ruins. By 1930, at almost sixty years of age, he had landed in Ouray in

9.18 Albert B. Reagan. Photo courtesy of L. Tom Perry Special Collections, Harold B. Lee Library, Brigham Young University, Provo.

9.19 This image appears to depict Albert B. Reagan chest-deep in an excavation pit. Reagan did not assist the Claflin-Emerson Expedition, although this photo is part of the Donald Scott Collection and is dated 1931. Courtesy of the Peabody Museum of Archaeology and Ethnology, Harvard University (PM No. 971-21-10/100162.1.1222, File 122410192).

the Uinta Basin as a teacher to the Utes. That same year he began investigating archaeological sites in Ashley–Dry Fork and Hill Creek with his friend and guide, Leo Thorne.

Reagan was clearly among the preeminent amateur archaeologists of his day (sometimes referred to as para-archaeologists or pseudoarchaeologists), all of them enthusiastic and often accomplished individuals who professed an adherence to the archaeological methods of the day but who were largely untrained in careful excavation techniques. Unfettered by the higher academic standards of their university counterparts, they sometimes speculated wildly on the origins of prehistoric cultures in the region. And they were particularly enamored of rock art, something many of their more esteemed academic colleagues eschewed as largely irrelevant.

Julian Steward, the scholar who had just assumed the helm of the University of Utah's anthropology department, afforded him some begrudging respect, coupled with backhanded criticisms. They were certainly acquainted, but they were hardly friends and even traded veiled insults about each other's excavation techniques.[56] In an April 1931 letter to Donald Scott, Steward described Reagan as "a rather strange man, egocentric in a way, but none the less intelligent." When Steward proposed his collaboration with Harvard, he included Reagan in the mix, saying that together they could "concentrate on an area somewhat larger than [Harvard] alone could undertake and that we could use the University's name and Reagan's knowledge of the Uintah basin."[57] As discussed earlier, this collaboration never occurred.

Reagan, who was granted an excavation permit by the Secretary of Interior, conducted numerous excavations in the region, although he never mentions why he believed himself to be qualified to do so, nor is there much indication of what became of most of the artifacts he recovered. In some instances, Reagan said that he had shipped artifacts to the Museum of Anthropology in Santa Fe. In other instances, they might have ended up in Thorne's collection.

Julianna Bratt, who has researched Reagan's legacy, believes that

> Reagan perceived himself as an archaeologist, as far as the term was conceived at the time. It was never his full-time interest though, unless you count his two years as a professor at BYU. He published frequently and seems to have been well read and aware of what was going on in the field. I don't think he considered archaeology as an entirely separate

distinction from the rest of the research he did. I don't believe that he ever thought of his work as amateur.[58]

When the Claflin-Emerson Expedition arrived in the Uinta Basin, they were in Reagan's territory. And in that day, archaeologists were a territorial bunch, eager to claim rights and disparage anyone who might jump their claim. There is no indication of any animosity on Reagan's part towards the expedition, even if they had spurned Steward's suggestion that they involve him in their project. Reagan did meet with Donald Scott and Dave Rust on July 30 to share his photo collection,[59] but there is no evidence that he offered to show Scott around to the sites he was investigating or offered assistance in any way. Beyond that single meeting, Reagan was on the outside looking in at his more esteemed colleagues from Harvard.

9.20 Albert B. Reagan was particularly enamored with the rock art of the Uinta Basin. Photo: Dan Bauer.

Mad Scramble to the End

September 3 was the last field day of the expedition, but it was also a mad scramble to settle accounts and investigate a few last sites. According to Rust's journal, they went on a wild goose chase into Dry Fork Canyon, then drove to Vernal, and finally Roosevelt. But the "goose chase," as Rust called it, was more likely the result of the budding friendship between Scott and Leo Thorne. For reasons not explained, Thorne had not taken Scott to Elizabeth Cave, the source of his most prized artifacts, during their earlier foray into the area. Or maybe they had not yet acquired landowner permission to go there (the receipt to Mrs. Shiner for "digging on property" is dated the day before, on August 2).

On August 3, Thorne finally took the crew to Elizabeth Cave (A6-6), his name for the site he had looted sometime in the past. Besides the famous

9.21 This rock art panel is located near Elizabeth Cave where Leo Thorne had earlier recovered a mummy. Photo: Dan Bauer.

"Elizabeth" mummy here, Thorne had recovered a cedar-bark blanket, dew-claw moccasins, rawhide, pumpkin shells dried into storage vessels, pumpkin seeds in a bark bag, and a buckskin bag. Was anything left? Wrote Scott, "We dug in several likely crevices, not deep, and along the back wall in one or two places left undug. One was very sterile, containing only rat refuse, the other was almost so, but one digging stick was found... in the rear corner of a rat's nest."[60]

Rust's journal for August 3 also mentions they paid a fellow named Pete Nelson for pasturage—an intriguing reference considering "Pete Nelson the father of Lee Sage," as Rust noted, was one of the last of the Robbers Roost outlaws still alive in 1931; the "Journal of Expenses" does not list this payment.

Pete Nelson (or Nielson) was, at one time, a typical Mormon cowboy living in Elsinore, Utah, with a wife, two children, and another on the way. But in March 1897, Pete rode off, deserting his family in search of something more adventurous than farming. He drifted to Robbers Roost where he took the name Pete Logan, and he soon garnered a reputation as a two-bit crook—one of dozens of Roosters, as the outlaws were known. In his home town, they called him Pete Thief.[61]

At Robbers Roost, Logan met C. L. "Gunplay" Maxwell and joined a gang of a "dozen or so" Roosters planning to rob a Provo bank—a plan that went awry when Nelson, in charge of the relay horses, never got word the holdup had been changed to Springville. One bandit was killed, and Maxwell went to prison. The next reference to Pete Logan was in 1909 when he was living in Nine Mile Canyon and working for Preston Nutter. A short time later he married Ada Slaugh, Gunplay Maxwell's widow. Nutter's business records indicate Pete was working for Nutter as late as 1918.[62]

9.22 Scenic view of Ashley–Dry Fork. Photo: Dan Bauer.

9.23 Elk pictograph in Jones Hole. Photo: Dan Bauer.

According to an account related by Don Wilcox, the grandson of rancher Jim McPherson who was known to have provided safe haven to many outlaws of that day, Pete Logan worked for Nutter as a ranch foreman, but Nutter found out there was an arrest warrant for Pete Logan. Nutter reportedly went to the county, told officials that he had found Pete Logan dead and his body deteriorated, and then he filled out a death certificate to that effect. A new ranch foreman was then introduced—Pete Nelson.[63] There is no hard evidence that Pete Nelson returned to his earlier lawlessness, although he tried unsuccessfully to nick the Claflin-Emerson Expedition for more money than it was willing to pay. They settled on a payment of fifty cents. Pete Nelson's exploits were later popularized in a quasi biography by his son, Lee Sage, who more than hints in *The Last Rustler* that his father never gave up his thieving ways.[64]

The Crimson Cowboys were by this point probably too tired to listen to Nelson's tall tales of the bandit life. There were trunks and crates to be packed, accounts to be settled, and goodbyes to be said. Rust and his son Nelson were paid $1,350 for personal services rendered, even if Rust, the official expedition guide, had done very little guiding the previous two months. The crew found time to get their hair cut, and Brew had the courtesy to pay twenty-five cents for a shower before getting on the train in Green River, Wyoming.[65]

The Uinta Basin investigations, which held so much promise seventeen days before, were over with little to show for it. Even the most ardent optimist would have to admit the looters had missed very little. Beyond a couple of baskets pulled from one alcove, they had precious little to show for their efforts here. They were simply too late: The spectacular artifacts the region once concealed were already on display in homes and shops throughout the area.

The Claflin-Emerson excavations here would soon be forgotten or relegated to footnotes in the archaeological history of the region. A few of the sites they investigated are known to archaeologists today, but most are not. And none of their observations here were of such monumental importance that anyone has really bothered to look.

There is certainly an ironic twist in that Albert Reagan—the amateur whose participation was summarily rejected by the expedition—still looms large in the history of the Uinta Basin. Archaeologists to this day continue to cite Reagan's reports, as well as Julian Steward's limited work here on the Uintah River, with hardly a mention anywhere of the Claflin-Emerson Expedition. The Crimson Cowboys would instead be remembered for their work in the Tavaputs Plateau—a place where they were the first archaeologists to venture.

10.1 Scenic view of the west entrance to the Jones Hole country. Photo: Dan Bauer.

Scholars and Cowboys

Afterwards

10

IT HAD BEEN A remarkable seven weeks in the Utah backcountry far from the civilized environs of Harvard Yard. And the Crimson Cowboys had acquitted themselves well in cowboy country. The boxes and crates were packed, and thoughts were undoubtedly turning to loved ones at home and the chores that awaited them. The six team members boarded the Union Pacific train in Green River, Wyoming, on August 4, bound for Boston. Four of the five students returned to school at Harvard and Donald Scott to the Peabody. Besides Scott, three of the crew would work part or all of their lives in archaeology or anthropology: J.O. Brew, Alfie Kidder, and Bill Bowers. Jim Dennison and Waldo Forbes, who remained close friends, followed very different career paths into family businesses. All, however, would be later honored for their scholarly contributions to Harvard's anthropology department.[1]

10.2 Donald Scott during his tenure as museum director. Courtesy of the Peabody Museum of Archaeology and Ethnology, Harvard University (Peabody Museum No. 2004.24.26810A, File 137710027).

New Museum Director

Donald Scott had a tremendous amount of work to do just catching up with tasks left undone in his absence. He also had to account for all the expedition expenses and inventory all the artifacts recovered on behalf of the Peabody Museum. Plus, law and practice required him to produce a preliminary report. His seventeen-page summary went to the Secretary of the Interior (Ray L. Wilbur), the secretary of the Smithsonian (Charles G. Abbot), and the director of the Laboratory of Anthropology in Santa Fe (Jesse L. Nussbaum), as well as to the expedition benefactors, Bill Claflin and Raymond Emerson. He supplemented that summary with more than a hundred pages of site descriptions and a catalog of artifacts.[2]

As Scott wrote to Emerson, his report was much more extensive than was usually submitted in that day. But Scott had heard that the Interior Department would soon be requiring more detailed reports, so he "considered it good policy to beat them to it."[3] He also informed all of the above-listed men that Henry B. Roberts, who directed the 1929 and 1930 expeditions, would be writing the formal, published report. Even as late as 1936, Scott was writing John F. Gillin at the University of Utah that a report was imminent.[4]

It never came.

Donald Scott certainly kept busy at the Peabody in the years after the expedition. The following year, in 1932, Edward Reynolds resigned as director, and Scott replaced him. He stayed in that post until he retired in 1948 at the age of sixty-nine. During his directorship he was also named Peabody Professor of American Anthropology, which bumped his status and his salary.

Scott worked some more in the Southwest in the 1930s, but he never finished his dissertation.[5] He had even talked to Dave Rust during the 1931 expedition about a 1932 field excursion that would target the Shivwits Plateau south of St. George, Utah, on the Arizona Strip, as well as the lower Green River to the confluence of the Green and Colorado Rivers.

10.3 Fremont rock art in the Jones Hole area. Photo: Dan Bauer.

Rust was very excited about both possibilities and even envisioned Bill Claflin and Raymond Emerson joining the crew for the river trip from Green River, Utah, down to the confluence and then motoring back to Moab. Three weeks later, on May 4, 1932, Scott wrote back that funds for such a trip were uncertain, that the men he wanted were not available, and that doing such trips in the extreme heat of July and August would be too difficult. "This is a disappointing letter to write, but we will have to look forward to 1933," Scott wrote.[6] The 1933 trip never materialized either. We searched the Peabody Museum records and correspondence, but found no references as to why the funding was terminated.

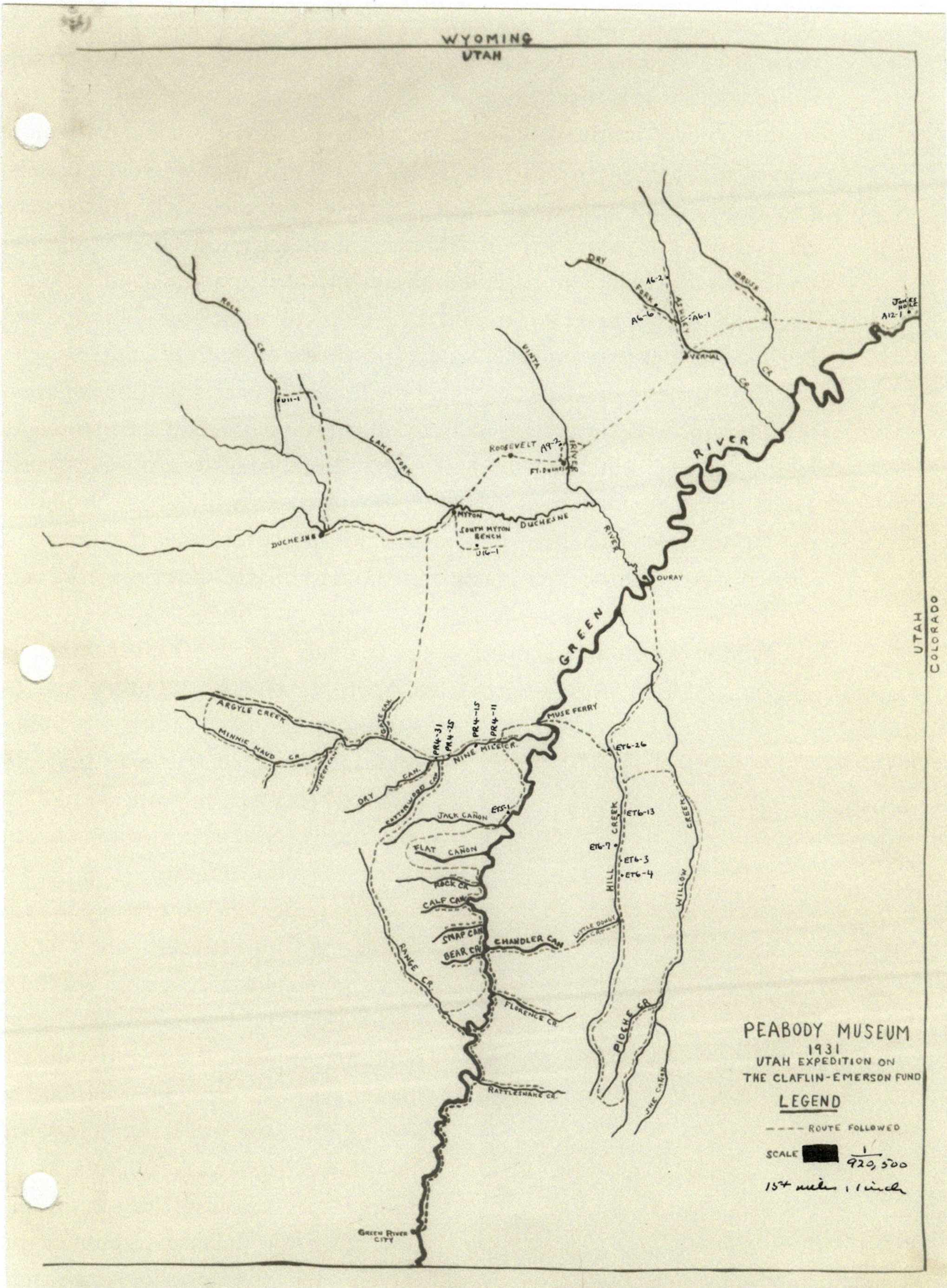

10.4 Hand-drawn map of the 1931 expedition route completed shortly after the crew returned to Harvard. The crew logged more than four hundred miles on horseback in six weeks. © President and Fellows of Harvard College, Peabody Museum of Archaeology and Ethnology (PM No. 33-2-10/100241.1.1.1, File 99310040).

Whether it was because of waning interest on the part of the benefactors or the cumulative effects of the Great Depression, the Claflin-Emerson Expeditions ended with the 1931 trip.

Scott never returned to the Tavaputs Plateau, but he maintained a life-long interest in the region's rock art. He corresponded with Utah photographers like Leo Thorne and Frank Beckwith, acquiring some of their rock art images for the Peabody Museum collection. He was still adding photos to the collection until a few days before his death. He always intended to write a monograph on Utah rock art, but never got around to it. Scott's photographic collection later became the foundation of Polly Schaafsma's classic *Rock Art of Utah*.[7]

During the Depression, Scott kept the Peabody afloat, reporting in 1940 to his fellow 1900 classmates that he loved "the freedom of action and of thought" which a university atmosphere encouraged—in contrast to the business world. He also encouraged his conservative classmates to get behind New Deal social legislation, which he called "long overdue." Finally, he told them that he and his wife tried to get up to New Hampshire often to hike or snowshoe from their small house there.[8]

10.5 Rock art scene on West Tavaputs Plateau. Photo: Dan Bauer.

During World War II, work at the Peabody shrank because of financial exigency. Staff members were cut, and Scott also worried about his students serving in the war, calling his undergraduate days "golden in retrospect." He lamented that he could not do more to serve the war effort. He was, however, enjoying his grandchildren.[9]

Two years after Scott retired in 1948, he suffered a heart attack, but he bounced back and remained active until the end of his life. He served as board director for publisher Appleton-Century-Crofts and for Harvard University Press. He and his wife typically spent at least three winter months in Arizona and California, mostly riding horses and being outside. He kept close ties with Harvard, establishing in 1955 the Harvard University Press Faculty Prize, "an annual award of two thousand dollars, to be given to that faculty member whose book, published by the Press...was judged to be the most significant contribution to scholarship."[10]

As his obituary in the *Harvard University Gazette* stated, "His final days were indicative of his energy and personality. After several miles of trail-riding in Arizona, he and Mrs. Scott drove to Santa Barbara. While building a fire to warm their ranch cottage, he suffered a severe heart attack and died almost immediately." At his death in 1967, Scott was eighty-seven years old. His former 1931 student from the expedition, J.O. Brew, headed the committee to write his mentor's obituary.[11]

The Missing Monograph

There were probably many reasons, perhaps interrelated ones, why Henry B. Roberts never completed the much-anticipated monograph to synthesize data derived from the expeditions of 1928 to 1931. The museum had even blocked out a title, date, and citation for Roberts's work: "Peripheral Cultures of the Southwest with Special Reference to the Archeology of Utah," to be published in 1931 in the *Papers of the Peabody Museum of American Archaeology and Ethnology* 12, no. 4.[12] No document draft by that name exists in the Peabody Museum archives.

One reason the manuscript was not completed might be that Roberts was simply too busy. In 1930, he took a position at the Carnegie Institution, although he was still allowed to work half-time at the Peabody to complete the monograph. In effect, he was doing two jobs and found himself pulled in two different directions. Another reason, it seems, was that his research interests got diverted from southern Utah to Panama and the Yucatan. In 1931, he was named director of a Peabody Museum expedition to Panama, also funded by William Claflin.[13] He must have returned in time to visit Scott's crew in the Uinta Basin by late summer of that year, or he left for Panama in the fall after visiting them. In 1932, he was in the Yucatan, working with Bowers.

The lack of funds during the Depression for the publication was probably another reason. Earlier in 1931, the museum published a monograph by Noel Morss, a member of the 1928 and 1929 Claflin-Emerson Expeditions. It articulated in remarkable clarity the Fremont Culture concept that Scott, Roberts, and Alfie Kidder's father, Alfred V. Kidder, had been talking about for years. The museum published the monograph only because Morss put up his own funds to do so.[14]

Archaeologist James H. Gunnerson says that Roberts got sick and thus could not finish the monograph.[15] Maybe he did get sick, but it never stopped him from his fieldwork, which continued uninterrupted in the years ahead. He lived another forty-eight years, working on projects throughout North and South America, often with his brother, Frank H.H. Roberts. Browman and Williams add that Roberts never finished his dissertation at Harvard and appeared to like "fieldwork more than he did the subsequent write-up and analysis."[16]

We will probably never know exactly why Roberts failed to deliver a manuscript to press. But we can surmise what Roberts's thoughts were as he mulled the manuscript. In 1929, Roberts wrote a brief, nine-page summary of that season's fieldwork in which he stated, "The evidence now at hand clearly proves this culture to be a peripheral variant of the early Pueblo types farther south. The localization and the distinct traits of this Fruita culture justify Mr. [Noel] Morss in calling it the Fremont Culture."[17]

10.6 Locomotive Rock in Range Creek. Photo: Dan Bauer.

A final reason he never completed the manuscript might very well relate to Morss's heralded monograph. Not only did Morss claim official bragging rights for naming the new culture, but his report was remarkably well written and reasoned for that period in time. In fact, his definition of the Fremont Culture (we call it the Fremont Complex today) stands up remarkably well even after the passing of eighty-five years. What more could Roberts say that Morss had not already said?

The Benefactors

The Peabody Museum's benefactors, Bill Claflin and Raymond Emerson, continued to support museum research projects in the years ahead. They appear not to have been burned too badly by the stock market crash in 1929 and subsequent Depression. As mentioned earlier, Claflin took over his father-in-law's sugar firm, Soledad Sugar Company. He traveled often to Cuba where the company operations were located near Cienfuegos. He had to give up the company in 1960 when Fidel Castro nationalized all such industries. He was a director of numerous banks, served as president of the Boston Stock Exchange in 1935–1936, and became treasurer of Harvard from 1938–1948, "The one job in all the world I really wanted," he said. During World War II he essentially ran Harvard while President James B. Conant was on leave, working with the Manhattan Project.[18]

Archaeology and history remained his dual passions the rest of his life, as did world travel and hunting. The 64,000 artifacts from his digs in the Southwest and Georgia ended up, not surprisingly, at the Peabody. He remained devoted to his wife, four children, and sixteen grandchildren, saying that his family gave him "the most pleasure and satisfaction."[19] Claflin died in 1982 at eighty-nine years of age. He inherited and acquired great wealth but also gave great service to his university and the science of archaeology.

Claflin's partner, Raymond Emerson, remained on the faculty at the Peabody until he retired in 1956. He served as a major in the army during World War II in his mid- to late fifties. He lived out his years in his native Concord,

10.7 Raymond Emerson was an avid equestrian throughout life. Photo courtesy of the Emerson Family Archives.

Massachusetts, while working at the prestigious Boston banking firm, J.M. Forbes. He traveled to Mexico, Scandinavia, the West Indies, and Alaska. Nature kept its allure for him, just like it did for his famous grandfather and father before him. In a class report in 1935, he wrote, "My chief recreations are riding, shooting, skiing, and canoeing. I find these pastimes have kept me so young in both body and spirit that it becomes apparent I shall never mature."[20] Besides his life-long devotion to the Peabody, he helped publish his grandfather's and father's writings. He died in 1977 at age ninety-one, the father of six children.

J.O. Brew

The winter following the expedition, in 1932, graduate student J.O. Brew felt a sense of nostalgia, perhaps coupled with obligation, to reach out to his compatriots from the summer of 1931. He sent photos to the families who had hosted the expedition members on that memorable trip. Accompanying the photos was a copy of Noel Morss's recently published report that defined the Fremont culture, *The Ancient Culture of the Fremont River in Utah* (1931). Brew explained to Elery Wild that the report would "give you some idea of what we do with the material and information we collect on our expeditions."[21] Brew included a personal note in each letter. Besides Wild, Brew sent similar posts to Austin and Hazel Wardle, Neal Hanks, Oliver Rasmussen, Dafton Thompson, Ivan Atwood, and Albert Pace. Clearly he had the most affection for the Wardles, saying, "I hope to see Hill Creek again and if I ever do come through the Uinta basin, I shall find some way to get down to see you."[22] He never did.

10.8 J.O. Brew's snow-covered "camp" at Alkali Ridge in the fall of 1931. Courtesy of the Peabody Museum of Archaeology and Ethnology, Harvard University (PM No. 990-7-10/100115.1.128, File 122550128).

Of all the student participants of the Claflin-Emerson Expedition, J.O. Brew had the most distinguished career as an archaeologist. After returning to Boston with the other expedition members, he promptly packed his bags and returned to Utah to initiate excavations at Alkali Ridge in southeastern Utah, just east of Blanding in San Juan County. It must have been late in the

10.9 Group portrait of the 1932 crew at Alkali Ridge. J.O. Brew is back row center and James Dennison is standing to his left. Courtesy of the Peabody Museum of Archaeology and Ethnology, Harvard University (PM No. 990-7-10/100115.1.139, File 99380254).

year because the photos from that project depict Brew's crew camped in deep snows. He continued his excavations there for the next two years.

As Richard B. Woodbury wrote, "His monumental report on the work, published in 1946, immediately became a landmark in southwestern archaeological literature."[23] Brew's second major archaeological project was directing the Peabody's dig at Awatovi in northeastern Arizona on the Hopi Reservation between 1936 and 1939. He designed a multidisciplinary project that ultimately yielded eleven reports.[24]

Besides directing significant archaeological excavations, Brew held numerous important posts at the Peabody: assistant curator of Southwestern archaeology from 1941–1946, curator of North American archaeology from 1946–1948, and director of the museum (succeeding Donald Scott) from 1948–1967. He oversaw many important exhibits during his tenure as well as a significant expansion of the Peabody's collections and activities.[25] According to anthropology scholar Don D. Fowler, his staff and friends affectionately called him "the D-Shaped Director," referring to his girth. "It fitted him and his sense of humor."[26]

10.10 Portrait of J.O. Brew, museum director 1948–1967. © President and Fellows of Harvard College, Peabody Museum of Archaeology and Ethnology (PM No. 2004.24.25825, File 99380206).

Brew's "third career" came after World War II with his increasing concern for salvage archaeology. He helped organize and chaired the Committee for the Recovery of Archaeological Remains (CRAR). The committee was active in preserving sites on the Missouri River, along the Nile, and in many other places around the world threatened by modern development. As scholar Richard D. Daugherty put it, "Without doubt, Jo has had more influence in the development of salvage archaeology, nationally and internationally, than any other man."[27]

Brew was a man who could cajole legislators in Congress and encourage graduate students to explore their interests. As Woodbury wrote, "He was gregarious, widely read...and generous of time and ideas with everyone."[28] The son of two poor, Irish immigrants died just before his eighty-second birthday in 1988. He had risen to the top of his profession.

Alfie Kidder

Another Claflin-Emerson alumnus who rose to the top of his profession—in Peruvian archaeology—was Alfred V. Kidder II, or Alfie. He graduated *magna cum laude* with his bachelor's degree in 1933, completed his master's in 1935, and his PhD in 1937. Kidder married Mary Barbour in 1934 and left immediately for Venezuela to conduct his doctoral fieldwork. It was the first Peabody-sponsored work in South America, although they had earlier sponsored work in Central America. Besides his dissertation and a monograph on his Venezuelan research, "he produced a highly regarded synthesis of Venezuelan archaeology for the *Handbook of South American Indians*" in 1948, according to Karen L. Mohr Chavez. She says, "His decision to specialize in South American archaeology was certainly influenced by a desire to distinguish his own career from that of his famous father," A. V. Kidder, the undisputed dean of Southwest archaeology. His wife, Mary, a full partner in his fieldwork, wrote a very readable account of their excavations in Peru, *No Limits but the Sky: The Journal of an Archaeologist's Wife in Peru* (1942).[29]

In addition to serving in World War II as an officer in the army, training foreign air force personnel, Kidder taught at Harvard from 1937 to 1950. During that time, his research interests shifted from Venezuela to Peru and Lake Titicaca. "He pioneered the use of thin-section analysis of Andean pottery, perhaps influenced by earlier work his father and Ann Shepard had carried out in the southwestern United States," wrote Chavez.[30]

Kidder left Harvard in 1950 to assume the assistant directorship of the University Museum at the University of Pennsylvania, all the while continuing active fieldwork in the Lake Titicaca region. He also took advantage of the recently discovered technologies of radiocarbon dating and pioneered its use in dating sites in the Incan highlands. By this time, he was known as "Ted," like his father, rather than "Alfie."

At the same time, and continuing for the next twenty years, he moderated the Peabody Award–winning CBS television show, *What in the World?* Produced in Philadelphia, this quiz show hosted a panel of mostly archaeologists who examined objects sent in by viewers. The experts then tried to identify them. Although Kidder never quite achieved the fame of his father, he carved out a niche for himself in Andean and South American archaeology and was one of the leaders in that field. He died at age seventy-three in 1984, an avid fisherman to the end.[31]

10.11 Alfred V. Kidder II and Wilton D. Krogman on *What in the World*, a television series that identified artifacts from around the world. Photo courtesy of the Penn Museum, Image # 148623.

The Crimson Cowboys

William Benton Bowers II also headed south of the border, first to the Yucatan Peninsula working with Roberts and later to Guatemala. In 1930 he married Rosamond Forbes, although they divorced sixteen years later. He had received his master's in 1931 based on his work with Kidder at Pecos Pueblo. He was a PhD graduate student with a bright future, but he dropped out of the program. This apparently deeply disturbed his father who had given substantial money to the Harvard anthropology program.[32] He stayed in the field of anthropology and sociology, however, lecturing some at the University of Chicago and in South Africa.

In 1946 he divorced Forbes and then married Katherine Harbison. But in Guatemala in the late 1950s, he met a native, Catherine Pellecer, while studying the mixed Spanish and Indian populations. He brought her to his Chicago home as a housekeeper, along with her three daughters. He subsequently divorced Harbison in 1961 and married Pellecer. Bowers worked with the Chicago Department of Urban Renewal, saying, "We deal with all sorts, especially

10.12 Bill Bowers drinking gin and tonics with his sister, Margaret Bowers Witt, on the front porch of her summer cottage in Scotland, Connecticut, sometime in the late 1950s or early 1960s. Photo courtesy of Lynn Bowers and the Bowers family.

Italians, Mexicans and Greeks, so my anthropological background is not wholly wasted."[33] He was still working there at age seventy-two. He never had children of his own, having contracted mumps at an early age.[34] But he told his classmates in their fiftieth anniversary report that "the sudden acquisition of three daughters...was certainly the best thing that ever happened to me." He suffered from anemia late in life and had to give up tennis. He also walked all his life with a limp from an unknown ailment or injury early in life. His relatives always considered him "a bit of a character." He died the day after his eightieth birthday in 1986. His three adopted daughters inherited his estate and "an important piece of family property in Scotland Valley."[35]

James Thurber Dennison lived, in many ways, the most conventional life of his fellow expedition members. He worked in 1932 for J.O. Brew at Alkali Ridge. Then in 1934, right after he graduated from Harvard, he employed Dave Rust to guide him, his father, Henry, his sister Mary, and her husband, David Stickney, around southern Utah. He wrote to Rust, saying he wanted "to disappear into the loneliest, ruggedest, most beautiful part of your wonderful state.... My principal desire is to get in some desolate, riotous canyon country and just meander around, climbing to granaries, messing in cave-dust, and exploring wild places." They began their horse-pack trip in Torrey, Utah, near Fish Creek Cove—the site Morss had excavated that led to his definition of the Fremont

Culture. From there they headed south up the Aquarius Plateau, or Boulder Mountain, the terrain the 1928 Claflin-Emerson Expedition had explored. The group then spent ten glorious days taking in some of the greatest views on the Colorado Plateau, including Powell Point at the far south end—all lands the Peabody Museum had investigated between 1928 and 1930.[36]

After graduation, Jim Dennison entered the family business, Dennison Manufacturing, for more than a hundred years the economic heart and soul of Framingham, Massachusetts. The company produced labels, crepe paper, wrapping paper, and packaging. It was a publicly owned company, so he did not inherit his position. He married Nancy Banister Williams of New Haven, Connecticut, a Principia College graduate, six years after graduation in 1940. The two of them loved to sing and were members of numerous choral groups through the years. They also were lifelong downhill skiers. Dennison took up gliding, and during World War II was a civilian glider instructor for the navy. In 1963, he left the family business because the board was abandoning many of the progressive policies his father had initiated. As his daughter Becky recalls, "This was an enormous heartbreak for him.... He quit before he had another job; this was when he had four teenagers and a myriad of responsibilities. I remember the house being very 'dark and quiet' during the year before he went to Washington."[37] There he joined NASA as an ombudsman and traveled the country introducing institutions, organizations, and businesses to NASA's innovations. He loved the job. Eventually he transferred to Massachusetts to work at a NASA research center in Cambridge.

During that time the Dennisons built a "country place" in Antrim, New Hampshire. They wanted a change, plus the town was close to skiing. They had three daughters and one son. Dennison had a hip replacement in 1983 at age sixty-six, which allowed him to keep skiing and playing tennis. The Dennisons

10.13 Jim Dennison became an avid skier and always wore an orange tie while skiing. New Hampshire, 1940. Photo: Dennison Family Archives.

lived in Antrim for more than twenty-five years, and Jim became involved in local politics. He kept in touch with Waldo Forbes until the latter's untimely death in 1955. Dennison's wife, Nancy, died in 1994 from complications from Alzheimer's; Dennison lived to age ninety and died in Antrim in 2002. He never had any association with archaeology or the West after 1934.[38]

Dennison's good friend and 1934 classmate Waldo Emerson Forbes led the most unusual life of all his fellow expedition members. He became a rancher—the only one of the Crimson Cowboys to actually become a cowboy.

Forbes family members had purchased a ranch in Sheridan, Wyoming, in 1899. The older brother, William Cameron Forbes, worried about his brother's lung problems and saw the ranch as a dry-air escape from the dank Massachusetts climate. They had watched their father, William Hathaway Forbes, die of tuberculosis. When Waldo was just sixteen, in 1928, he spent the summer working at the ranch, and the lifestyle got in his blood. In 1932 he went back to Utah and chased wild horses with Dafton Thompson and Sam Adams, a local horse wrangler and trader.[39] It took him less than a year after graduation from Harvard in 1935 to find his way back to Wyoming.[40]

But during his college years studying anthropology, he helped Harvard teams excavate in Ireland, Ethiopia, and the southern Arabian Peninsula. He was a research associate at the Peabody in 1935–1936 after graduation and took graduate classes in business administration at M.I.T. During this time he also applied to Columbia Law School and Columbia's graduate program in meteorology.[41] Clearly Forbes, like many college graduates, was searching for his path. One imagines, though, that the West kept calling him.

10.14 Waldo Forbes and his wife Sarah "Sal" Cushing Paine on their Wyoming ranch. Photo courtesy of Charlotte Forbes Wunderlich.

In the winter of 1936 he moved to Sheridan, Wyoming, and began his ranching life. Originally, the Forbes ranch had included a post office and flour mill, built by George Beck in the 1880s. Known as Beckton Stock Farm (after Beck), its cattle operation expanded under Waldo's guidance. Also, for the first time, a Forbes family member was living there full-time. Waldo married Sarah (Sal) Cushing Paine of Weston, Massachusetts, in 1939, and she became a full partner in the ranching operation, and continued to operate the spread well past Waldo's death.

Forbes used the new ideas of genetic breeding to build up his herd of Hereford cattle. After World War II he bought some Red Angus calves from registered Black Angus herds, hoping to establish a new breed based on selection by performance traits of economic importance as well as by eye evaluation. He also began crossbreeding with a number of different breeds, an uncommon approach at the time. In 1954, he helped found the Red Angus Association of America, the first registry to use performance testing. Waldo Forbes—no surprise—served as the association's first president until his death.[42]

10.15 Fremont ruins in Range Creek. Photo: Dan Bauer.

During his years in Wyoming, Forbes made sure his family of seven children knew their Forbes, Emerson, and Paine roots. They took many trips east to visit their large families there. Forbes did not forget his Claflin-Emerson Expedition brethren either. He named the small bunkhouse by his first ranch house "Robbers Roost," in memory of the area where he first surveyed in 1930. Forbes was known as a quietly gregarious man who loved baseball (especially the Red Sox) and square dancing. He made a game out of every ranch activity, and he had an easy charm that attracted people to him.[43]

Waldo Forbes contracted lung cancer in 1953 and sought treatment at Massachusetts General Hospital in Boston. In 1955, the last year of his life, he, Sal, and their daughter Cherry drove to Teasdale, Utah, near the site of his first Claflin-Emerson expedition. He went to visit Sam Adams and they talked about the old days, about surveying and excavating around the Capitol Reef area, and chasing wild horses. The Utah trip was followed by more cancer treatment in Boston; he died at age forty-three. His family scattered his ashes on a hill overlooking the Wyoming ranch.[44]

Rust Never Sleeps

The expedition guide, Dave Rust, continued to guide horse-pack trips around the Colorado Plateau for another decade after he said goodbye to the Harvard boys in 1931. He also led river trips in Glen Canyon during the 1930s. His last guiding, however, came in the spring of 1941 at age sixty-seven when he took friend and frequent client Dodge Freeman to the Escalante River–Waterpocket Fold country. Even if Rust had wanted to keep guiding after that, World War II's travel restrictions effectively ended such activities; Rust had no client base to draw from. He took a job as a night watchman at the Geneva Steel Plant in Provo, all the while keeping physically active and reading books. In August 1944, he received a telegram informing him and his wife that their son Nelson, a wrangler on the 1931 trip, had died in action in France. Nelson was buried at the Normandy American Cemetery overlooking Omaha Beach.[45]

Following World War II, recreation boomed around the Colorado Plateau, and Dave Rust watched as guides like Norman Nevills and Bus Hatch began taking groups down the region's rivers. Likewise, visitation to the area's national parks exploded. Rust's last visit to the canyon country came in 1948, a car trip which his son Richard organized. They revisited some of Rust's old haunts: Capitol Reef, the Aquarius Plateau, and Bryce Canyon. He continued an active correspondence with former clients like Donald Scott and Dodge Freeman and with fellow river adventurer Emery Kolb. His wife, Ruth, died in the fall of 1962, and Dave Rust followed her in January 1963 at age eighty-nine.[46]

During his post-expedition years at the Peabody, Donald Scott had maintained a sporadic but warm correspondence with Rust. It says much about his love of the western wilderness and his time working with Rust. For example, in 1957 Scott learned about Glen Canyon Dam and the reservoir that would drown many of the places where they explored and worked. He wrote Rust, "I read with some horror of the plans for Glen Canyon Dam and the roads and towers that will intrude upon that lovely wilderness, to say nothing at the flooding of that beautiful canyon."[47]

Then four years later as the dam was rising, he expanded on his elegiac mood, telling Rust, "When I think of what the land was like when I first met you…it seems incredible that bulldozers, uranium, and moving pictures and tourists should so completely have changed the world we knew."[48] Both men lived long lives into their late eighties and kept up a friendship, nurtured by a love of the incomparable landscape of the Colorado Plateau. Much of that wilderness and cultural landscape remains as it was for Rust and Scott, but much has been utterly changed.

Rust's remarkable life, memorialized in *Dave Rust: A Life in the Canyons*, by Fred Swanson, can be summarized by the man himself: "A thorough traveler must be something of a geologist, something of a botanist, an archaeologist, an ornithologist, an artist, a philosopher, and so on. Through it all he is likely to be friendly with a camera. He must be agreeable in society, contented in solitude, enthusiastic, and patient as a fisherman."[49] He died a very "thorough" traveler.

Legacy Revisited

It might seem presumptuous to refer to the "legacy" of the Claflin-Emerson Expeditions of 1928–1931: The expeditions' findings were largely ignored and forgotten until decades later. Yet the project stands as a hallmark of archaeological inquiry. It was the first major exploration of the most remote regions of Utah north and west of the Colorado River. It resulted in a definition of the Fremont Complex that remains largely intact. It established the archaeological importance of the northern Colorado Plateau—something that successive generations of researchers—Julian Steward, John Gillin, Jesse Jennings, and others—built upon in the years to come. But it was, and still is to some extent, a largely forgotten legacy.

The expedition field notes were never published and were stored away in the Peabody Museum archives. And James Gunnerson, who examined the notes as part of his doctoral dissertation at Harvard University, summarized only a portion of them, ignoring scores of sites described in the field journals.[50] Until recently, the location of most 1931 sites remained unknown.

In 2003, the Colorado Plateau Archaeological Alliance (CPAA) embarked upon a multiyear project to reidentify and thoroughly document the expedition's 1931 sites. Working closely with the Peabody Museum, and through generous grants from the Utah Division of State History and the National Park Service, CPAA has now identified more than a hundred Claflin-Emerson Expedition sites in the region, including almost all of the sites they visited in Range Creek, Desolation Canyon, and Nine Mile Canyon.[51]

By comparing historic photographs taken in 1931 (there are hundreds of them in the Peabody's archives) to a site's current condition, we can evaluate the rate of site degradation over time. We can begin to understand which sites are at risk to vandals and looters, and we can even estimate when past looting might have occurred. These efforts will assist land managers and private property owners to better protect the region's rich archaeological legacy for future generations.

Donald Scott's decision not to return to the northern Colorado Plateau in 1932 punctuated the end of the Peabody's grand expeditions into the American West. The Peabody returned periodically in the years to come, but always on a much smaller scale and never with such a grand geographic vision, as evidenced by Brew's work at Alkali Ridge. Gone were the days of horseback archaeology—crews dispatched for weeks on end into the wilderness in search of the unknown and undiscovered. In a very real sense, the 1931 Claflin-Emerson Expedition marked the end of one era and the beginning of another.

10.16 A 1931 view of a large red elk figure inside Rasmussen Cave. Courtesy of the Peabody Museum of Archaeology and Ethnology, Harvard University (PM No. 971-21-10/100162.1.288, File 99380222).

10.17 Recent view of the same large red elk figure. Photo: Dan Bauer.

It was the end of what we call "adventure" archaeology, or exploration for the sake of discovery. Throughout the nineteenth century, there was a mounting appreciation of the sciences in general as America pushed ever deeper into unexplored regions of the West. As Willey and Sabloff wrote, it was "an intellectual climate in which anthropology and archaeology could flourish." This climate was stimulated by the publication of Charles Darwin's *Origin of Species*, the emergence of geology as a scientific discipline, and a growing appreciation of the natural world that did not conform to religious dogma.[52] That same climate led to the rise of the Transcendentalist thinkers such as Emerson and Thoreau, all of which inspired scientific explorers like John Wesley Powell and Clarence King.

The study of past cultures was certainly part of that intellectual renaissance, but

10.18 Scenic view of tower ruins in Hill Creek. Photo: Dan Bauer.

archaeology as a science did not exist until the late 1800s. It emerged in response to the unabashed race by museums and private collectors to acquire spectacular and exotic artifacts. As early scholar Warren K. Moorehead observed in 1892, "They do not care to make primitive man a study, but are mere curiosity hunters, such as ones seen about the ruins of a city swept by a cyclone or flood."[53]

Not surprisingly, the Peabody Museum pioneered the efforts in those days to cultivate a different attitude towards archaeology, one focused on scientific inquiry rather than artifacts. The effort was led by Frederic Ward Putnam, the curator of the Peabody Museum from 1874 to 1909, who is widely considered to be the father of American archaeology. He demanded rigid methods for scientific excavation and collection.[54]

America's first scholars trained in archaeology studied at Putnam's feet, or at the very least were profoundly influenced by his scientific approaches. And among these was A.V. "Ted" Kidder, who arrived at Harvard in 1904 at age nineteen. Like a sponge, he soaked up the emerging theories and methods of the day espoused by Old World archaeologists George Chase and George Reisner, and then applied those principles to his studies in the American Southwest. His work at Pecos Pueblo in New Mexico from 1915 to 1929 is considered the first large-scale, thoroughly systematic excavation in American archaeology.[55]

As Curator of Southwestern Archaeology at the Peabody, Kidder wielded enormous influence over a rising generation of archaeologists, the first to be formally trained in the new science. He instilled in them the values of sound theory and research questions, and the importance of each and every artifact to understanding the people who left them. He set standards of careful excavation documented by detailed field notes, and he saw the importance of understanding prehistory from a broader geographic context. The Claflin-Emerson Expedition into the unknown regions north of the Colorado River was his idea, and Donald Scott, J.O. Brew, Noel Morss, Henry B. Roberts, and the rest of the Crimson Cowboys were his acolytes. The Fremont Culture concept, articulated so brilliantly in Morss's monograph, was Kidder's paradigm.

FIGURE 10:19: Scenic view of Desolation Canyon. Photo: Dan Bauer.

Despite all this, it would be a mistake to assume that archaeologists in that day of emerging method and theory suddenly became uninterested in collecting artifacts. Artifacts were instead viewed as a means to understanding prehistory, and artifact collecting and museum exhibits remained an ever-present influence. In that respect, some might consider the Claflin-Emerson Expedition a failure because they collected relatively few museum-quality artifacts.

The real value of the expedition to archaeology today lies not so much in the artifacts themselves, but in the detailed journals of the young scholars and in the hundreds of photographs now curated at the Peabody Museum. Many of the sites they visited in 1931 no longer exist or have been damaged beyond recognition, sometimes through natural erosion but more often by the thoughtless acts of individuals. A few of those sites are exactly the same today as they were in 1931, each representing a book in the prehistoric library of the American West waiting to be opened by future generations of archaeologists.

Instead of merely describing archaeological remains—and the Crimson Cowboys were certainly good at that—the next generation of archaeologists refocused their scholarly efforts toward explaining how and why prehistoric humans behaved the way they did. In a way, as archaeology became more and more of a science in the years after 1931, it also became more and more clinical, perhaps even boring to most. At least it was by the standards of the Crimson Cowboys who thought nothing of a four-hundred-mile horseback trip into the Utah wilderness armed only with notepads, trowels, and cameras.

Notes

Preface

1. Patricia Thompson, "Excavations in Nine Mile Canyon from 1892–1990: A Study in Cultural Diversity" (Master's thesis, Brigham Young University, 1993).
2. James H. Gunnerson, "The Fremont Culture: A Study in Cultural Dynamics on the Northern Anasazi Frontier," *Papers of the Peabody Museum of Archaeology and Ethnology* 59, no. 2 (Cambridge: Peabody Museum, 1969).
3. Jerry D. Spangler, K. Renee Barlow, and Duncan Metcalfe, "A Summary Report of the 2002–2003 Intuitive Surveys of the Wilcox Acquisition and Surrounding Lands, Range Creek Canyon, Utah," *Utah Museum of Natural History Occasional Papers* 2004-1 (Salt Lake City: University of Utah, 2004).
4. Jerry D. Spangler, Shannon Arnold, and Joel Boomgarden, "Chasing Ghosts: A GIS Analysis and Photographic Comparison of Vandalism and Site Degradation in Range Creek Canyon, Utah," *Utah Museum of Natural History Occasional Papers* 2006-1 (Salt Lake City: University of Utah, 2006).
5. James M. Aton, *The River Knows Everything: Desolation Canyon and the Green* (Logan: Utah State University Press, 2009).
6. Gordon R. Willey, "Prehistoric Settlement Patterns in the Viru Valley, Peru," *Bureau of American Ethnology Bulletin* 155 (1953): 1.
7. Jerry D. Spangler, "Site Distribution and Settlement Patterns in Lower Nine Mile Canyon: The Brigham Young University Surveys of 1989–91" (Master's thesis, Brigham Young University, 1993).

Chapter 1: An Elephantine Endeavor

1. Don D. Fowler, the foremost expert on the history of Western archaeology, correctly observes that the Glen Canyon Project—the archaeological investigations done in advance of the Glen Canyon Dam construction in southern Utah and northern Arizona in the late 1950s and early 1960s—probably surpassed the geographic scope of the 1931 Claflin-Emerson Expedition, but it did not begin to approach it in terms of logistical difficulty. The Glen Canyon crews used jeeps, motor boats, and rubber rafts to complete their surveys, occasionally resorting to horses, mules, and backpacks to access certain roadless areas like the Kaiparowits

Plateau. The 1931 expedition, conducted almost exclusively with horses and mules, benefited only rarely from any motorized vehicle support.

2. Gunnerson, "Fremont Culture."
3. Amelia Forbes Emerson, *Recollections and Ramblings of Amelia Forbes Emerson* (Boston: Thomas Todd Co., 1968), 119–26.
4. Gunnerson, "Fremont Culture," 23. See also Donald Scott Collection, Peabody Museum of Archaeology and Ethnology, Harvard University, Cambridge, Massachusetts.
5. Daniel J. Coolidge, "William Henry Claflin, Jr.," *Massachusetts Historical Society* 94(1982): 85; "Harvard's Military Record in the World War," *U.S. Adjutant General Military Records, 1631–1976*, 1921, p. 182, Ancestry.com.
6. "William Henry Claflin," *Harvard Class of 1915 Fiftieth Anniversary Report* (Cambridge: President and Fellows of Harvard College, 1965), 100–101; David L. Browman and Stephen Williams, *Anthropology at Harvard: A Biographical History, 1790–1940* (Cambridge: Peabody Museum Press, 2013), 374–75.
7. Browman and Williams, *Anthropology at Harvard*, 375.
8. Ibid.; Bill Claflin to Dave Rust, May 12, 1927, MS 1143, Reel 2, David Dexter Rust Papers 1870–1963, The Church of Jesus Christ of Latter-day Saints, Church History Library, Salt Lake City, Utah; Gunnerson, "Fremont Culture," 23.
9. Claflin to Rust, March 20, 1978, Reel 2, David Dexter Rust Papers.
10. Edward Waldo Emerson, *Henry Thoreau, As Remembered by a Young Friend* (1917; Concord, MA: Thoreau Foundation, 1968), v.
11. "Emerson, Raymond, S.B. 1910 (11)," UA 1115.88.10, 1890–1968, Box 1383, HA 1751, Harvard University Archives, Pusey Library, Harvard University, Cambridge, Massachusetts.
12. "Raymond Emerson," *Harvard Class of 1910, Vicennial Report* (Cambridge: President and Fellows of Harvard College, 1930), 45; Browman and Williams, *Anthropology at Harvard*, 376; Claflin to Rust, May 12, 1927, MS 1143, Reel 2, David Dexter Rust Papers.
13. Frederick H. Swanson, *Dave Rust: A Life in the Canyons* (Salt Lake City: University of Utah Press, 2007), 222.
14. "Donald Scott," *Harvard University Gazette* (November 4, 1967): 62. *Harvard College Class of 1900: Twenty-Fifth Anniversary Report* (Cambridge: President and Fellows of Harvard College, 1925), 605.
15. *Harvard College Class of 1900: Secretary's Ninth Report* (Cambridge: President and Fellows of Harvard College, 1940), 230.
16. Browman and Williams, *Anthropology at Harvard*, 340.
17. Ibid., 370–71.
18. Ibid., 371.
19. Donald Scott to Rust, April 9, 1931, Box 31-16, folder 4, Peabody Museum; Year: *1910*; Census Place: *Malden Ward 5, Middlesex, Massachusetts*;

Roll: *T624_601*; Page: *15A*; Enumeration District: *0900*; FHL microfilm: *1374614* Ancestry.com; New England Historic Genealogical Society; Boston, Massachusetts; *Massachusetts Vital Records, 1911–1915* Ancestry.com; United States, Civil War Soldier Records and Profiles, 1861–1865," Ancestry .com; Year: *1920*; Census Place: *Malden Ward 5, Middlesex, Massachusetts*; Roll: *T625-713*; Page: *2B*; Enumeration District: *278*, Ancestry.com. Michael P. Brew emigrated from Ireland, but in the 1910 and 1920 censuses he listed himself as Irish English. He may have come from Northern Ireland.

20. Richard B. Woodbury, "John Otis Brew, 1906–1988," *American Antiquity* 55, no. 3 (July 1990): 452; Browman and Williams, *Anthropology at Harvard*, 372–73.
21. Lynn Bowers, email to Jerry D. Spangler, June 8, 2017.
22. Browman and Williams, *Anthropology at Harvard*, 426; "William Benton Bowers, II," Harvard University Archives, Box 7, UAV 161.201.11, Harvard University Archives; Scott to Rust, April 9, 1931, Box 31-16, folder 4, Peabody Museum; Scott to Julian Steward, May 5, 1931, Box 31-16, folder 4, Peabody Museum; Scott to Henry S. Bowers, June 18, 1931, Box 31-16, folder 4, Peabody Museum.
23. Browman and Williams, *Anthropology at Harvard*, 413; Richard B. Woodbury, *Alfred V. Kidder* (New York: Columbia University Press, 1973), 35.
24. Swanson, *Dave Rust*, 231–33; Browman and Williams, *Anthropology at Harvard*, 413; Karen L. Mohr Chavez, "Alfred V. Kidder II, 1911–1984," *Expedition* 30, no. 3 (1988): 4; Scott to Rust, April 9, 1931, Box 31-16, folder 4, Peabody Museum; J.O. Brew to John Walcott, June 25, 1931, Box 31-16, folder 4, Peabody Museum.
25. Swanson, *Dave Rust*, 240.
26. Scott to Rust, April 9, 1931, Box 31-16, folder 4, Peabody Museum.
27. Ellen Forbes to Dean A. C. Hanford, August 9, 1930, "Waldo Emerson Forbes, 1934," UA 1115.88.10, 1890–1968, Box 1586, HA 170Y, Harvard University Archives.
28. Swanson, *Dave Rust*, xv.
29. Ibid.
30. Ibid., xvii, 113.
31. Ibid., xiii–xv, 187, 221; Claflin to Rust, May 12, 1927, Reel 2, MS 1143, David Dexter Rust Papers.
32. Rust was also an accomplished photographer, and he shot scores of images for the 1928 expedition, some of which are on file with the Peabody Museum and others with the LDS Church History Library. There is no indication he took any photographs on the 1931 expedition.
33. Gunnerson, "Fremont Culture," 23.
34. "Fremont Complex" is used by Utah archaeologists as an umbrella term to describe farmers and foragers north of the Colorado River, although there are distinct differences in adaptations from region to region. In some areas, the

Fremont peoples were highly dependent on cultivated maize, and in other areas they depended more on wild plants, especially marsh resources. A hallmark of the Fremont was their ability to shift adaptive strategies between farming and foraging as conditions warranted.

35. Donald Scott to Julian H. Steward, February 26, 1931, Box 31-16, folder 4, Scott Expedition NE Utah 1931, Peabody Museum.
36. Expenses of Scott Expedition NE Utah 1931, Box 31-16, folder 3, Peabody Museum. He purchased the topos in these quantities: East Tavaputs (7), Price River (7), Ashley (2), San Rafael (4), Gilbert Peak (1), Abayo (5), Henry Mountains (5), Sunnyside (5), Fish Springs (2), Uinta (9), Jensen (5), Vernal (4), La Sal (4), and Hayden Peak (1). He also bought state topographical maps of Utah (7) and Colorado (4). The Utah topos and Colorado state maps were ten cents per copy; the Utah state maps were twenty-five cents each.
37. Donald Scott Correspondence with Neil Judd, W. H. Bradley, W. H. Mendenhall, Frank Roberts, and E. M. Speiker, Box 31-16, folder 4, Peabody Museum. Dave Rust to Scott, March 16, 1931, Box 31-16, folder 4, Peabody Museum. Bradley studied oil shale on the east Tavaputs in the mid-1920s. His 1927 dissertation at the Yale Sheffield School of Science was published by the US Geological Survey and remains a standard work today, *Origins and Microfossils of the Oil Shale of the Green River Formation of Colorado and Utah*, US Geological Survey Professional Paper 168 (Washington, DC: Government Printing Office, 1931). It should also be noted here that the term "Fremont Culture" is commonly attributed to Noel Morss's 1931 manuscript, but in reality that term had been used by Morss, Roberts, and Scott since 1928.
38. Donald Scott–Julian H. Steward Correspondence, February 28, April 6, and May 5, 1931, Box 31-16, folder 4, Peabody Museum.
39. C. N. Strevell and C. S. Pulver, *Report of the Utah State Museum Association Archaeological Expedition* (Salt Lake City: Utah State Historical Society, 1935), page c.
40. Scott kept suggesting that Rust hire Ned Chaffin who had worked on previous Claflin-Emerson trips. After a little back-and-forth on the subject, Rust finally stated his case about Chaffin, saying, "Ned Chaffin, as you say, is a hustling wrangler, but he is rather reckless and inefficient as a packer." Scott deferred to Rust, and Chaffin stayed home (see Rust to Scott, June 8, 1931, Box 31-16, folder 4, Peabody Museum). One of Chaffin's descendants, Barry Scholl, told the authors that Rust and Chaffin were rivals in the guiding business and that some bad blood existed between the two.
41. Donald Scott–David Rust Correspondence, April 9 and May 6, 1931, Box 31-16, folder 4, Peabody Museum.
42. Our attempts to identify any films shot during the course of the 1931 field season were entirely unsuccessful. If they carried a movie camera into the field, there is no reference anywhere in the journals that they used it, and the Peabody Museum

has none of the film footage on file. And yet, J.O. Brew wrote Henry B. Roberts in 1932 to say that the crew had met at Scott's house to watch movies of the expedition. Perhaps Scott kept it and somehow the film went into the trash after he died. See J.O. Brew to Henry B. Roberts, April 18, 1932, Box 31-16, folder 4, Peabody Museum.

43. Expenses of Scott Expedition NE Utah 1931, Box 31-16, folder 3, Peabody Museum.
44. http://www.usinflationcalculator.com/.
45. Expenses of Scott Expedition NE Utah 1931, Box 31-16, folder 3, Peabody Museum; David Rust Journal 1931, MS 1143, Reel 2, David Dexter Rust Papers.

Chapter 2: The Adventure Begins

1. Green River, Utah, has endured countless boom-and-bust cycles over the decades, although the booms were always less than promised and the busts much longer than ever anticipated. The main drag through town is littered with the carcasses of businesses whose owners have arrived expecting "the next big thing," only to shutter their doors in a year or two. At one point, city fathers even looked the other way when an adult film studio briefly set up shop. Any business was good for the town. Today, the city is pinning its hopes and prayers on a nuclear power plant still in its planning stages—a project that could suck the Green River to a trickle and which faces ferocious opposition from conservationists across the country.
2. Gregory C. Crampton and Steven K. Madsen, *In Search of the Spanish Trail: Santa Fe to Los Angeles, 1829–1848* (Salt Lake City: Gibbs Smith, 1994), 54–57.
3. Solomon Nunes Carvalho, *Incidents of Travel and Adventure in the Far West with Col. Fremont's Last Expedition* (Philadelphia: Jewish Publication Society of America, 1857), 167–73; Ferol Egan, *Fremont: Explorer for a Restless Nation* (Reno: University of Nevada Press, 1985), 499–501.
4. Carvalho, *Incidents*, 168.
5. "Green River News," *Times Independent*, July 9, 1931.
6. Dave Rust, "Journal 1931 Claflin Emerson Expedition," Reel 1 MS 1143 (1931): 1, David Dexter Rust Papers, 1870–1963, The Church of Jesus Christ of Latter-day Saints, Church History Library, Salt Lake City, Utah.
7. "Journal of Expenses, Utah 1931," Claflin-Emerson Expedition Records, 31-16-10/100240.1.7. Box 31-16, folder 3, Peabody Museum of Archaeology and Ethnology, Harvard University, Cambridge, Massachusetts.
8. Rust, "Journal," 1.
9. Year: *1930*; Census Place: *Green River, Emery, Utah*; Roll: *2415*; Page: *2A*; Enumeration District: *0012*; Image: *500.0*; FHL microfilm: *2342149*, Ancestry.com.
10. Year: *1920*; Census Place: *Emery, Emery, Utah*; Roll: *T625_1862*; Page: *1B*; Enumeration District: *69*; Image: *879*. Year: *1930*, Ancestry.com; Census Place: *Vernal, Uintah, Utah*; Roll: *2424*; Page: *10A*; Enumeration District: *0017*; Image: *143.0*; FHL microfilm: *2342158*, Ancestry.com.

11. "Journal of Expenses," 3.
12. A note on one of the earliest photographs (U-31-501) indicates it was taken at the Hastings Ranch and depicts a "power dam" on the Green River. If accurately labeled, the Hastings Ranch would have been about nine miles upriver at what is today known as the Tusher Dam. It also means Rust was pasturing the pack animals on July 10 and 11 a considerable distance from the town of Green River where the Harvard crew was staying at the Midland Hotel.
13. E. C. Larue, "The Colorado River and Its Utilization," *US Geological Survey Water Supply Paper* 395 (Washington, DC: Government Printing Office, 1916), 134. See also Roy Webb, "Coal Creek Dam Site," *Confluence: The Journal of Colorado Plateau River Guides* 27 (December 2003): 11–12.
14. Aton, *The River Knows Everything*, 146.
15. The Colorado Plateau Archaeological Alliance later investigated this drainage, but surprisingly very little evidence of prehistoric occupation was found, despite the presence of a permanent stream. There is a granary at the mouth of the canyon and a few scatters of lithic artifacts, but little to suggest a major prehistoric farming presence here.
16. Curry was rumored to have been carrying a fortune in purloined gold, which he hid before being killed by the posse. Treasure hunters have been exploring every nook and cranny in this area since 1900 looking for the gold, but to no avail.
17. Ralf R. Woolley, "A Boat Trip Down Green River from Green River, Wyoming, to Green River, Utah, July 10–September 14, 1922," US Geological Survey Field Records Library, Denver, Colorado. For a more complete history of the Cradle M Ranch at Florence Creek, see Aton, *The River Knows Everything*, 103–12.
18. George W. McCall testimony, *The Heirs of Joseph E. Wing v. John Darioli*, October 24–28, 1922, National Archives, Washington, DC, Records at Division H, US Department of the Interior, RG-49.
19. Aton, *The River Knows Everything*, 108.
20. Pearl Baker, *The Wild Bunch at Robber's Roost* (1965; repr., Lincoln: University of Nebraska Press, 1989), 68–69, 75–78; Ray "Budge" Wilcox, interview by Bill Belknap and Loie Belknap Evans, 1974, Belknap Collection, Cline Library, Northern Arizona University, Flagstaff.
21. Waldo Wilcox, interview by James M. Aton and Steve Gerber, January 10, 2004, Green River, Utah; James A. Bennett, *Hereford History in Utah* (Salt Lake City: Utah Hereford Association, 1946), 12–13, 24; June Seamount Orm, interview by Steve Gerber and Paul Phillips, July 15, 2003, Salt Lake City; Ellsworth Kolb, *Through the Grand Canyon from Wyoming to Mexico* (New York: Macmillan, 1940), 103; Waldo Wilcox, interview by James M. Aton, Steve Gerber, and Paul Phillips, July 16, 2003, Green River, Utah; Woolley, "A Boat Trip."
22. Kolb, *Through the Grand Canyon*, 103–4; Zelpha McPherson McClurg, interview by Steve Gerber and Paul Phillips, July 2, 2003, Grand Junction, Colorado;

Waldo Wilcox interview, January 10, 2004. After using the land for more than forty years, McPherson finally filed a land-entry claim in 1929 to gain official title. See the land records, Bureau of Land Management, Salt Lake City, Utah. McPherson may have been trying to tidy up his affairs before selling to his son-in-law.

23. Waldo Wilcox, interview by James M. Aton, May 31, 2005, Green River, Utah.
24. Cows must be milked every day or they stop lactating, and they will not resume producing milk until after their next calf is born. That crew members had access to fresh milk suggests that someone was on hand to milk a cow (or cows) every day. Milk cows were important assets to every self-sufficient farmer and rancher in the West, providing food staples such as milk, cream, butter, and cheese.
25. Aton, *The River Knows Everything*, 112.
26. The Hill Creek Extension: A Portfolio of Primary Documents, Utah Division of State History, https://heritage.utah.gov/history/uhq-sum-2015-hill-creek-extension.
27. Waldo Wilcox, interview by James M. Aton, December 17, 2015, Green River, Utah.
28. Roland McCook Sr., Ute Tribe historian and former Ute Tribe chairman, interview by James M. Aton, August 8–12, 2007, Arcadia, Utah.
29. Rick Chapoose, Ute Tribe river guide, interview by James M. Aton, August 8–12, 2003, Fort Duchesne, Utah.
30. The expedition's journal of expenses indicates that the Wilcoxes were to be paid 15 cents a day for pasturage, but the expense total was left blank. This suggests the Wilcoxes were never actually paid for pasturing the horses and mules, which became a recurring theme in the weeks ahead as other ranchers also were not paid.
31. This would be the only occasion on the entire expedition where Donald Scott, the senior fellow of the archaeologists, split off to investigate something on his own. In all subsequent instances (Range Creek, Desolation, Argyle, and Willow Creek) he sent the students to do the exploring.
32. Repeated attempts by Peabody Museum staff to find the Scott journal proved unsuccessful, and all Claflin-Emerson Expedition sites can be found in the other five journals. One possibility is that Scott did not keep a journal. Scott's subsequent report to the Department of Interior, however, contains substantially more detail than is found in the journals themselves, as if Scott was pulling additional information from his own notes or perhaps from memory. James H. Gunnerson refers to the journal in his monograph, "The Fremont Culture: A Study in Cultural Dynamics on the Northern Anasazi Frontier, Including the Report of the Claflin-Emerson Expedition of the Peabody Museum" (1969). It is possible the journal disappeared into Gunnerson's personal papers, which now reside at the University of Nebraska, but no one there could locate Scott's journal.

33. Waldo Forbes, "Field Journal of the 1931 Claflin Emerson Expedition," Donald Scott Collection, Peabody Museum of Archaeology and Ethnology, Harvard University, Cambridge, Massachusetts (1931), 2.
34. Scott says this about the site numbering system: It "is based upon the topographical maps of the United States Geological Survey. The number is composed of three elements: the letter or letters indicating the name of the topographical sheet: the number indicating in which of the sixteen divisions of the map the site lies, counting from the top left-hand corner: and the third number which is the actual numerical indicator of the site. Thus ET 6-6 signified a site on the East Tavaputs sheet; second section from the left in the second row from the top (there being four rows of four sections each); and the sixth site encountered in that section. The exploration covered parts of four sheets: East Tavaputs, Price River, Uinta, and Ashley." Donald Scott, "The Claflin-Emerson Field Notes," Donald Scott Collection, 1–2.
35. Albert B. Reagan, "Some Ancient Indian Granaries," *Proceedings: Utah Academy of Sciences, Arts and Letters* 11 (1934): 39–40.
36. John Wesley Powell, *The Exploration of the Colorado River and Its Canyons* (1895; repr., New York: Dover Publications Inc., 1961), 191.
37. For information on Julien's life around the Colorado Plateau, see James H. Knipmeyer, "The Denis Julien Inscriptions," *Utah Historical Quarterly* 64, no. 1 (1996): 52–69. George E. Stewart Jr. "discovered" the DJ inscription at Chandler around 1967. Because the J is different from Julien's initials elsewhere, some experts like Blaine Miller, formerly the Price BLM archaeologist, have suggested that perhaps Stewart might have scratched it himself. It has faded some in recent years. Blaine Miller, interview by James M. Aton, July 8, 2005, Price, Utah.
38. Baker, *Robber's Roost*, 67–70.
39. Brownie Tomlinson, interview by James M. Aton, December 16, 2015, Vernal, Utah.
40. Waldo Wilcox, interview by James M. Aton, July 27, 2004, Green River, Utah. For a short time, there was a ferry at Chandler Creek which connected to the Seamount brothers' cattle trail on the west side of the river. That trail provided access to railheads at Woodside.
41. Alfred Kidder II, "Field Journal of the 1931 Claflin Emerson Expedition," Donald Scott Collection, 4.
42. Kidder, "Field Journal," 5.
43. Forbes, "Field Journal," 9–11.
44. James Dennison, "Field Journal of the 1931 Claflin Emerson Expedition," Donald Scott Collection, Peabody Museum of Archaeology and Ethnology, Harvard University, Cambridge, Massachusetts (1931), 4–6.
45. Kidder, "Field Journal," 5.
46. Rust, "Journal," 1. Chandler Creek features numerous major side canyons on both the north and south sides, and it is easy to get disoriented as to which is the

main canyon. The trail would have been in the bottom of the main canyon until a split almost at the headwaters where the trail veers left into East Fork and finally onto the top of the plateau. The "south" fork that Rust referred to could be any of three major side drainages on the south side of Chandler Creek.

47. Rust, "Journal," 1.
48. The journals refer to this as Little Doggie Canyon, but the topographic maps today call it Big Doggie, with no references to a Little Doggie.
49. Donald Scott, "The 1931 Claflin-Emerson Expedition," Donald Scott Collection, Peabody Museum of Archaeology and Ethnology, Harvard University, Cambridge, Massachusetts (1931), 2.
50. Gunnerson, "Fremont Culture."
51. Shannon Arnold-Boomgarden, "An Application of ARCGIS Viewshed Analysis in Range Creek Canyon, Utah," *Utah Archaeology* 22, no. 1 (2009): 15–30.
52. Reagan, "Indian Granaries," 40.

Chapter 3: Divide and Conquer

1. Topographic maps today refer to it as Big Doggie Canyon, but the journals actually refer it as "Little Doggie Canyon."
2. Technically, the Book Cliffs define the southern perimeter of the Tavaputs Plateau and are visible to every passing motorist for roughly one hundred miles of US Highway 6 and Interstate 70 between Price, Utah, and Grand Junction, Colorado. Hill Creek and Willow Creek originate on the East Tavaputs Plateau above the Book Cliffs and drain north to the Uinta Basin. Locals refer to everything behind the Book Cliffs escarpment as the "Books."
3. George Long, "A Narrative History of Uintah County, As Told to and Recounted by George Long," self-published manuscript in authors' possession, p. 48, 70.
4. Scott, "Claflin-Emerson," 5–6.
5. Gunnerson, "Fremont Culture," 114–16.
6. John D. Barton, "Antoine Robidoux and the Fur Trade of the Uinta Basin" (Master's thesis, Brigham Young University, 1989), 59–66.
7. Aton, *The River Knows Everything*, 70–71.
8. The US Geological Survey, the official keeper of place names, spells it Uinta Basin, but locals prefer Uintah Basin and can be quite adamant about it. The proper spelling of place names in this area can be confusing. For example, there are the Uinta Mountains and the Uinta Basin, and there is a Uintah River and a Uintah County. We prefer to use the official spelling of place names. Our apologies to our friends in the basin who would prefer the Uintah Basin spelling.
9. Aton, *The River Knows Everything*, 58–59.
10. Gilsonite is a trade name for the mineral more generally known as asphaltum. It was named after Deputy US Marshal Sam Gilson, who, in partnership with Bert Seaboldt, locked up the most valuable claims before the Indian lands had even

been removed from the reservation by Congress. Gilson sold out within a couple of years, and legend has it that a condition of the sale was that the mineral continue to bear his name (see Jerry D. Spangler and Donna Kemp Spangler, *Back Country Byway: The History of Nine Mile Canyon* (Salt Lake City: University of Utah Press, 2016), 40–63.

11. Doris Karren Burton, *Settlements of Uintah County: Digging Deeper* (Vernal, UT: Uintah County Library, 1998), 487.
12. James H. Beckstead, *Cowboying: A Tough Job in a Hard Land* (Salt Lake City: University of Utah Press, 1991), 86.
13. Rust, "Journal."
14. Beckstead, *Cowboying*, 87–88. Nutter's sale to his hated rival was part of a condition the federal government attached to a lease whereby Nutter acquired rights to graze his herds on tribal lands in the Uinta Mountains and Strawberry Valley—lands far better suited to grazing than the East Tavaputs. The lease stipulated that Nutter could hold no other properties or holdings in Utah during the tenure of the lease. In addition to the Strawberry Valley lands, he then established by hook and crook a massive ranch operation on the Arizona Strip just outside the Utah border. Between the two operations, it was rumored that the cattle baron ran as many as 100,000 head of cattle, although this is probably an exaggeration.
15. Beckstead, *Cowboying*, 172; Burton, *Digging Deeper*, 507.
16. Utah Law Enforcement Memorial, "In Honor of Utah's Fallen Officers," https://www.utahsfallen.org/archives/687.
17. Beckstead, *Cowboying*, 88; Burton, *Digging Deeper*, 507.
18. Forbes, "Field Journal," 14.
19. Donald Scott–Dave Rust Correspondence, May 6, 1931, Box 31-16, folder 4, Peabody Museum.
20. Waldo Wilcox, interview, December 17, 2015.
21. Craig Woods Fuller, "Land Rush in Zion: Opening of the Uncompahgre and Uintah Indian Reservations" (PhD diss., Brigham Young University, 1990), 100–101; Virginia N. Price and John T. Darby, "Preston Nutter: Utah Cattleman, 1886–1936," *Utah Historical Quarterly* 32, no. 3 (summer 1964): 240.
22. Willow Creek, Utah. 1930 Federal Census, ancestry.com.
23. Pawwinnee's daughters, interview, Ute Indian Oral History Project Collection, accn. 0883, Special Collections, Marriott Library, University of Utah, Salt Lake City, Utah, 71.
24. George Emery Stewart Jr., *Tales from Indian Country: Authentic Stories and Legends from the Great Uintah Basin* (Sandy, UT: Mary Ellen Stewart Gardner, 1997), 7; Long, "A Narrative History," 71–73.
25. There are inconsistencies in the mileage traveled. Forbes indicates the first site (ET9-1) was twelve miles from Webster City, whereas Scott's summary indicates it was fifteen miles. Forbes indicated the second site (ET9-2) was twelve and a half

miles above Webster City, whereas Dennison indicated the second site was only ten miles from Webster City, and Scott's report indicated it was fifteen miles, or the same distance as ET9-1. Given that Forbes was an experienced cartographer, we usually defer to his mileage estimates here.

26. Kidder, "Field Journal," 6–7. In 1962, the University of Utah recorded a rock shelter in this general area (42Gr381) that is similar to ET9-1 and ET9-2, but the description of this site is insufficient for positive identification and no photos were taken in 1962 whereby they could be compared to the 1931 photos. Excavating in 1931 was primitive by today's standards, but it was light years beyond the first digs in the nineteenth century which focused on finding "cool" artifacts. Following the lead of Alfred V. Kidder, who introduced the new techniques in the west with his work at Pecos Pueblo, the Claflin-Emerson crew did excavate by stratigraphic levels.
27. Dennison, "Field Journal," 7–8.
28. Kidder, "Field Journal," 6–7.
29. Ibid., 7. Scott's report attributes this site description to James Dennison, but it is actually in Kidder's journal. The field notes and Scott's version indicate the site is eighteen to twenty miles above the Webster City Ranch, whereas Forbes's mileage log places it fifteen to sixteen miles above the ranch (see Scott, "Claflin-Emerson," 14).
30. Forbes, "Field Journal," 16.
31. Kidder, "Field Journal," 8.
32. Dennison, "Field Journal," 8.
33. Ibid., 9.
34. Kidder, "Field Journal," 8; Dennison, "Field Journal," 10.
35. Forbes's job on this expedition was to create an accurate mileage log and map of the route. But he apparently did not communicate well with Dennison and Kidder, both of whom offered mileage estimates quite different than Forbes. The problem with the July 23 sites is that Forbes's mileage estimates would place several of them upstream from the mouth of Pioche Canyon, whereas the estimates provided by Dennison and Kidder would place them downstream from the mouth. The journals are consistent that the sites were below Pioche Canyon. In the absence of field verification of these sites, the locations offered here should be considered gross estimates.
36. Kidder, "Field Journal," 19.
37. Ibid., 10–11.
38. Dennison, "Field Journal," 10–11.
39. Kidder, "Field Journal," 11–12.
40. Ibid., 12.
41. Ibid., 12–13.
42. Ibid., 14.

43. Ibid., 14–15.
44. Pauline Hazelbush Oral History, Pauline Hazelbush file, no. 1055, Uintah County Regional History Center, Uintah County Library, Vernal, Utah, p. 13.
45. Ibid., 28–30.
46. Ibid., 13, 30, 35.
47. Ibid., 36–37.
48. "Pauline, Book Cliff Pioneer," Pauline Hazelbush file; "Walter R. Hazelbush," Death Certificate, ancestry.com; "Pauline Hazelbush buried in Colorado," Pauline Hazelbush file.
49. Pauline Hazelbush Oral History, 42–43.
50. Kidder, "Field Journal," 16–17.
51. Ibid., 18.
52. Ibid., 18–19.
53. Ibid., 19.

Chapter 4: Castles in the Sky

1. J. Walter Fewkes, "Archaeological Investigations in New Mexico, Colorado, and Utah," *Smithsonian Miscellaneous Collections* 68, no. 1 (1917): 1. See also J. Walter Fewkes, "Prehistoric Remains in New Mexico, Colorado, and Utah," *Smithsonian Miscellaneous Collections* 66, no. 17 (1917): 76–92.
2. Fewkes, "Investigations," 23.
3. Ibid., 33–34. Fewkes suggested the possibility that the towers functioned as kivas, or ceremonial rooms, and that the multiple towers evident at any single site were representative of different families or clans. In the hundred years since Fewkes floated the idea, kivas have not yet been documented as such anywhere in the Tavaputs Plateau region or elsewhere among the Fremont Complex that occupied most of Utah north of the Colorado Plateau.
4. From the 1880s through the 1920s, the most prestigious museums in the world dispatched crews to the Southwest to harvest rich collections of artifacts with little or no thought to understanding the people behind the artifacts. In some instances, the museums even paid locals to hunt their collections for them, which led to the rural tradition of pot hunting. The preoccupation with artifacts gave way to the emergence in the 1910s of archaeology as a scientific discipline oriented towards careful attention to detail, record keeping and reporting, and attempts to place archaeological resources in spatial and temporal context. Alfred Kidder's father was at the forefront of this paradigm shift, and the Claflin-Emerson Expedition of 1928–1931 represented one of the earliest attempts to implement these new practices on a grand scale.
5. Year: *1930*; Census Place: *Willows, Uintah, Utah*; Roll: *2424*; Page: *1B*; Enumeration District: *0022*; Image: *196.0*; FHL microfilm: *2342158*, Ancestry.com.
6. Burton, *Digging Deeper*, 489.

7. Year: *1900*; Census Place: *Brookline, Norfolk, Massachusetts*; Roll: *669*; Page: *16A*; Enumeration District: *1024*; FHL microfilm: 1240669, Ancestry.com; Earnest Wild, *Utah, Death and Military Certificates, 1904–1961*, Ancestry.com.
8. Waldo Wilcox interview, December 17, 2015.
9. Number: *529-50-3583*; Issue State: *Utah*; Issue Date: *1955*, Ancestry.com.
10. Waldo Wilcox interview, December 17, 2015; Expenses of Scott Expedition NE Utah 1931, Box 31-16, folder 3, Peabody Museum of Archaeology and Ethnology, Harvard University, Cambridge, Massachusetts.
11. John Otis Brew, "Field Journal of thc 1931 Claflin Emerson Expedition," Donald Scott Collection, Peabody Museum of Archaeology and Ethnology, Harvard University, Cambridge, Massachusetts (1931): 5. Gunnerson's synthesis indicates the site is two miles above Horsecorn Canyon.
12. Scott, "Claflin-Emerson," 29. Brew, "Field Journal," 6–7.
13. Brew, "Field Journal," 9–10.
14. Scott, "Claflin-Emerson," 5.
15. Some of the photographic images are quite vivid and many of them appear to have been chalked to enhance contrast. Chalking of rock art images is today categorically unacceptable, but it was a common practice in the 1930s. It is not known if the Harvard crew chalked the images themselves or whether they had been chalked by an earlier photographer, perhaps Leo Thorne of Vernal who had a renowned collection of high-quality rock art photos and typically accompanied Albert Reagan on his investigations.
16. Burton, *Digging Deeper*, 489; Randlett, Utah, 1910 Federal Census, ancestry.com; "Austin Wardle, Find a Grave Memorial," ancestry.com.
17. Hazel Wardle, Fort Duchesne interview by Norma Denver, Doris Duke, MS 0417, Box 21 Number 790, Western History Center, Special Collections, Marriott Library, University of Utah, Salt Lake City, Utah; Hazel Wardle interview, Ute Indian Oral History Project Collection, 1.
18. Hazel Wardle interview, Ute Indian Oral History, 2, 68.
19. Ibid., 34.
20. Ibid., 18–19, 45–50; Tomlinson, interview by Aton.
21. Hazel Wardle interview, Ute Indian Oral History, 15.
22. There is no Tom's Canyon on today's topographic maps anywhere in the area. Brew's notes indicate it was two miles above the Wild Ranch, which is itself about a mile above the mouth of Horsecorn Canyon. In this area, there is Wilcox Canyon on the west side and Oil Sand Canyon on the east side of Hill Creek.
23. Fewkes, "Investigations," 31–32.
24. Albert Reagan, "Some Archaeological Notes on Hill Canyon in Northeastern Utah," *El Palacio* 31, no. 4 (1931): 235.
25. Brew, "Field Journal," 18.
26. Scott, "Field Notes," 20.

27. Brew, "Field Journal," 11.
28. Ibid., 12.
29. Scott, "Claflin-Emerson," 20. It should be noted that Scott's report contains a lot more detail than is found in Brew's journal, suggesting that Scott might have kept a journal that has since been lost. Based on an illustration in Fewkes's report, this might be what Fewkes referred to as the Inverted Cone Ruins (see Fewkes, "Investigations," 31).
30. Scott, "Claflin-Emerson," 21. Reagan was told there was a granary near Pedestal Rock, but he did not investigate further (see Reagan, "Notes," 235).
31. Brew, "Field Journal," 14.
32. Bowers's journal indicates they began excavations here on July 21, but this is probably in error and it is not consistent with Brew's journal. The only way this date would be accurate is if Bowers began working here by himself while all the others were at Pedestal Rock and the other sites in the same area.
33. This site was revisited in 1954 by James Gunnerson and assigned the site number 42Un120.
34. Brew, "Field Journal," 16.
35. Fewkes, "Investigations," 27–28.
36. Reagan, "Notes," 233–36.
37. Ibid., 243.
38. Ibid., 244.
39. Albert Reagan, "Utah: Report of Investigations," *American Anthropologist* 35, no. 1 (1933): 508.
40. Scott, "Claflin-Emerson," 23.
41. Ibid., 23–24.
42. Ibid., 24.
43. Edmund Schulman, "Dendrochronology in Northeastern Utah," *Tree-Ring Bulletin* 15 (1948): 2–14.
44. Reagan, "Notes," 234–35.
45. Reagan's 1931 three-page description of the site is actually far more detailed than the Claflin-Emerson field notes and Scott's later summary. Although not formally trained in archaeology, Reagan usually tried to hold himself to high professional standards.
46. Dennison, "Field Journal," 12–14.
47. Gunnerson, "Fremont Culture," 111.
48. It is possible this site is the "cliff house" referred to by Reagan.
49. Kidder, "Field Journal," 20.
50. William Bowers, "Field Journal of the 1931 Claflin Emerson Expedition," Donald Scott Collection, Peabody Museum of Archaeology and Ethnology, Harvard University, Cambridge, Massachusetts (1931): 5.
51. Black-on-white potsherds are good temporal indicators of occupations after about AD 1000, when this tradition flourished in northern Arizona and ce-

ramic vessels made their way north into Utah by way of trade. The Fremont Complex did not have a black-on-white pottery tradition, but they imitated it by painting black designs on their grayware pottery. The presence of true black-on-white pottery is seen as evidence of trade with distant Puebloan peoples. Black-on-white pottery and other painted ceramics are fairly common in Nine Mile Canyon and Range Creek Canyon, but they seem to have been rare in Hill Creek.

52. Rust, "Journal."
53. Brew, "Field Journal," 17. This site was redocumented in 2004 by Montgomery Archaeological Consultants and assigned the number 42Un3794.
54. Scott, "Claflin-Emerson," 30.
55. Kidder, "Field Journal," 23–25.
56. Fewkes, "Investigations," 32–33.
57. Reagan, "Notes," 230.
58. This site was later revisited in 2004 by Montgomery Archaeological Consultants (MOAC) and assigned the number 42Un3728. The structures on top of the pinnacle were not accessible at that time.
59. Kidder, "Field Journal," 25–26.
60. This site was redocumented in 2004 by Montgomery Archaeological Consultants. It had earlier been assigned the number 42Un105.
61. Fewkes, "Investigations," 24–26. Reagan, "Notes," 226–30.
62. Scott, "Claflin-Emerson," 32. Bowers, "Field Journal," 6–9.
63. Reagan, "Investigations," 228.
64. Scott, "Claflin-Emerson," 33. This site is probably 42Un3722, documented in 2004 by Montgomery Archaeological Consultants, although the descriptions are somewhat different. MOAC described it as a two-room structure.
65. "Journal of Expenses," 3.
66. Rust, "Journal," 1.
67. Virginia Kerns, *Scenes from the High Desert: Julian Steward's Life and Theory* (Urbana: University of Illinois Press, 2003), 115–24. Steward's salary was $3,000 (about $49,700 in 2018 dollars) and his research budget was $800 (just over $13,200 in 2018 dollars).
68. Donald Scott to Julian H. Steward, February 28, 1931, Donald Scott Papers.
69. Ibid.; Steward to Scott, April 6, 1931, Donald Scott Papers.
70. Ibid.
71. Steward to Scott, April 6, 1931; Scott to Steward, May 5, 1931; Steward to Scott, May 20, 1931, Donald Scott Papers.
72. Steward to Scott, August 16, 1931; Scott to Steward, October 2, 1931, Donald Scott Papers; Kerns, *Scenes*, 133.
73. Kerns, *Scenes*, 131–36.
74. Ibid. Kilgor Stewart, the brother of Omer Stewart (who later achieved fame for his work in Native American anthropology) introduced Steward to Cannon at

Whiterocks that summer. He also arranged for the three of them, along with Cannon's friend, to meet for drinks at a speakeasy in Salt Lake following their Bear Dance meeting.

75. Ibid., 138–45, 192.
76. Ibid., 107, 119, 127, 157–58.
77. Ibid., 177.
78. "Journal of Expenses," 3.
79. Rust, "Journal," 1.
80. This site is today recognized by its official designation of 42Un104 in the state archaeological database.
81. "Victims of Gun Play at Hill Creek Monday Brought to Vernal Severely Wounded," *Vernal Express*, February 13, 1930; "Party to Shooting Affray Released from Hospital and Put Under Bond," *Vernal Express*, February 21, 1930; "Criminal and Civil Cases Disposed of by Judge Watkins at April Term of D.C.," *Vernal Express*, April 17, 1930; Ken Sleight to Otis R. "Doc" Marston, March 12, 1962, Otis R. Marston Collection, Huntington Library, San Marino, California; Doris Karren Burton, "Memorable Character: Ben Morris–Josie Bassett's Fifth," *Outlaw Trail Journal* (summer 1999): 35–41; Frank McKnight, *A Family Remembered* (Salt Lake City: Ponderosa Printing, 1994), 82–84.
82. For a longer account of Morris's colorful life, see Aton, *The River Knows Everything*, 137–40. In 2008, Aton traveled to the cemetery in Dinosaur, Utah (formerly Artesia) and found two unmarked graves, one of which he presumed to be that of Morris.
83. Bowers, "Field Journal," 10–11. Scott, "Claflin-Emerson," 40–41. This site was later revisited in 1954 by James Gunnerson, but it has not been redocumented since that time.
84. Brew, "Field Journal," 20–21.
85. Reagan, "Notes," 226.
86. Donald Scott to David Rust, April 9, 1931, Donald Scott Papers.
87. Ibid., May 6, 1931.
88. Arden Stewart, "This Story Was Told to Me," Arden Stewart File, Uintah County Regional History Center, Vernal, Utah; Arden Stewart, interview by James M. Aton, January 8, 2004, Vernal, Utah; Arden Stewart, interview by Kathleen Irving, April 19, 2002, Uintah County Regional History Center; Arden Stewart, "Ferries," lecture to the Uintah County Historical Society, July 10, 1993, Uintah County Regional History Center; For a complete history of Hank Stewart and the Sand Wash ferry, see Aton, *The River Knows Everything*, 130–37.
89. Ibid.
90. "Journal of Expenses."
91. James H. Gunnerson, "An Archaeological Survey of the Fremont Area," *University of Utah Anthropological Papers* 28 (Salt Lake City: University of Utah, 1957).

Chapter 5: Into the Thick of It

1. Peabody Museum, expense memorandum dated May 18, 1931, entitled "David Rust, Utah." Claflin-Emerson Expedition Records, 31-16-10/100240.1.7, Box 31-16, folder 3, Peabody Museum of Archaeology and Ethnology, Harvard University, Cambridge, Massachusetts.
2. To date, about 1,500 archaeological sites have been documented in Nine Mile Canyon with only about 10 percent of the canyon formally investigated. More than half are rock art sites.
3. Scott, "Claflin-Emerson," 10.
4. Rust, "Journal," 2.
5. "Journey to Ashley," *Deseret News*, May 17, 1890.
6. Henry Montgomery, "Prehistoric Man in Utah," *The Archaeologist* 2, nos. 8, 10, and 11 (1894): 227–34, 298–306, 335–42.
7. Jerry D. Spangler, *Nine Mile Canyon: The Archaeological History of an American Treasure* (Salt Lake City: University of Utah Press, 2013), 34–35.
8. Noel Morss, "The Ancient Culture of the Fremont River in Utah," *Peabody Museum of American Archaeology and Ethnology* 12, no. 3 (1931): 28. Clarence Mumford's name was etched into a cliff face just outside of Rasmussen Cave where it is still visible today.
9. "Journal of Expenses."
10. "Preston Nutter Ranch at Nine Mile Burns," *Vernal Express*, June 30, 1955.
11. Dennison, "Field Journal," 14. Bowers, "Field Journal," 12.
12. Dennison, "Field Journal," 14. This site is now known as 42Dc681.
13. Year: *1930*; Census Place: *Harper, Duchesne, Utah*; Roll: *2415*; Page: *1A*; Enumeration District: *40*; Image: *1118.0*; FHL microfilm: *2342149*. Year: *1930*; Census Place: *Price, Carbon, Utah*; Roll: *2415*; Page: *10B*; Enumeration District: *22*; Image: *273.0*; FHL microfilm: *2342149*, Ancestry.com.
14. Norma Dalton, interview by Jerry D. Spangler and James M. Aton, June 8, 2016, Sunset, Utah; Spangler and Spangler, *Last Chance Byway*, 260.
15. The expedition described PR4-1 on July 31 on their way to the Pace Ranch, and it appears that site numbers PR4-9 and PR4-10 were skipped as they do not appear in any of the journals (or the descriptions were later lost). In other words, they might have only described seven sites over the course of August 1.
16. Dennison, "Field Journal," 17. This site is now known as 42Dc671.
17. Ibid., 19.
18. Forbes, "Field Journal," 36.
19. Dennison, "Field Journal," 20–21.
20. Spangler, "Site Distribution," 261–63. This site is formally known as 42Dc699.
21. Forbes, "Field Journal," 26–27. This site is now known as 42Dc653.
22. Ibid., 39.
23. Ibid., 40–41.

24. Dennison, "Field Journal," 21–22. This site is now known as 42Dc664. PR4-6 and PR4-7 have not yet been reidentified. Sites PR4-9 and PR4-10 are not described in any of the field journals, nor are they mentioned in Gunnerson's 1969 synthesis. It would have been highly unusual for the expedition to simply skip over those site numbers, but the next numerical reference is to PR4-11.
25. This is inferred from the "Journal of Expenses" that indicates Dafton Thompson remained with the expedition through its duration, and from Dave Rust's journal, which indicates he had arrived at the Pace Ranch on July 31 after getting supplies in Roosevelt.
26. Brew, "Field Notes," 22. This site is known today as 42Dc5.
27. Ibid., 23. PR4-12 has not yet been reidentified. PR12-13 is now known as 42Cb769.
28. Kidder, "Field Notes," 28. This site is now known as 42Cb778.
29. Scott, "Claflin-Emerson," 6.
30. Brew, "Field Notes," 24–25. This site was later divided into three sites now known as 42Dc618, 42Dc619, and 42Dc620.
31. Scott, "Claflin-Emerson," 66.
32. Ibid., 7.
33. Ibid.
34. Thompson, "Cultural Diversity," 86.
35. Scott, "Claflin-Emerson," 10.
36. "Journal of Expenses," 3.
37. The crew probably had access to a motorized vehicle. Dave Rust had arrived by rented pickup truck at the Pace Ranch with supplies on July 31. We are uncertain how Scott traveled from Roosevelt to Salt Lake City, but by the time the expedition left Nine Mile Canyon they had a pickup truck and an automobile.
38. Kidder, "Field Journal," 44–45.
39. Brew, "Field Notes," 26.
40. Ibid.
41. Scott, "Claflin-Emerson," 68.
42. Thompson, "Cultural Diversity." This site is formally known as 42Cb770.
43. Brew, "Field Notes," 26.
44. Ibid., 27.
45. Ibid., 27–28.
46. Spangler, "Site Distribution." Thompson, "Cultural Diversity." Archaeologist James Gunnerson visited Nordell's Fort (42Dc5) in 1955, but there is no evidence he investigated any other sites in this area.
47. Gunnerson, "Fremont Culture."

Chapter 6: Unnoticed Treasures

1. Scott, "Claflin-Emerson," 10.
2. Leonard L. Leh, "Prehistoric Pueblo Ruins in Range Creek Canyon, Utah," *Uni-*

versity of Colorado Studies 23, no. 2 (1937): 159–68; Gunnerson, "Archaeological Survey," 69–73.

3. Note: Ownership of the figurines remained in dispute for years, something that undoubtedly would have inhibited Pilling's efforts to sell the figurines, if he ever really intended to do so. Pilling willingly allowed experts to study the figurines over the years, and he later took federal land managers to the site where he found the figurines. It was determined the site, located in Turtle Canyon, a tributary to Range Creek, was on federal lands administered by the Bureau of Land Management. The figurines are on permanent display at the Prehistoric Museum, Utah State University Eastern, in Price, Utah.
4. Coauthor Jerry D. Spangler was the lead archaeologist on the 2002 expedition, the first archaeological exploration of the canyon in forty-seven years.
5. One of the more colorful although embellished accounts is offered by David Roberts, *The Lost World of the Old Ones* (New York: W. W. Norton, 2016).
6. Duncan Metcalfe, interview by James M. Aton, July 14, 2003, Range Creek, Utah. Transcript in the possession of the authors.
7. Joseph E. Wing, "The Story of Lonesome Creek II," *The Breeder's Gazette* (March 26, 1919): 209. For a complete history of Euro-American ranching in Range Creek, see Steven L. Gerber and James M. Aton, "Empires and Homesteads: Making a Living in Range Creek," *Utah Historical Quarterly* 79, no. 1 (Winter 2011): 20–41.
8. Edward A. Geary, *A History of Emery County* (Salt Lake City: Utah State Historical Society and Emery County Commission, 1996), x; William J. Tidwell Testimony, *The Heirs of Joseph E. Wing v. John Darioli*, October 24–28, 1922, Records at Division H, US Department of the Interior, RG-49, National Archives, Washington, DC; Decision of Register and Receiver, September 13, 1926, Entry #2021 A, *Patented Serial Case Files*, 1907–1975; Record Group 49, Bureau of Land Management, Serial Land Patent #950962 (Salt Lake City 019896) issued to John Darioli by the General Land Office.
9. Joseph E. Wing, *Alfalfa Farming in America* (Chicago: Sanders Publishing Company, 1916), 16–17.
10. For a dissection of the legal complications of Range Creek, see Gerber and Aton, "Empires and Homesteads," 34–40; for a lengthy discussion of Preston Nutter's ranching experience, mostly about Nine Mile Canyon, see Spangler and Spangler, *Last Chance Byway*, 153–87.
11. "Young Rancher Found Dead on Farm," *Sun Advocate*, January 13, 1944.
12. Bud Pilling, interview by Steven L. Gerber, September 17, 2004, Price, Utah; Lloyd Gerber, *Heroes Are Made, Not Born: Stories of the Life of Lloyd M. Gerber* (Eagle, ID: Red Canyon Corporation, 1998), 316–23; *Gerber v. Wilcox, et al.*, Preston Nutter Corporation, Preston Nutter, Katherine Nutter, and H. Byron Mock, box 40, folders 26–35, Nutter Collection, Marriott Library, University of Utah, Salt Lake City.

13. Year: *1900*; Census Place: *Sunnyside, Carbon, Utah*; Roll: *1682*; Page: *15A*; Enumeration District: *0086*; FHL microfilm: *1241682*, Ancestry.com.
14. Registration State: *Utah*; Registration County: *Carbon*; Roll: *1983883*, Ancestry .com.
15. Dalton, interview.
16. Bowers, "Field Journal," 17. This site might be 42Cb2089 about 4.5 miles up Cottonwood Canyon.
17. Ibid.
18. Ibid., 17–18.
19. Ibid., 13. Bowers labeled this site Range Pictograph A. It is now known by the site number 42Cb1704. It was redocumented in 2002.
20. Dennison, "Field Journal," 23. Dennison labeled this site Range Pictograph B. It is now known by the site number 42Em2825. It was redocumented in 2002.
21. Forbes, "Field Journal," 50.
22. Ibid., 52. Forbes labeled this site PR12-1, known today as 42Em2827 or Donna's Alcove. It was redocumented in 2002. There is no remaining trace of the test pit, unlike other expedition test pits that have remained visible after more than eight decades.
23. Bowers, "Field Journal," 14. Bowers labeled this site Range Pictograph C, known today as 42Em2828. It was redocumented in 2002.
24. Forbes, "Field Journal," 48.
25. Bowers, "Field Journal," 19. Bowers labeled this site PR12-2, known today as 42Em2835 or the Fat Man Site for its depiction of a rotund anthropomorph with a blue lower torso akin to blue jeans. It was redocumented in 2002.
26. Dennison, "Field Journal," 24–25. Dennison labeled this site PR12-3, known today as 42Em3210. It was redocumented in 2004.
27. Bowers, "Field Journal," 21–25. Bowers labeled this site PR12-4, known today as 42Em2841. It was redocumented in 2002 using the same technique as in 1931, a vantage point from an adjacent tree.
28. Ibid., 26. Bowers labeled this site PR12-5, known today as 42Em3110. It was redocumented in 2004.
29. Forbes, "Field Journal," 53. This site was erroneously labeled Range C, when in fact Range Pictograph C was at the location of their camp the night before. This site is known today as 42Em3107, located at the north edge of Nelson Canyon.
30. Dennison, "Field Journal," 25–31. Dennison labeled this site PR12-6, known today as 42Em741. It was redocumented in 2002, but only from a vantage point to the north. The rock art on the interior described by Dennison could not be observed from this point. This remarkably preserved site remains a popular stop for Range Creek tourists today. A wood sample was later recovered and radiocarbon dated to about AD 1080.
31. Bowers, "Field Journal," 27. Bowers labeled this site Range Pictograph D, known today as 42Em2844 and 42Em2845, two separate clusters of petroglyphs next to the modern road. These were redocumented in 2002.

32. Ibid. Bowers labeled this site PR12-7, known today as 42Em3215. It was redocumented in 2004.
33. Ibid., 18.
34. Ibid., 36.
35. Gerber and Aton, "Empires and Homesteads," 20–41.
36. Dennison, "Field Journal," 32–33. Bowers, "Field Journal," 28–30. This site was labeled PR12-20, now known as 42Em761. It was redocumented in 2004. Later investigations at the lower granary revealed that it had been filled with wild Great Basin rye seeds, which produced a radiocarbon date of about AD 1000.
37. Bowers, "Field Journal," 33. Bowers labeled this site PR12-19, known today as 42Em760. It was redocumented in 2004 by Uinta Research.
38. Dennison, "Field Journal," 34. Forbes, "Field Journal," 64–65. The first of the three sites was labeled PR12-18, now known as 42Em759. The second was labeled PR12-17, now known as 42Em758. And the third site was labeled PR12-16, now known as 42Em757. All three sites, which are highly visible from the trail in the bottom of the canyon, were redocumented in 2004. PR12-16 and PR12-18 were also observed in 1934 by Leonard Leh, but he offered little description.
39. Bowers, "Field Journal," 36.
40. Dennison, "Field Journal," 33–34. Forbes, "Field Journal," 60–63. The first site was labeled PR12-15, now known as 42Em756, and the second site was labeled PR12-14, now known as 42Em755. Both sites were redocumented in 2004.
41. Bowers, "Field Journal," 37–38. These sites are known today as 42Em751, 42Em752, and 42Em753, respectively. These sites were redocumented in 2002 and 2004.
42. Dennison, "Field Journal," 31–36. Dennison labeled these sites Range Pictograph E, Range Pictograph F, and Range Pictograph G, known today as 42Em2879, 42Em2882, and 42Em2883, respectively. All three sites were redocumented in 2002.
43. Forbes, "Field Journal," 66. This site was labeled PR12-12, now known as 42Em2892. It was redocumented in 2002.
44. Ibid., 67–69. This site was labeled PR12-13, now known as 42Em2891. It was redocumented in 2002.
45. Bowers, "Field Journal," 38–40. This site was labeled PR12-11, now known as 42Em2881. It was redocumented in 2002. A corncob from this site later produced a radiocarbon date of about AD 920.

Chapter 7: Wildest Desolation

1. W. H. Bradley letter to Donald Scott, March 5, 1931, Claflin-Emerson Expedition Records, 31-16-10/100240.1.7, Peabody Museum of Archaeology and Ethnology, Harvard University, Cambridge, Massachusetts.
2. David Rust letter to Donald Scott, May 5, 1931, Claflin-Emerson Expedition Records. River runners today would never drink water from the Green River without excessive boiling or chemical treatment, and only after letting the copious sand settle out. We tend to side more with Bradley on this one.

3. Ibid.
4. Powell, *Exploration*. Frederick S. Dellenbaugh, *A Canyon Voyage: The Narrative of the Second Powell Expedition Down the Green-Colorado River from Wyoming, and the Explorations on Land, in the Years 1871–1872* (New Haven: Yale University Press, 1908).
5. National Park Service, *Eligibility of Desolation Canyon, Utah, for Designation as a National Historic Landmark*, Memorandum from the director of the National Park Service to the commissioner of the Bureau of Indian Affairs (Denver: National Park Service), 1968.
6. Bowers, "Field Journal," 51. As discussed in chapter 2, the mysterious Trapper Jack drowned in the Green River and was buried on one of these three islands.
7. Ibid., 43.
8. Ibid.
9. Dennison, "Field Journal," 36–38.
10. Bowers, "Field Journal," 49.
11. Ibid., 41–42.
12. Ibid., 43.
13. David Rust letter to Donald Scott, May 5, 1931, Donald Scott Collection.
14. For addition historical context regarding Shed Lunt, see Spangler and Spangler, *Last Chance Byway*, 96–97. For a more detailed history of ranching at Rock Creek see Aton, *The River Knows Everything*, 112–19.
15. McClurg interview; Billie Seamount McRich, interview by Steve Gerber and Paul Phillips, July 13, 2003, Salt Lake City; Leona Seamount Moon, interview by Steve Gerber and Paul Phillips, July 2, 2003, Grand Junction, Colorado; Orm interview; Fern Seamount Nelson, interview by Paul Phillips, July 2, 2003, Grand Junction, Colorado; Bill and Mrs. Seamount, interview by Otis R. "Dock" Marston, January 1, 1966, Salt Lake City, Marston Collection, Huntington Library, San Marino, California.
16. Flossie Taylor Seamount, "Journal," in possession of James M. Aton.
17. Bill and Mrs. Seamount interview; McRich interview; Ed F. Harmston, "Diary and Report of Ed F. Harmston, Engineer, on Feasibility of Line for Railroad from Green River on Denver and Rio Grande R.R. to Roosevelt in Uintah Basin, State of Utah. September 6th, 1913," Marston Collection.
18. Preston Nutter to Katherine F. Nutter, September 11, 1923, box 1, book 5, Nutter Collection, Marriott Library, University of Utah, Salt Lake City, Utah. Nutter writes to his wife that the Seamounts had been looking to sell to a man named Nielsen as early as 1923 but they could not agree on a price (see Dan Seamount Jr. to Paul Phillips, email to James M. Aton, March 19, 2007).
19. Bill and Mrs. Seamount interview; Billie Seamount McRich Interview; Jean Seamount Orm interview; Fern Seamount Nelson interview; Dan Seamount Jr. to Paul Phillips.

20. Year: *1900*; Census Place: *Spring City, Sanpete, Utah*; Roll: *1685*; Page: *15A*; Enumeration District: *0119*; FHL microfilm: *1241685*, Ancestry.com.
21. Gerber, *Heroes Are Made*, chap. 36.
22. Butch Jensen, interview by James. M. Aton, August 1–2, 2006, Tavaputs Ranch, Utah; see land records, Bureau of Land Management, Salt Lake City.
23. Trail Canyon, Flat Canyon, and Jack Canyon can have flowing water in exceptionally wet years, and the upper reaches of these canyons often have flowing water in not-so-wet years. These creeks typically go underground long before they reach the Green River.
24. Jerry D. Spangler, "Nine Mile, Minnie Maud, and the Mystery of a Place Name," *Utah Historical Quarterly* 79, no. 1 (2011): 42–51.
25. Jerry D. Spangler, "The Archaeology of Desolation Canyon, Utah," in *An Archaeological Legacy: Essays in Honor of Ray T. Matheny*, edited by Deanne G. Matheny, Joel C. Janetski, and Glenna Nielsen, Museum of Peoples and Cultures Occasional Paper 18 (Salt Lake City: University of Utah Press, 2013), 99–124. This site is now known as 42Cb224.
26. Dennison, "Field Journal," 39–40.
27. Bowers, "Field Journal," 48.
28. Ibid., 50.
29. Ibid.
30. Spangler and Spangler, *Last Chance Byway*, 96.
31. Bowers, "Field Journal," 50.
32. Gerber, *Heroes Are Made*, 241.
33. Bowers, "Field Journal," 50–51.
34. Ibid., 53.
35. Ibid., 53–54.
36. In the 1970s, federal land managers authorized a natural gas well head in the bottom of Jack Canyon at the point the two major forks come together. A rough two-track road was built to service this well—a road also used by looters to access archaeological sites in the upper Jack Canyon area.
37. Bowers, "Field Journal," 54.
38. Dennison, "Field Journal," 40.
39. Ibid., 41.
40. Powell, *Exploration*, 191.
41. BLM River ranger Jim Wright knows of a small spring in the Peter's Point area up an unnamed side canyon, but it is well hidden. It is possible that Rasmussen knew of this spring, although we consider this unlikely.
42. Bowers, "Field Journal," 55.
43. Ibid., 56–57.
44. Dennison, "Field Journal," 42.
45. Scott, "Claflin-Emerson," 91; Gunnerson, "Fremont Culture," 82.

46. Forbes, "Field Journal," 70–71.
47. Scott, "Claflin-Emerson," 1–2.
48. Rust, "Journal."
49. Scott, "Claflin-Emerson," 10.

Chapter 8: Dirty Shovels

1. Brew, "Field Journal," 29. This site has not been redocumented.
2. Ibid. This site has not been redocumented.
3. Ibid. The lower rubble mound is now known as 42Cb3242 and the upper rock shelter is 42Cb3245.
4. Spangler and Spangler, *Last Chance Byway*, 93–94. Three of the six rock art sites have been identified and documented (42Cb3240, 42Cb3241, and 42Cb3244).
5. Rust, "Journal."
6. Brew, "Field Journal," 30. This site is now known as 42Cb3174 and the neighboring rock art panel is 42Cb3175.
7. Scott, "Claflin-Emerson," 8.
8. Brew, "Field Journal," 30–35. This site is now known as 42Cb3162.
9. Scott, "Claflin-Emerson," 77.
10. Jerry D. Spangler, *Devil's Playground: Site Documentation and Comparative Analysis of 42Cb3162 with Complete 1931 Claflin Emerson Expedition Field Notes* (Ogden, UT: Colorado Plateau Archaeological Alliance, 2013).
11. Through photographic comparisons, these rock art sites have been positively identified as 42Cb2896 (Family Panel) and 42Cb3024.
12. Brew, "Field Journal," 36. This site is now known as 42Cb3192.
13. Mildred Miles Dillman, *Early History of Duchesne County* (Springville, UT: Art City Publishing, 1948), 281.
14. Spangler and Spangler, *Last Chance Byway*, 245–46.
15. Rust, "Journal," 2.
16. Jerry D. Spangler, *Dust Up: A Baseline Site Condition Assessment and Analysis of Dust Accumulation and Vandalism of Cultural Resources in the Cottonwood Canyon Confluence Area, Nine Mile Canyon* (Ogden, UT: Colorado Plateau Archaeological Alliance, 2008).
17. Brew, "Field Journal," 42. PR4-32 is actually a series of sites that extend from the toe of the ridge just above the Hanks cabin several hundred meters to the north to the second cliff level. They are now known as 42Cb2650, 42Cb2651, and 42Cb2652.
18. Kidder, "Field Journal," 48. Brew, "Field Journal," 36. This site is now known as 42Cb903.
19. Rust, "Journal," 2.
20. Brew, "Field Journal," 37. This site is now known as 42Cb2068.
21. Scott, "Claflin-Emerson," 80.

22. Brew, "Field Journal," 37, 40. This site is now known as 42Cb48. The mud bricks, when wet, are laid on a flat surface to dry. The bottom dries flat and the wet top becomes rounded, like a turtleback.
23. Ibid., 38. This site is now known as 42Cb2218.
24. Scott, "Claflin-Emerson," 81.
25. Spangler and Spangler, *Last Chance Byway*, 257.
26. Scott, "Claflin-Emerson," 82.
27. Frank Beckwith, "Some Interesting Pictographs in Nine Mile Canyon, Utah," *El Palacio* 31, no. 14 (1931): 221–22.
28. Rust mentions in his journal that Snyder was one of the treasure hunters looking for hidden Spanish gold. His name and a 1931 date are also etched on a cliff wall behind a large granary very near Devil's Playground.
29. Albert Reagan, "Some Archaeological Notes on Nine Mile Canyon, Utah," *El Palacio* 31, no. 4 (1931): 45–71; Reagan, "Anciently Inhabited Caves of the Vernal (Utah) District, with Some Additional Notes on Nine Mile Canyon, Northeast Utah," *Transactions of the Kansas Academy of Sciences* 36 (1933): 41–70.
30. Alfred E. Gaumer, "Basketmaker Caves in Desolation Canyon, Green River, Utah," *Masterkey* 11 no. 5 (1937): 160–65.
31. Ibid.
32. Spangler, *Nine Mile Canyon*, 65–69.
33. Scott, "Claflin-Emerson," 82.
34. Gunnerson, "Fremont Culture," 97.
35. Scott, "Claflin-Emerson," 83.
36. Ibid., 83–84.
37. Ibid., 84–85.
38. Ibid., 84.
39. Ibid., 85.
40. Ibid.
41. Ibid., 86.
42. Gunnerson, "Fremont Culture," 101.
43. Richard K. Talbot and Lane D. Richens, "Steinaker Gap: An Early Fremont Agriculture Farmstead," *Brigham Young University Museum of Peoples and Cultures Technical Series* 94, no. 18 (1996).
44. James D. Wilde and Deborah E. Newman, "Late Archaic Corn in the Eastern Great Basin," *American Anthropologist* 91, no. 3 (1989): 712–20. Recent research by Heidi Roberts at Jackson Flats near Kanab has not yet been formally reported, but numerous radiocarbon dates support maize farming as early as 1000 BC.
45. David Yoder, email communication with Jerry D. Spangler, December 7, 2016. The child burial dated to AD 108, +21 years, with a 2 Sigma range of AD 124 to 237 (D-AMS 011271). The maize from the west side of the cave returned a date of AD 867, +24 years, with a 2 Sigma range of AD 895 to 1016 (D-AMS 010871).

46. Ibid. The rawhide below the skeleton returned a date of AD 360, +26 years, with a 2 Sigma range of AD 421 to 534 (D-AMS 010872) and bone from the Basketmaker-like skeleton dated to AD 743, +21 years, with a 2 Sigma range of AD 768 to 886 (D-AMS 011270).
47. "Journal of Expenses," 3.
48. Utah State Archives and Records Service; Salt Lake City, UT; *Utah State Archives and Records Service*; File Number #: *1947005073*, Ancestry.com.
49. Year: *1930*; Census Place: *Green River, Emery, Utah*; Roll: *2415*; Page: *1B*; Enumeration District: *0012*; Image: *499.0*; FHL microfilm: *2342149*, Ancestry.com.

Chapter 9: Out with a Whimper

1. "Journal of Expenses," 4.
2. *Roosevelt Standard*, August 16, 17, and 18, 1931.
3. "Journal of Expenses," 4, 6.
4. Dave Rust to Donald Scott, May 23, 1931. Claflin-Emerson Expedition Records.
5. Donald Scott to Walter E. Atwood, May 24, 1932, Claflin-Emerson Expedition Records.
6. Year: *1910*; Census Place: *Crescent, Salt Lake, Utah*; Roll: *T624_1605*; Page: *11B*; Enumeration District: *0087*; FHL microfilm: *1375618*, Ancestry.com.
7. Utah State Archives and Records Service; Salt Lake City, Utah; *World War I Service Questionnaires, 1914–1918*; Creating Agency: *State Historical Society*; Series: *85298*; Reel: *1*, Ancestry.com.
8. Year: *1920*; Census Place: *Precinct 8, Salt Lake, Utah*; Roll: *T625_1864*; Page: *2B*; Enumeration District: *54*; Image: *1093* City Directories, 1922–1995, Salt Lake City Directory, 1920, Ancestry.com.
9. US City Directories, 1822–1995, Salt Lake City, 1927, Ancestry.com.
10. John D. Barton, *A History of Duchesne County* (Salt Lake City: Utah Historical Commission, 1998), 254–58.
11. Year: *1940*; Census Place: *Roosevelt, Duchesne, Utah*; Roll: *T627_4212*; Page: *9A*; Enumeration District: *7-3*, Ancestry.com.; The National Archives at St. Louis; St. Louis, Missouri; Record Group Title: *Records of the Selective Service System, 1926–1975*; Record Group Number: *147*, Ancestry.com; Walter Edward Atwood, *U.S. Social Security Death Index*, 1935–2014, Ancestry.com.
12. Scott, "Claflin-Emerson," 11.
13. Ibid.
14. Scott to Atwood, May 24, 1932, Claflin-Emerson Expedition Records.
15. Ibid.
16. Brew, "Field Journal," 47. Bowers, "Field Journal," 66.
17. "Journal of Expenses," 5.
18. Ibid., 5–6.
19. Rust's journal says this happened on August 28, but the "Journal of Expenses" indicates it was on August 30.

20. Scott, "Claflin Emerson," 13.
21. Ibid., 13–14.
22. The crew had earlier photographed small circular holes bored into the bedrock at Devil's Playground in Nine Mile Canyon, but these had not warranted much comment in the field notes at that time.
23. "Journal of Expenses," 7.
24. Doris Karren Burton, *Uintah County Prominent People: Leo Thorne's Story* (Vernal, UT: Uintah County Library, 2005), 44.
25. Ibid., 62.
26. Bowers, "Field Journal," 86. Burton, *Uintah County*, 103.
27. Government Property Seizure Notice, July 30, 1932, Leo Thorne File, Regional History Center, Uintah County Library, Vernal, Utah; Archie D. Ryan to Leo Thorne, August 4, 1932, Leo Thorne File, Regional History Center.
28. Donald Scott to Leo C. Thorne, June 30, 1932, Leo Thorne File, Regional History Center.
29. The exceptionally high quality of the rock art images is immensely valuable to researchers because they depict details which are not readily apparent today or which have eroded away. The quality of the images was enhanced using a technique called "chalking," where the petroglyphs were traced and sometimes colored in with white chalk to increase the contrast. This practice was common in the 1930s. Chalking is no longer acceptable due to the corrosive nature of the chalk itself, which can accelerate the erosion and degradation of the images. Traces of white chalk can still be seen on many of the images, remnants of the early photographers. The Crimson Cowboys did not chalk.
30. Scott, "Claflin-Emerson," 109–10. Brew, "Field Journal," 52.
31. Brew, "Field Journal," 53. Axes were a common stone tool in prehistoric contexts among Ancestral Puebloan peoples, but they are extremely rare among the Fremont Complex north of the Colorado River.
32. Bowers, "Field Journal," 80.
33. Ibid., 83–85.
34. Rust, "Journal."
35. Billie Ruple Untermann, "History of the Island Park Area," file folder 542, Regional History Center (RHC), Uintah County Library, Vernal, Utah; Wanda Ruple Staley, "Henry Case Ruple and May Coon Ruple," file folder 1149, Regional History Center; Billie Ruple Untermann, "Island Park," *The Outlaw Trail Journal* (Winter 2003): 2–10.
36. It is unclear from the journal entries and expense logs whether the entire Harvard crew stayed at the Ruple Ranch or whether only Dennison and Scott stayed there while the others camped in Brush Creek.
37. Rust, "Journal"; Arthur L. Crawford, "Foreword," *Geology of Dinosaur National Monument and Vicinity*, by G. E. Untermann and B. R. Untermann (Salt Lake City: Utah Geological and Mineral Survey, 1954), ix–xi.

38. Crawford, "Foreword," x.
39. "Historical Note," G. Ernest Untermann Papers, 1936–1975, MS 0118, Special Collections, Marriott Library, University of Utah, Salt Lake, Utah.
40. "Historical Note." Mark W. T. Harvey, *Symbol of Wilderness: Echo Park and the American Conservation Movement* (Albuquerque: University of New Mexico Press, 1994), 161.
41. Scott's report indicates they were gone two days, but Rust's journal is explicit that they returned to the base camp the same day. The following day was spent traveling by car to Roosevelt and Vernal.
42. Ellen S. Kiever, "Historic Landmark: A Place to Hide: 'Jones Hole,'" *The Outlaw Trail Journal* (Winter 2015): 27.
43. Ibid., 27–28.
44. Ibid., 28.
45. Ibid.
46. Ibid.
47. Dennison, "Field Journal," 43.
48. Ibid., 44–48. The crew had photographed and sketched rock art throughout the Tavaputs Plateau, but on arriving in the Uinta Basin—which has a remarkable suite of images—they ignored the rock art with a brief explanation that it had already been photographed and described by Albert B. Reagan. The Jones Hole rock art sketches were an exception, perhaps because Reagan had not yet made it this far into the backcountry.
49. Rust, "Journal," 3.
50. Larry L. Leach, "Archaeological Investigations at Deluge Shelter (42Un1)," (PhD diss., University of Colorado, 1970).
51. Dennison, "Field Journal," 48–49.
52. Ibid., 49–50.
53. Brew, "Field Journal," 55–56. Scott, "Claflin-Emerson," 114.
54. Brew, "Field Journal," 57–58.
55. James Allison, "Julian Steward's Uintah River Mounds," paper presented at the Great Basin Anthropological Conference, Layton, Utah (2010).
56. Ibid.
57. Ibid.
58. Julianna Bratt, email communication with Jerry D. Spangler (2011), cited in Spangler, *Nine Mile Canyon*, 72.
59. Rust, "Journal," 1.
60. Scott, "Claflin-Emerson," 112. See also Bowers, "Field Journal," 86–87.
61. Joel Frandsen, "In Search of Lee Sage, Pete Logan's Son," *Outlaw Trail Journal* (Winter 2008): 38.
62. Ibid., 47.
63. Ibid., 48.

64. Lee Sage, *The Last Rustler: The Autobiography of Lee Sage* (Boston: Little, Brown, 1930).
65. "Journal of Expenses," 6–7.

Chapter 10: Scholars and Cowboys

1. Browman and Williams, *Anthropology at Harvard.*
2. Scott, "Claflin–Emerson."
3. Donald Scott to Raymond Emerson, November 13, 1931, Claflin-Emerson Expedition Records.
4. Donald Scott to John F. Gillin, August 19, 1936, Claflin-Emerson Expedition Records.
5. Browman and Williams, *Anthropology at Harvard*, 340–41.
6. David Rust to Donald Scott, April 13, 1932; Donald Scott to David Rust, May 4, 1932, Claflin-Emerson Expedition Records.
7. J.O. Brew, "Donald Scott and His Collection," in Polly Schaafsma, *Rock Art of Utah: A Study from the Donald Scott Collection* (1971; repr., Salt Lake City: University of Utah Press, 1994), xv.
8. "Donald Scott," *Harvard College—Class of 1900* (Cambridge: President and Fellows of Harvard College, 1940), 230.
9. "Donald Scott," *Harvard College—Class of 1900* (Cambridge: President and Fellows of Harvard College, 1945), 223.
10. "Donald Scott," *Harvard University Gazette* 63, no. 8 (November 4, 1967): 63; "Donald Scott, *Harvard College—Class of 1900* (Cambridge: President and Fellows of Harvard College, 1955), 155.
11. "Donald Scott," *Harvard University Gazette*, 62.
12. Browman and Williams, *Anthropology at Harvard*, 370–71.
13. Ibid.
14. Spangler, *Nine Mile Canyon*, 51.
15. Gunnerson, "Fremont Culture," 24.
16. Browman and Williams, *Anthropology at Harvard*, 371.
17. Henry B. Roberts, "Summary of the 1929 Field Seasons," Claflin-Emerson Expedition Records, 1.
18. Coolidge, "Claflin," 85–86.
19. "William Henry Claflin," 98–101.
20. Browman and Williams, *Anthropology at Harvard*, 376; "Raymond Emerson," *Harvard Class of 1910 Twenty-Fifth Anniversary Report 1935* (Cambridge: President and Fellows of Harvard College, 1935), 125–26.
21. J.O. Brew to Ellery Wilds [*sic*], March 24, 1932, SE Utah Exp. Records, Box 33-2, Peabody Museum.
22. J.O. Brew to Mr. and Mrs. Austin Wardle, March 25, 1932, SE Utah Exp. Records, Box 33-2, Peabody Museum.

23. Woodbury, "John Otis Brew," 452–53. See also J.O. Brew, "The Archaeology of Alkali Ridge, Southeastern Utah, with a Review of the Prehistory of the Mesa Verde Division of the San Juan and Some Observations on Archaeological Systematics," *Papers of the Peabody Museum of American Archaeology and Ethnology* 21 (Cambridge: Harvard University Press, 1946); Browman and Williams, *Anthropology at Harvard*, 372–73.
24. Woodbury, "Brew," 453.
25. Ibid., 454.
26. Don D. Fowler communication to authors, August 13, 2017.
27. Woodbury, "Brew," 454–55.
28. Ibid., 456.
29. Karen L. Mohr Chavez, "Alfred V. Kidder II, 1911–1984," *Expedition* 30, no. 3 (1988): 4–5. See also Browman and Williams, *Anthropology at Harvard*, 413; Mary B. Kidder, *No Limits but the Sky: The Journal of an Archaeologist's Wife in Peru* (Cambridge: Harvard University Press, 1942).
30. Chavez, "Kidder," 5; Browman and Williams, *Anthropology at Harvard*, 413; "Alfred V. Kidder II," *Harvard College Class of 1933, Quindecennial Report* (Cambridge: President and Fellows of Harvard College, 1948), 202.
31. Chavez, "Kidder," 6–7.
32. Lynn Bowers, email to Jerry D. Spangler, August 11, 2017.
33. "William Benton Bowers," *Harvard Class of 1928, Thirty-Fifth Anniversary Report* (Cambridge: President and Fellows of Harvard College, 1963), 34; "William Benton Bowers," *Harvard Class of 1928, Fiftieth Anniversary Report* (Cambridge: President and Fellows of Harvard College, 1978), 75.
34. Lynn Bowers, email to Jerry D. Spangler, August 11, 2017.
35. Lynn Bowers, emails to Spangler, June 7 and 8, 2017.
36. Swanson, *Dave Rust*, 239–42.
37. Becky Dennison Sakellariou, email to James M. Aton, October 16, 2017.
38. "James Thurber Dennison," *Harvard Class of 1934, Twenty-Fifth Anniversary Report* (Cambridge: President and Fellows of Harvard College, 1959), 131; "James Thurber Dennison," *Harvard Class of 1934, Thirty-Fifth Anniversary Report* (Cambridge: President and Fellows of Harvard College, 1969), 55; "James Thurber Dennison," *Harvard Class of 1934, Fiftieth Anniversary Report* (Cambridge: President and Fellows of Harvard College, 1984), 135–36; Sakellariou to Aton.
39. Charlotte Forbes Wunderlich, email to James Aton, March 15, 2018.
40. Charlotte Forbes Wunderlich, phone interview by James Aton, July 9, 2015.
41. Browman and Williams, *Anthropology at Harvard*, 426–27; "Waldo Emerson Forbes C3978 1934," UA III 1588.10, 1890–1968 Box 1586, HA 170Y, Harvard University Archives, Pusey Library, Harvard University, Cambridge, Massachusetts.

42. "Waldo Forbes Emerson," *Harvard Class of 1934, Twenty-Fifth Anniversary Report* (Cambridge: President and Fellows of Harvard College, 1959), n.p.; "The Beckton Story: How the Foundation Herd Came into Being," www.becktonredangus.com (accessed June 11, 2018).
43. Wunderlich interview.
44. Ibid.
45. Swanson, *Dave Rust*, 264–81.
46. Ibid., 282–91.
47. Donald Scott to Dave Rust, June 29, 1957, MS 1143, Reel 2, David Dexter Rust Papers.
48. Donald Scott to Dave Rust, August 24, 1961, MS 1143, Reel 2, David Dexter Rust Papers.
49. Dave Rust, https://uofupress.lib.utah.edu/dave-rust/ (accessed June 11, 2018).
50. Gunnerson, "Fremont Culture."
51. Jerry D. Spangler, K. Renee Barlow, and Duncan Metcalfe, "A Summary of the 2002–2003 Intuitive Surveys of the Wilcox Acquisition and Surrounding Lands, Range Creek Canyon, Utah," *Utah Museum of Natural History Occasional Papers* 2004-1 (Salt Lake City: University of Utah, 2004); Jerry D. Spangler, Shannon Arnold, and Joel Boomgarden, "Chasing Ghosts: A GIS Analysis and Photographic Comparison of Vandalism and Site Degradation in Range Creek Canyon, Utah," *Utah Museum of Natural History Occasional Papers* 2006-1 (Salt Lake City: University of Utah, 2006); Jerry D. Spangler and Kevin T. Jones, *Land of Wildest Desolation: Final Report of the Desolation Canyon Intuitive Surveys and Baseline Site Condition Assessments of 2006 to 2008* (Ogden, UT: Colorado Plateau Archaeological Alliance, 2009). The Nine Mile Canyon sites were documented over the course of many years and are reported in more than fifteen different technical reports by the Colorado Plateau Archaeological Alliance.
52. Gordon R. Willey and Jeremy A. Sabloff, *A History of American Archaeology* (New York: W. H. Freeman, 1980), 4.
53. William K. Moorehead, quoted in Joel C. Janetski, "150 Years of Utah Archaeology," *Utah Historical Quarterly* 65, no. 2 (1997): 100–133.
54. Alfred M. Tozzer, "Biographical Memoir of Frederic Ward Putnam, 1839–1915," *National Academy of Sciences Biographical Memoirs* 16, Fourth Memoir (1933).
55. Browman and Williams, *Anthropology at Harvard*, 325.

Bibliography

Manuscript Collections

Cambridge, MA

Harvard University, Peabody Museum of Archaeology and Ethnology
    Claflin-Emerson Expedition Field Records, 31-16-10/100240.1.7.
    Donald Scott Collection.
Harvard University, Pusey Library
    Harvard University Archives.

Denver, CO

US Geological Survey Field Records Library
    US Geological Survey Field Records.

Salt Lake City, UT

Bureau of Land Management
    Patented Serial Case Files, 1907–1975, Record Group 49.
The Church of Jesus Christ of Latter-day Saints Church History Library
    David Dexter Rust Papers, 1870–1963, MS 1143.
Special Collections, J. Willard Marriott Library, University of Utah
    Doris Duke American Indian Oral History Project Audio Recordings, 1949–1972, Collection, MS 0417.
    G. Ernest Untermann Papers, 1936–1975, MS 0118.
    The Records of the Preston Nutter Corporation, MS 289.
    Ute Indian Oral History Project Collection, accn. 0883.
Utah State Archives and Records Service
Utah State Historical Society

San Marino, CA

The Huntington Library
    The Otis R. Marston Collection

Vernal, UT

Uintah County Library, Regional History Center (RHC)

Leo Thorne File, folder 0455.

Pauline Hazelbush file, folder 1055.

Henry Case Ruple and May Coon Ruple, folder 1149.

"History of the Island Park Area," folder 542.

Arden Stewart. Interview by Kathleen Irving. April 19, 2002.

Washington, DC

National Archives

Records at Division H, US Department of the Interior, RG-49.

Newspapers and Magazines

The Breeder's Gazette (Chicago)

Deseret News (Salt Lake City, UT)

Harvard University Gazette (Cambridge, MA)

Sun Advocate (Price, UT)

Times Independent (Moab, UT)

Vernal Express (Vernal, UT)

Published Books, Articles, Papers, and Essays

Allison, James. "Julian Steward's Uintah River Mounds." Paper presented at the Great Basin Anthropological Conference. Layton, Utah (2010).

Arnold-Boomgarden, Shannon. "An Application of ARCGIS Viewshed Analysis in Range Creek Canyon, Utah." *Utah Archaeology* 22, no. 1 (2009): 15–30.

Arnold-Boomgarden, Shannon, Duncan Metcalfe, and Corinne Springer. "Prehistoric Archaeology in Range Creek Canyon, Utah: A Summary of the Activities of the Range Creek Field Station." *Utah Archaeology* 27, no. 1 (2014): 9–32.

Aton, James M. *The River Knows Everything: Desolation Canyon and the Green*. Logan: Utah State University Press, 2009.

Baker, Pearl. *The Wild Bunch at Robber's Roost*. 1965; repr., Lincoln: University of Nebraska Press, 1989.

Barton, John D. "Antoine Robidoux and the Fur Trade of the Uinta Basin." Master's thesis, Brigham Young University, 1989.

——. *A History of Duchesne County*. Salt Lake City: Utah Historical Commission, 1998.

Beckstead, James H. *Cowboying: A Tough Job in a Hard Land*. Salt Lake City: University of Utah Press, 1991.

Beckwith, Frank. "Some Interesting Pictographs in Nine Mile Canyon, Utah." *El Palacio* 31, no. 14 (1931): 220–22.

Bennett, James A. *Hereford History in Utah*. Salt Lake City: Utah Hereford Association, 1946.
Brew, J.O. "Donald Scott and His Collection." In Polly Schaafsma, *Rock Art of Utah: A Study from the Donald Scott Collection*, xv–xvii. 1971; repr., Salt Lake City: University of Utah Press, 1994.
Browman, David L., and Stephen Williams. *Anthropology at Harvard: A Biographical History, 1790–1940*. Cambridge: Peabody Museum Press, 2013.
Burton, Doris Karren. "Memorable Character: Ben Morris—Josie Bassett's Fifth." *Outlaw Trail Journal* (Summer 1999): 35–41.
——. *Settlements of Uintah County: Digging Deeper*. Vernal, UT: Uintah County Library, 1998.
——. *Uintah County Prominent People: Leo Thorne's Story*. Vernal, UT: Uintah County Library, 2005.
Carvalho, Solomon Nunes. *Incidents of Travel and Adventure in the Far West with Col. Fremont's Last Expedition*. Philadelphia: Jewish Publication Society of America, 1857.
Chavez, Karen L. Mohr. "Alfred V. Kidder II, 1911–1984." *Expedition* 30, no. 3 (1988): 4–7.
Coolidge, Daniel J. "William Henry Claflin, Jr." *Proceedings of the Massachusetts Historical Society* 94 (1982): 85–87.
Crampton, Gregory C., and Steven K. Madsen. *In Search of the Spanish Trail: Santa Fe to Los Angeles, 1828–1848*. Salt Lake City: Gibbs Smith Books, 1994.
Crawford, Arthur L. "Foreword." In *Geology of Dinosaur National Monument and Vicinity*, by G. E. Untermann and B. R. Untermann, ix–xi. Salt Lake City: Utah Geological and Mineral Survey, 1954.
Dellenbaugh, Frederick S. *A Canyon Voyage: The Narrative of the Second Powell Expedition Down the Green-Colorado River from Wyoming, and the Explorations on Land, in the Years 1871–1872*. New Haven: Yale University Press, 1908.
Dillman, Mildred Miles. *Early History of Duchesne County*. Springville, UT: Art City Publishing, 1948.
Dimock, Brad, ed. *Every Rapid Speaks Plainly: The Salmon, Green, and Colorado River Journals of Buzz Holmstrom*. Flagstaff: Fretwater Press, 2003.
"Donald Scott." *Harvard College Class of 1900: Twenty-Fifth Anniversary Report*. Cambridge: President and Fellows of Harvard College, 1925.
"Donald Scott." *Harvard College—Class of 1900*. Cambridge: President and Follows of Harvard College, 1940.
"Donald Scott." *Harvard College Class of 1900*. Cambridge: President and Fellows of Harvard College, 1945.
"Donald Scott." *Harvard College Class of 1900*. Cambridge: President and Fellows of Harvard College, 1955.
"Donald Scott." *Harvard University Gazette* (November 4, 1967): 62.

Egan, Ferol. *Fremont: Explorer for a Restless Nation*. Reno: University of Nevada Press, 1985.

Emerson, Amelia Forbes. *Recollections and Ramblings of Amelia Forbes Emerson*. Boston: Thomas Todd Co., 1968.

Emerson, Edward Waldo. *Henry Thoreau, As Remembered by a Young Friend*. 1917; Concord, MA: Thoreau Foundation, 1968.

Fewkes, J. Walter. "Archaeological Investigations in New Mexico, Colorado, and Utah." *Smithsonian Miscellaneous Collections* 68, no. 1 (1917): 1–38.

——. "Prehistoric Remains in New Mexico, Colorado, and Utah." *Smithsonian Miscellaneous Collections* 66, no. 17 (1917): 76–92.

Frandsen, Joel. "In Search of Lee Sage, Pete Logan's Son." *Outlaw Trail Journal* (Winter 2008): 36–55.

Fuller, Craig Woods. "Land Rush in Zion: Opening of the Uncompahgre and Uintah Indian Reservations." PhD diss., Brigham Young University, 1990.

Gaumer, Alfred E. "Basketmaker Caves in Desolation Canyon, Green River, Utah." *Masterkey* 11, no. 5 (1937): 160–65.

Geary, Edward A. *A History of Emery County*. Salt Lake City: Utah State Historical Society and Emery County Commission, 1996.

Gerber, Lloyd. *Heroes Are Made, Not Born: Stories of the Life of Lloyd M. Gerber*. Eagle, ID: Red Canyon Corporation, 1998.

Gerber, Steven L., and James. M. Aton. "Empires and Homesteads: Making a Living in Range Creek." *Utah Historical Quarterly* 79, no. 1 (Winter 2011): 20–41.

Gunnerson, James H. "An Archaeological Survey of the Fremont Area." *University of Utah Anthropological Papers* 28. Salt Lake City: University of Utah, 1957.

——. "The Fremont Culture: A Study in Cultural Dynamics on the Northern Anasazi Frontier, Including the Report of the Claflin-Emerson Expedition of the Peabody Museum." *Papers of the Peabody Museum of Archaeology and Ethnology* 59, no. 2. Cambridge: Peabody Museum, 1969.

Harvard Class of 1928, Thirty-Fifth Anniversary Report. Cambridge: President and Fellows of Harvard College, 1963.

Harvard Class of 1928, Fiftieth Anniversary Report. Cambridge: President and Fellows of Harvard College, 1978.

Harvard Class of 1934, Twenty-fifth Anniversary Report. Cambridge: President and Fellows of Harvard College, 1959.

Harvard Class of 1934, Thirty-fifth Anniversary Report. Cambridge: President and Fellows of Harvard College, 1969.

Harvard Class of 1934, Fiftieth Anniversary Report. Cambridge: President and Fellows of Harvard College, 1984.

Harvard College—Class of 1900: Secretary's Ninth Report. Cambridge: President and Fellows of Harvard College, 1940.

Harvard College Class of 1900: Twenty-Fifth Anniversary Report. Cambridge: President and Fellows of Harvard College, 1925.

Harvard College Class of 1933, Quindecennial Report. Cambridge: President and Fellows of Harvard College, 1948.

Harvey, Mark W. T. *Symbol of Wilderness: Echo Park and the American Conservation Movement*. Albuquerque: University of New Mexico Press, 1994.

Janetski, Joel C. "150 Years of Utah Archaeology." *Utah Historical Quarterly* 65, no. 2 (1997): 100–133.

Kerns, Virginia. *Scenes from the High Desert: Julian Steward's Life and Theory*. Urbana: University of Illinois Press, 2003.

Kidder, Mary B. *No Limits But the Sky: The Journal of an Archaeologist's Wife in Peru*. Cambridge: Harvard University Press, 1942.

Kiever, Ellen S. "Historic Landmark: A Place to Hide: 'Jones Hole,'" *The Outlaw Trail Journal* (Winter 2015): 25–30.

Kolb, Ellsworth. *Through the Grand Canyon from Wyoming to Mexico*. New York: Macmillan, 1940.

La Rue, E. C. "The Colorado River and Its Utilization." *US Geological Survey Water Supply Paper* 395. Washington, DC: Government Printing Office, 1916.

Leach, Larry L. "Archaeological Investigations at Deluge Shelter (42Un1)." PhD Diss., University of Colorado, 1970.

Leh, Leonard L. "Prehistoric Pueblo Ruins in Range Creek Canyon, Utah." *University of Colorado Studies* 23, no. 2 (1937): 159–68.

Long, George. "A Narrative History of Uintah County, As Told to and Recounted by George Long." Self-published manuscript in author's possession.

McKnight, Frank. *A Family Remembered*. Salt Lake City: Ponderosa Printing, 1994.

Montgomery, Henry. "Prehistoric Man in Utah." *The Archaeologist* 2, nos. 8, 10, and 11 (1894): 227–34, 298–306, 335–42.

Morss, Noel. "The Ancient Culture of the Fremont River in Utah." *Papers of the Peabody Museum of American Archaeology and Ethnology* 12, no. 3. Cambridge: Peabody Museum of American Archaeology and Ethnology, 1931.

Powell, John Wesley. *The Exploration of the Colorado River and Its Canyons*. 1895; repr., New York: Dover Publications Inc., 1961.

Price, Virginia N., and John T. Darby. "Preston Nutter: Utah Cattleman, 1886–1936." *Utah Historical Quarterly* 32, no. 3 (Summer 1964): 232–51.

"Raymond Emerson." *Harvard Class of 1910, Vicennial Report*. Cambridge: President and Fellows of Harvard College, 1930.

"Raymond Emerson." *Harvard Class of 1910, Twenty-Fifth Anniversary Report 1935*. Cambridge: President and Fellows of Harvard College, 1935.

Reagan, Albert B. "Anciently Inhabited Caves of the Vernal (Utah) District, with Some Additional Notes on Nine Mile Canyon, Northeast Utah." *Transactions of the Kansas Academy of Science* 36 (1933): 41–70.

——. "Some Ancient Indian Granaries." *Proceedings: Utah Academy of Sciences, Arts and Letters* 11 (1934): 39–40.

——. "Some Archaeological Notes on Hill Canyon in Northeastern Utah." *El Palacio* 31, no. 4 (1931): 223–44.

——. "Some Archaeological Notes on Nine Mile Canyon, Utah." *El Palacio* 31, no. 4 (1931): 45–71.

——. "Utah: Report of Investigations," *American Anthropologist* 35, no. 1 (1933): 508.

Roberts, David. *The Lost World of the Old Ones*. New York: W. W. Norton, 2016.

Sage, Lee. *The Last Rustler: The Autobiography of Lee Sage*. Boston: Little Brown, and Company, 1930.

Seamount, Flossie Taylor. "Journal." In possession of James M. Aton.

Schulman, Edmund. "Dendrochronology in Northeastern Utah." *Tree Ring Bulletin* 15 (1948): 2–14.

Spangler, Jerry D. "The Archaeology of Desolation Canyon, Utah." In *An Archaeological Legacy: Essays in Honor of Ray T. Matheny*, edited by Deanne G. Matheny, Joel C. Janetski, and Glenna Nielsen, 99–124. *Museum of Peoples and Cultures Occasional Paper* 18. Salt Lake City: University of Utah Press, 2013.

——. *Devil's Playground: Site Documentation and Comparative Analysis of 42Cb3162 with Complete 1931 Claflin Emerson Expedition Field Notes*. Ogden, UT: Colorado Plateau Archaeological Alliance, 2013.

——. *Dust Up: A Baseline Site Condition Assessment and Analysis of Dust Accumulation and Vandalism of Cultural Resources in the Cottonwood Canyon Confluence Area, Nine Mile Canyon*. Ogden, UT: Colorado Plateau Archaeological Alliance, 2008.

——. *Nine Mile Canyon: The Archaeological History of an American Treasure*. Salt Lake City: University of Utah Press, 2013.

——. "Nine Mile, Minnie Maud, and the Mystery of a Place Name." *Utah Historical Quarterly* 79, no. 1 (2011): 42–51.

——. "Site Distribution and Settlement Patterns in Lower Nine Mile Canyon: The Brigham Young University Surveys of 1989–91." Master's thesis, Brigham Young University, 1993.

Spangler, Jerry D., Shannon Arnold, and Joel Boomgarden "Chasing Ghosts: A GIS Analysis and Photographic Comparison of Vandalism and Site Degradation in Range Creek Canyon, Utah." *Utah Museum of Natural History Occasional Papers* 2006-1. Salt Lake City: University of Utah, 2006.

Spangler, Jerry D., K. Renee Barlow, and Duncan Metcalfe. "A Summary Report of the 2002–2003 Intuitive Surveys of the Wilcox Acquisition and Surrounding Lands, Range Creek Canyon, Utah." *Utah Museum of Natural History Occasional Papers* 2004-1. Salt Lake City: University of Utah, 2004.

Spangler, Jerry D., and Kevin T. Jones. *Land of Wildest Desolation: Final Report of the Desolation Canyon Intuitive Surveys and Baseline Site Condition Assessments of 2006 to 2008*. Ogden, UT: Colorado Plateau Archaeological Alliance, 2009.

Spangler, Jerry D., and Donna Kemp Spangler. *Last Chance Byway: The History of Nine Mile Canyon*. Salt Lake City: University of Utah Press, 2016.

Stewart, George Emery, Jr. *Tales from Indian Country: Authentic Stories and Legends from the Great Uintah Basin*. Sandy, UT: Mary Ellen Stewart Gardner, 1997.

Strevell, C. N., and C. S. Pulver. *Report of the Utah State Museum Association Archaeological Expedition*. Salt Lake City: Utah State Historical Society, 1935.

Swanson, Frederick H. *Dave Rust: A Life in the Canyons*. Salt Lake City: University of Utah Press, 2007.

Talbot, Richard K., and Lane D. Richens. "Steinaker Gap: An Early Fremont Agriculture Farmstead." *Brigham Young University Museum of Peoples and Cultures Technical Series* 94, no. 18 (1996).

Thompson, Patricia. "Excavations in Nine Mile Canyon from 1892–1990: A Study in Cultural Diversity." Master's thesis, Brigham Young University, 1993.

Tozzer, Alfred M. "Biographical Memoir of Frederic Ward Putnam, 1839–1915." *National Academy of Sciences Biographical Memoirs* 16, Fourth Memoir (1933).

Untermann, Billie Ruple. "Island Park." *The Outlaw Trail Journal* (Winter 2003): 2–10.

US National Park Service. "Eligibility of Desolation Canyon, Utah, for Designation as a National Historic Landmark." Memorandum from the Director of the National Park Service to the Commissioner of the Bureau of Indian Affairs. Denver: National Park Service, 1968.

Webb, Roy. "Coal Creek Dam Site." *Confluence: The Journal of Colorado Plateau River Guides* 27 (December 2003): 11–12.

Wilde, James D., and Deborah E. Newman. "Late Archaic Corn in the Eastern Great Basin." *American Anthropologist* 91, no. 3 (1989): 712–20.

"William Henry Claflin." *Harvard Class of 1915 Fiftieth Anniversary Report*. Cambridge: President and Fellows of Harvard College, 1965.

Willey, Gordon R. "Prehistoric Settlement Patterns in the Viru Valley, Peru." *Bureau of American Ethnology Bulletin* 155. Washington, DC: Smithsonian Institution, 1953.

Willey, Gordon R., and Jeremy A. Sabloff. *A History of American Archaeology*. New York: W. H. Freeman, 1980.

Wing, Joseph E. *Alfalfa Farming in America*. Chicago: Sanders Publishing Company, 1916.

Woodbury, Richard B. "John Otis Brew, 1906–1988." *American Antiquity* 55, no. 3 (1990): 452–56.

Woodbury, Richard B. *Alfred V. Kidder*. New York: Columbia University Press, 1973.

Interviews/Correspondence

Chapoose, Rick. Interview by James M. Aton. August 8–12, 2003. Fort Duchesne, Utah.
Cooper, Hayden E. "Bud." Interview by James M. Aton. October 22, 2007. Myton, Utah.
Dalton, Norma Rich. Interview by James M. Aton and Jerry D. Spangler. June 8, 2016. Sunset, Utah. Transcript in the possession of the authors.
Jensen, Butch. Interview by James. M. Aton. August 1–2, 2006. Tavaputs Ranch, Utah.
McClurg, Zelpha McPherson. Interview by Steve Gerber and Paul Phillips. July 2, 2003. Grand Junction, Colorado.
McCook, Roland, Sr. Interview by James M. Aton. August 8–12, 2007. Arcadia, Utah.
McRich, Billie Seamount. Interview by Steve Gerber and Paul Phillips. July 13, 2003. Salt Lake City, Utah.
Metcalfe, Duncan. Interview by James M. Aton. July 14, 2003. Range Creek, Utah.
Miller, Blaine. Interview by James M. Aton. July 8, 2005. Price, Utah.
Moon, Leona Seamount. Interview by Steve Gerber and Paul Phillips. July 2, 2003. Grand Junction, Colorado.
Mott, Alice Sands. Phone interview by James M. Aton. October 10, 2007.
Nelson, Fern Seamount. Interview by Paul Phillips. July 2, 2003. Grand Junction, Colorado.
Orm, June Seamount. Interview by Steve Gerber and Paul Phillips. July 15, 2003; July 15, 2007. Salt Lake City, Utah.
Pilling, Bud. Interview by Steven L. Gerber. September 17, 2004. Price, Utah.
Seamount, Bill and Mrs. Interview by Otis R. "Dock" Marston. January 1, 1966. Salt Lake City, Utah. Otis R. Marston Papers, Huntington Library, San Marino, California.
Smith, Donald A. Interview by James M. Aton. August 15, 2007. Vernal, Utah.
Stewart, Arden. Interview by James M. Aton. January 8, 2004; March 25, 2006. Vernal, Utah.
Tomlinson, Brownie. Interview by James M. Aton. December 16, 2015. Vernal, Utah.
Wilcox, Ray "Budge." Interview by Bill Belknap and Loie Belknap Evans, 1974, Belknap Collection, Cline Library, Northern Arizona University, Flagstaff.
Wilcox, Waldo. Interview by James M. Aton. July 27, 2004; May 31, 2005; December 17, 2015. Green River, Utah.
Wilcox, Waldo. Interview by James M. Aton and Steve Gerber. January 10, 2004. Green River, Utah.
Wilcox, Waldo. Interview by James M. Aton, Steve Gerber, and Paul Phillips. July 15–16, 2003. Green River, Utah.
Wunderlich, Charlotte Forbes. Phone interview by James M. Aton. July 9, 2015.

Audiovisual and Electronic Sources

Ancestry.com.

"The Beckton Story: How the Foundation Herd Came into Being." www.beckton redangus.com.

The Hill Creek Extension: A Portfolio of Primary Documents. Information available online at https://heritage.utah.gov/history/uhq-sum-2015-hill-creek-extension.

Deputy Samuel F. Jenkins. Information available online at https://www.utahsfallen .org/archives/687.

US Inflation Calculator. Information available online at http://www.usinflation calculator.com/.

Index

Note: page numbers printed in *italics* indicate figures or illustrations